D1163179

Prince of Carpetbaggers

Other books by Jonathan Daniels

* * *

THE END OF INNOCENCE

THE MAN OF INDEPENDENCE

FRONTIER ON THE POTOMAC

TAR HEELS: A PORTRAIT OF NORTH CAROLINA

A SOUTHERNER DISCOVERS NEW ENGLAND

A SOUTHERNER DISCOVERS THE SOUTH

CLASH OF ANGELS

GENERAL MILTON S. LITTLEFIELD

. . . His uniform, at least, was as immaculate as Lee's . . .

(*See page 16*)

First Edition

Library of Congress Catalog Card Number 58-9534
Printed in the United States of America

Prince of Carpetbaggers

by

Jonathan Daniels

J. B. LIPPINCOTT COMPANY
Philadelphia and New York

To

Jonathan Worth

Governor of North Carolina, 1865–1868

* * *

He opposed Secession, saying, "I think the South is committing suicide, but my lot is cast with the South, and being unable to manage the ship I intend to face the breakers and go down with my companions."

Elected by his companions after the war, he was removed from the Governorship by the military to make way for Congressional Reconstruction. He was old, twice tried and tired. But he did not mistake the character of the new madness, nor think of it as the evil of one section alone.

"Money has become the God of this country," he wrote in 1869, "and men, otherwise good men, are almost compelled to worship at her shrine. The evidence of this is found in the facility by which the National Legislature and all the State Legislatures are bribed by money or controlled by corrupt rings."

He died that same year and left little but a record of integrity in the war and the peace.

I am proud to bear his name. I place it with honor in this story of his times in which arrogance and avarice made equal havoc. They are not qualities and dangers which have disappeared.

Table of Contents

Preface to Perfidy

WITHOUT THE AID of Helen or Homer, we Americans have made of our Civil War a story more satisfying to ourselves than any tale of Troy. Our native *Iliad* grows in the books that accumulate as we approach that war's centennial. Our *Odyssey* lags behind. Yet when Odysseus got back to far-seen, rocky Ithaca, he told no stranger tales than some which have been widely accepted about those years during which the North and South, through Reconstruction, managed to come home uneasily together as one nation.

We have only the reports of Homer to support the opinion of Odysseus about the insolence of the suitors for Penelope's hand whom he found in his house. And we have generally accepted a similarly single-sided story from the Southerners about the carpetbaggers. Many of them surely were insolently devouring the substance of the South. They took arrogant places in its halls. There were thieves among them. And some of the sanctimonious were even less welcome than the rogues. Least pleasant of all may have been those who came confidently counting on gratitude for superior Yankee skill, which was the current equivalent of American know-how.

It is possible that some of the doomed suitors, who seemed only insolent to Odysseus, really loved Penelope. And it is even possible that some of the carpetbaggers really loved the South. Even General Sherman found it an enchantress. Sometimes it was, like Penelope, tearful but slightly coquettish.

Penelope was a popular name in the classical South, though often its wearer became Miss Neppie as she aged. And all things can happen to Penelope in all the ages. After the centuries there are still disagreements as to whether the first Penelope was always all she should have been. The preferred story about her, of course, is that in shrewd fidelity she put off her importunate suitors by promising to choose one of them when the web she was weaving should be finished. Then at night she secretly unraveled what she had woven through the day. The South, too, has spent much time reweaving its unraveled web.

There is another story (Cicero, as a Latin, later, picked it up and passed it on) that a less prim Penelope became the mother of a lively offspring by all the suitors together. And certainly something of the same sort happened to the South, where old graces did not completely satisfy new hungers or rectify old mistakes. The South which erectly followed Lee also saw the equipment—and the commissary—of Grant's armies. Materialism did not come like a Minié ball to those who had righteously regarded slaves as property. There were Southerners, even before Appomattox, who preferred hard money, when they could get it, to the most patriotic Confederate paper. Not all the natives were naïve or innocent. There was shrewdness as well as sadness in the South after General Grant declined to accept General Lee's sword. There was corruption in the late Confederacy, some not alien or black.

Not all need was met by the Freedmen's Bureau. Perhaps, indeed, the conquered South's longest lasting need was to find another cause for its plight than its own folly. And however much the carpetbaggers carried away with them, it was not so precious as the enduring excuse for the South which they brought in their little satchels of carpeting when they came.

The North needed more. It required adequate foundation for the respectability which apparently always follows excesses in acquisition or idealism, or both. Having lost the zeal for freedom which once had prodded even a reluctant Lincoln, the North needed an elegant explanation for retreat. Its idealism had already languished, by no fault of the carpetbaggers. But the carpetbagger was at hand. His personal guilt was often apparent. His sacrifice seemed both sanitary and serviceable. Perhaps he got what he deserved when the same Northerners who had dispatched him repudiated him. That made it possible at low cost for them to sacrifice what they had sought in order to get what they wanted.

In all history, North and South, it is difficult to find so nationally useful a man as a scapegoat for everybody. Certainly no man from the belated abolitionism of Lincoln to the theft of the Presidency for Hayes touches all the aspects of the carpetbagger story as well as General Milton Smith Littlefield of New York and Illinois. He was not Odysseus. Undoubtedly he sometimes seemed an insolent suitor for the South's regard. Personally, he seems more like a man named Gatsby who came home from another war. But as a human figure who comes home from all wars, even our best beloved one, he should be well remembered if not always remembered well.

Prince of Carpetbaggers

CHAPTER I

Prince of Bummers

PEACE WAS POLITENESS at Appomattox. No tears were shown. Elation was curbed. Two armies composed mostly of boys were tired of dying. And the rations promptly issued to the hungry Confederates made the occasion for many of them more like barbecue than heartbreak. Men were allowed to ride their horses home to hitch to the plows in hard fieldrows, so many of which had grown up with pines. Only the very arrogant were unsubdued. Only the very righteous seemed unsatisfied. War came to an end like a clean wound ready for healing.

But Charleston, which had shaken the first fist, fell like a palsied hand. That city, General William Tecumseh Sherman thought, as he blazed and burned through upcountry South Carolina, was "not worth the time it would take to starve it out." Its condition, he said, was "retribution decreed by heaven itself." And when the Lieutenant Colonel of a Negro regiment landed in a rowboat to receive its surrender, it was a place of widowed women and rotting wharves, of buzzards perched in melancholy rows upon the roofs of deserted warehouses, of weed-grown gardens and miles of grass-grown streets. Indeed, Harriott Horry Rutledge Ravenel, who became the city's great lady and tender historian and who was then thirty-three, tall, fair and slender, reported that "not grass merely, but bushes grew in the streets. The gardens looked as if Sleeping Beauty might be within."

The awakening was not arranged with a kiss. Still afterward the South made a prince—though in a peerage of pillage—of the officer, just a year older than young Mrs. Ravenel, who came to preside over the first, spontaneous ceremonial of Charleston's fall. He became the Prince of Carpetbaggers. His specific title, bestowed by a Southern editor who gave him his anger and admiration at the same time, was "the Prince of Bummers." In the sharp Southern slang of the time, that phrase undertook to tie his eminence among carpetbaggers to a disreputable, ravening, wartime company of rogues.

Not even a Rutledge or a Ravenel would have mistaken General Milton Smith Littlefield then, however, for any of the ring-snatching, spoon-stealing bummers on the fiery fringes of Sherman's army. The General, who hurried up to Charleston from the golden Sea Islands to which Lincoln had sent him, was one of the President's Illinois friends and military protégés. In that March of 1865 his uniform at least was as immaculate as Lee's at Appomattox.

Littlefield was then, as he was regarded afterward in North Carolina before that state offered a reward for his apprehension, "a man of singular courtesy and intelligence." And in Florida, where he required two mansions in the manipulation of the state's railroads, he was remembered even by Hamilton Jay, a disapproving witness from the North, as "in the full flush of a magnificent manhood, the handsomest man in the State, and of wonderful magnetic power . . . tall, well-proportioned, with dark hair and dark, close-cropped beard, rosy cheeks and genial laughing eyes."

The South, which has always honored audacity, kept a hidden admiration for Milton Littlefield even when it hated him most. He came to seem only ominous to such a Yankee of Yankees as John Greenleaf Whittier. As ardent abolitionist and passionate pacifist, Whittier during the war wrote special, sweet verses for some of those with whom Littlefield served on the Sea Islands where freedom on the marshy land was lit by the flickering hope of forty acres and a mule. But, as a waspish spokesman for a flickering idealism, Whittier put Littlefield in his position of eminence as "carpet-bagger." As Reconstruction ended in the Presidential bargain of 1877, the aging poet described the handsome General as the kind of "knavish, unprincipled & low minded republican" from whom Rutherford B. Hayes, now that he no longer needed him, must escape.

All that was afterward. But a full month before Appomattox, on March 3, 1865, Littlefield's prominence in Charleston, where Secession began with dramatics, gave the Reconstructionist a ceremonial entrance, too. It was in terms of Charleston that Lincoln, harassed in his own household, plagued by politicians of his own party, troubled by dark dreams, and already marked for assassination, made it plain that he planned no peace so forgiving that it could soon be forgotten.

Clearly the gaunt Lincoln understood that while Richmond was the Union's military objective, Charleston was its emotional target. The city's strategic irrelevance saved it from Sherman and the salt which leaders in Washington had suggested that the General, when he was finished with it, sow where it had stood. But weeks before the politeness at the courthouse crossroads in Virginia, the President helped plan a pageant of retribution in Charleston on the anniversary of the fall of Fort Sumter. Chosen as orators for the occasion were William Lloyd Garrison and Henry Ward Beecher. They were the two men in America whose triumph was most calculated to humiliate those described by the sharp-eyed and sharp-tongued journalist, Whitelaw Reid, as the "haughty Southrons who scorned the Yankee scum" and had "dashed into revolution as they would into a waltz."

Jubilee was in a hurry, too. Two weeks after the city fell and six weeks before the planned national dramatization of once-defiant Charleston's desolation, the freed multitude applied its own variety of salt to the city which had been spared the torches, but still, according to Mrs. Ravenel, had lost its old life. With shouting and singing, in multi-colored concourse, the freed people and those who had set them free staged their own celebration. Spruce and smart town Negroes had been joined by hundreds who had come from the plantations, some of whom shouted and sang in a Gullah dialect supposed to contain African as well as corrupted English words. Many seemed scarcely altered this side of Gambia and Guinea.

Some white people, abandoned by retreating Confederates, that day watched behind closed shutters. They were filled with old-time fears of slave insurrections, not realizing that law enforced by arms was in the crowded streets and that all that was left of insurrection was with them in the shadows behind the shutters. Some bolder ones watched from the sidewalks and piazzas. A Northern correspondent complained that some patricians who remained were a little too eager to set themselves up quickly as loyal Union men.

The Negroes moved to jubilee as they customarily marched to church, solemn if seldom silent. Even Mrs. Frances J. Porcher, an unhappy aristocrat, found the day orderly, complaining only that some white people were turned back from the parade ground by "nicely dressed black sentinels" because their passes were not correct. But a multitude, varying in color from magnolia to midnight, were passed as they paraded to the grounds of the Citadel—"a military college," explained Correspondent Berwick of *The New York Tribune* for the benefit of Northern readers, "founded for the purpose of destroying the Union and erecting on its ruins an empire whose cornerstone should be Negro slavery."

No bushes grew on that ground, Berwick wrote, and the grass was new and green. A warm sun shone in a cloudless sky. The "Flag of the Free" flew from the turrets of the tall, castle-like building. Beneath it a long line of erect black soldiers in blue and scarlet extended across the whole front of the Citadel. At right angles to them, less impressive, was another line of "new recruits, fresh from the plantations." A third side of the hollow square before the building was filled by "a multitude of men, women and children." The whole crowd sang with one tremendous voice:

> "Sound the loud timbrel o'er Egypt's dark sea!
> Jehovah has triumph'd,—his people are free."

Then, at three o'clock promptly, General Littlefield, accompanied by Lieutenant Colonel A. G. Bennett of the 21st Regiment U. S. Colored Troops, who had accepted Charleston's surrender, marched into the hollow square. The "tall and handsome" General, Berwick reported, "advanced toward the center, where thirteen colored ladies, tastefully dressed, were waiting to receive him." For decades the Negro seamstresses in Charleston had made the gowns which added to the charm of the select at St. Cecilia balls. They had made the costumes, too, in which the thirteen women, Berwick said, represented the Thirteen Original States. With special care they had made the dress of the young woman in the group who held a large flag to be presented for them by the General to the 21st Regiment which he had trained and still nominally commanded.

Berwick gave no description of the girl except that she was of distinguished white and comely colored parentage. She had been chosen by all the freed women of Charleston to represent them best pictorially. She was well poised in her rôle. In his newspaper dispatch the correspondent quoted her in a language free of dialect. "God bless you all forever and ever," she said. She passed the staff to General Littlefield. Then soldier and girl turned together toward the array of solemn black troops. The General praised the soldiers. He spoke of a peaceful, prosperous happy Reconstruction "teeming with schools where every child is educated and churches where all are blest." He put the flag's staff into his Lieutenant Colonel's hands. The cheers rose around them almost like a chant.

"General Littlefield was proud of his day's work," the admiring Berwick said, "and has good cause to be."

It was a significant day and the eve of a still more consequential one. The sunlit afternoon in Charleston was the same as that upon which, in Washington, the drizzle and cold, gusty wind set in which were to make Lincoln's second inauguration, next day, a damp, chill and mud-bedaubed occasion. Much more attention, of course, has been given in history to the "motley democratic"—but apparently less orderly—crowd then gathering in Washington. Indeed, it was the Washington crowd in the White House the next evening which a guard there said left that mansion looking "as if a regiment of Rebel troops had been quartered there, with permission to forage." In Charleston Mrs. Porcher was only sarcastic about "young ladies of color" and sharply critical of the fact that a Negro caterer had "provided magnificently for a miscegenat dinner, at which blacks & whites sat on an equality, & gave toasts and sang songs for Lincoln & freedom."

Nothing in the Charleston jubilation mocked the spirit of Lincoln's address the following noon. And nothing in his address rebuked the almost religious rite of retribution on the South Carolina shore. In that famous speech Lincoln, with little more than a month to live, put "malice toward none" and "charity for all" directly following and dependent upon the sentence in which he promised that "if necessary every drop of blood drawn with the lash shall be paid by another drawn with the sword."

Neither the lash nor the sword was to be forgotten soon in Charleston or in the South around it. Both were already in bright remembrance on General Littlefield's proud day. But in the crowd around him and the costumed girls, an old woman, with long arms uplifted, shouted a prayer to the cloudless sky, and dark children skipped and danced. Some recruits shuffled in their places. Then, as a signal for the completion of the ceremony, the slim girl in the center of the square lifted her hand again and the great crowd quieted. Others of the costumed women moved toward the General with tokens for him, too. One brought him a great bouquet of flowers already blooming in Charleston—and "in all our hearts today"—before even the lilacs had begun to show in Washington dooryards. And finally he was given a present to take to the President for Mrs. Lincoln. It was a fan made from the pure white feathers of a swan.

Mrs. Lincoln never received the fan and Lincoln himself died before Littlefield ever saw him again. The General did not linger long in Charleston. At his headquarters on Hilton Head Island he was needed to say much in rejoicing and instruction to more thousands of black folk whom Mr. Lincoln had freed. But that was soon interrupted. When jubilee there suddenly shifted to lamentation, he sailed down the shore to Savannah. Littlefield's personal loss in Lincoln's death was understood in the Department of the South and his gift as orator was recognized all along the occupied coast. He spoke beneath great black banners at the mourning meeting attended by one of the largest crowds which had ever gathered in Savannah.

"Our father, our leader, our friend has gone to rest," he said. "Spirits of the Patriots, bid him welcome as he comes fresh from the fields of glory. Pilgrims, in your dusty beds make room for him, our country's idol."

There was not to be any room for Littlefield in the Lincoln legend. It is possible that before Lincoln died Littlefield's career as the Prince of Bummers had already secretly begun. Afterward that career was all that was remembered of him when anyone troubled, after the General's money gave out, to remember him at all. The quality of the man before he became the most noted of carpetbaggers has been regarded as irrelevant by historians who have dismissed him briefly in distaste. What happened to him after he had moved like a princely plunderer through the South seems to have been unworthy of anybody's search. The North has been content to reject him in silence. And in the South there is some evidence that those who set up the loudest hue and cry did not really want to catch him and bring him back to tell his whole story, even in a Southern court.

Some of his associates among Southern respectables kept more loot than he carried away. They made almost a vocation of forgetting him as did his colleagues in the North, including members of the patriotic Union League when they no longer required him in their practical operations. His own descendants were intimidated by the steady insistence upon his sinister eminence from the Republican Whittier to the melodramatically Democratic Claude G. Bowers, who described the carpetbaggers' time, in terms the South liked best, in *The Tragic Era.* Anna Elizabeth Shull, the girl Milton Littlefield brought as wife with him from Illinois, was silent in the faith she kept even after she had to learn the occasional necessity for flight from process servers and would-be reward seekers. She stayed quiet even when another lady, who did not carry a carpetbag but moved with a bonnet box and a Saratoga trunk, seemed all too eager to tell about the General and herself, or about bribes and bonds. Even the General's own son, a minister who became a famous compiler of hymnbooks, tore much material out of the scrapbook his father kept. A writ of attainder seemed almost to run against Littlefield's blood.

"My father told me," said the General's granddaughter, "that he never addressed any audience (which he did many times all over the U.S.A.) that he didn't have a dreadful fear that someone would recognize him or identify him as the son of M.S.L., Sr. And he loved his father so much—enough to tear out all the pages from the scrapbook so that even I would never know."

He did not tear out all the pages. Much of the General's scrapbook remains as he kept it. Perhaps in the pages which were ripped out the younger Littlefield destroyed evidence which, if available, would damn the General with a darker reputation than his ghost wears now. Enough information remains to establish his sinister eminence as carpetbagger-in-chief, though he had much high company in that corps.

General Grant was complaining vociferously before he took Vicksburg of speculators who "come in with their carpet-sacks" while Littlefield was still one of Sherman's chief police officers in Memphis. But Littlefield qualified for the application of the term after the war. Then Northern men, sometimes with no more property of their own to hazard than the contents of their carpet-sacks, came south. Among other activities, and often only incidental to them, they labored to organize the enfranchised Negroes for the Republican Party, or, as they insistently put it, to protect the Negroes in the rights of freedom the North had fought to give them.

That was not quite as simple a black and white problem, North or South, as it has been pictured. The termination of slavery meant the abrupt increase in the Southern States of the number of citizens counted for Congressional representation and Presidential voting. Under the Constitution slaves had been counted as only three-fifths their actual number for such representation. Thus, if the Negroes were not allowed to vote that would mean that the white men, most of whom had been in the Secession army, would have more weight in the Congress and the Electoral College of the Union, which they had fought to leave, than they had had before the war. And that, said the journalist Whitelaw Reid, then a young observer on the scene in the summer after surrender, "would be putting a reward on treason that we can hardly afford to pay."

That logical and political situation underlying Radical Republicanism was served by the carpetbaggers. They were men of all grades of personal integrity and honesty of purpose from sincere old-fashioned abolitionists to headlong adventurers. Sometimes abolitionists and adventurers were the same men. The abolitionist was still often an adventurer when he moved into the South, which in large part had abandoned its rebellion but not its recalcitrance.

Adventurers understood that abolition provided the basis of their power, which endeared them to both the Republican Party and those realistic men of business, North and South, who Dr. C. Vann Woodward in *Reunion and Reaction* has suggested later made a deal to end Reconstruction. Actually, some such gentlemen, as men calculating in chaos, were ready to make—and in many ways did make—such a deal when Reconstruction began.

Sometimes the carpetbagger came south by invitation, sometimes by accident. There were even those who came back homesick for a warm, flowering South which had enchanted them in war. Some undoubtedly came with a sense of the special superiority of the conqueror which has been well-known and well-hated from the time when Romans went out to instruct the barbarians to the days when later Americans were distributing know-how to the world. Others in classic and current times were only the technicians of resident operators who knew very well how they wanted things to go. Also, like the Romans and later Americans, the carpetbaggers picked up bargains among the conquered from trinkets to transportation systems, took the best jobs, had the most money, occupied the best houses or lived in the best hotels. Often they rode in carriages, while natives walked in the dust. Some were surprised that they were not loved. Some carpetbaggers undoubtedly trampled down the fragile South with ruthless boots. But the tracks of many and of their Southern coadjutors or principals (scalawags, as they were called) are hard to follow. It is increasingly clear that it does not suffice in telling the story of such a carpetbagger as General Littlefield to say that he went south on an individual errand of larceny.

If he looted the treasuries of sovereign states, stole railroads, debauched legislatures, bribed Negroes and white men, too, cheated European bond buyers (and took time out of that business as veteran of Shiloh to watch the Prussian bombardment of Metz), lived like a king and jumped his hotel bill, that was not all he accomplished. From first to last, from idealism to partisanship for profit, from courage to connivance, he embodied the story and character of the Reconstructionist who is not now easily reconstructed. He is a skeleton in a closet not merely of Northern—or

Southern—but of continental dimensions. Patriotism was his stock in trade. Loot may have been his specialty, even when he called it "development." But he combined both good and evil, like aspiring and sinful Man.

Littlefield was no Lucifer. Perhaps he was no angel of any sort to begin. But if he fell far, he was an appealing member of the company of the damned to the end—and an instructive one. He became the very image of the scoundrel, but it is at least possible that he was also the epitome of the scapegoat. In many ways he embodied complex factors in the personality of the nation which produced the carpetbagger and made that American figure less a private criminal than a national symbol. Perhaps such a symbol deserves the forgetfulness in crowded history which Milton Littlefield has received in his unmarked grave in much-monumented Kensico Cemetery near New York. To forgetfulness, however, it is possible that America, seeking understanding of its story and its spirit, could better spare some better men.

CHAPTER II

Shoulders for Lincoln

THE *Forest Queen* steamed smoothly up the green-rimmed Grand River. The white ship provided the kind of sparkling service which made it brightly clear that Grand Rapids was no longer merely a village in the great woods of Michigan. From the flag at her masthead to the white ripple at her bow the *Queen* was made for the company she carried that day in the eighteen-fifties, not for the grim duty to which she was to be put in less than a decade. Between the forested shores the ship was going home, and no one in the gay company aboard her dreamed that the time might soon come when the *Forest Queen* would be carrying William T. Sherman on the Mississippi to join Ulysses S. Grant in the fighting about Vicksburg. Certainly there was no such notion then in the young, gay head of Milton Smith Littlefield.

This particular trip provided the occasion for the best description available of Milton Littlefield on the Grand Rapids scene. Though it was made when he was about to leave that scene forever, Littlefield himself considered the account so good a picture of himself at a pleasant time that he pasted it in the scrapbook which he began then and was to keep for the rest of his life. It appeared in a brief item from *The Grand Rapids Herald*, signed simply "G," written by one who called Milton by his first name.

The steamer sailed happily along, "G" wrote, "with the ever-obliging Captain Merchant as commander; and one of the good-looking Sargeant boys as Master-of-Amusements." "G" commented with some timidity about the card-playing and heartily commended the food in terms of both quality and price.

"But the most attractive of all," he said, "was the Vocal and Instrumental Music, furnished by the charming Mrs. S., and two or three other talented ladies, assisted by Mr. M. S. Littlefield." Milton, he added, was coming home singing "from St. Louis at which place he has formed business relations which will cause our city to lose the light of his presence."

The young man, smiling and singing with the ladies, had been an undoubted light—illuminating Grand Rapids with learning, liveliness and, particularly, the culture which became more and more important to New Englanders and New Yorkers as they moved westward. Like so many other things in his early life, the facts about Milton Littlefield's education are obscure. In his boyhood there were, of course, plenty of schools back in New York State where he was born in Ellisburgh, Jefferson County, on July 19, 1830. He grew up in Onondaga County, at Cicero, near Syracuse, where John Brown's friend Gerrit Smith and other abolitionists rescued from the police station a fugitive slave named Jerry, who got almost as much attention as Dred Scott. This was in the same year that Milton left for the West.

Such an event, of course, was not a part of Milton's formal education. It was an aspect of the atmosphere in which he grew and received a schooling sufficient to permit him to start teaching, almost immediately after he arrived in Michigan in 1851, in "the old Grand Rapids School on the west side of the river." He was twenty-one, six feet tall and weighed nearly two hundred pounds. He looked more like one of the bold log drivers on the Grand River than the conventional image of the teacher. But the quality of his teaching, as judged by his colleagues, was shown by his election as recording secretary of the Kent County Teachers' Institute when it was organized in 1854.

In the same year he became one of the three original curators of the Grand Rapids Museum of Natural History (now the Grand

Rapids Public Museum), the opening of which indicated the feeling of the community in the first year of its incorporated existence that even in the forests of Michigan man could not live on logs alone. Obviously, however, Milton was no mere book-bound or museum-keeping improver of the public mind. The teacher and the curator marched as soldier, too, as sergeant in the Grand Rapids Light Guards Militia after that regiment was formed in July 1855.

Young man in the city, Milton found in Grand Rapids a pleasant and secure place. His father, James Pennell Littlefield, who as a patriarch of nearly sixty had led his big family west, was an alderman. The Littlefields, who had been settled in America since 1637, coming from Titchfield in Hampshire were the same kind of New York and New England folk as their neighbors who had been pouring into the Middle Country since the Erie Canal was opened in 1825. Back in New York State, Milton's father, old James, had been "licensed" as a Baptist preacher in 1820, but as a man of a people who never found it necessary to neglect the material while serving the spirit, he engaged in milling and politics on the side. Appropriately, he married Phoebe Smith, daughter of a member of the New York Stock Exchange, who as a young woman wrote down for herself a set of "sollom and pious resolutions" which her only son Milton preserved, if he did not always keep, all his life.

Phoebe Smith died young, leaving Milton an infant with four adoring older sisters. Then by a second marriage old James provided him with brothers. Significantly, the oldest of them, John Harrison Littlefield, was sent soon after the family arrived in Michigan to Oberlin College in Ohio, which with even-handed radicalism admitted both coeds and colored people. With the Littlefields such approval of advanced ideas was the radicalism of respectability. No member of the family showed the qualities of a crank. They were patriots with a possessive sense about America. James's father, Edmund, had been at Bunker Hill. And all his life Milton, remembering that, liked to give resounding recitals of "The Sword of Bunker Hill." Old James Littlefield's three younger sons, boys when they arrived in Michigan, all lived and died in the patterns of propriety Grand Rapids prescribed.

They were not the patterns of Middle Border pioneer struggles but of the Northeast transplanted—of well-fed idealism and practical piety; often, of the intellectual and the speculator, the poet and the politician walking hand in hand. Sometimes equal values were put on sentimental verses and well-located real estate, on timber tracts and patriotic oratory. It was the country in which, and the time when, the Republican Party was born to blossom as the enduring combination of hard heads and romantic hearts, of missionary purposes and the main chance. As the darling of his older sisters, curator of culture, teacher of the future and marcher with the Guards, Milton Littlefield was a natural light in such a place. Only his restlessness there was strange.

His father, old James, had given his younger sons the names of his American heroes. Daniel Webster, as a young cavalryman, was to die of smallpox near the front in the Civil War. Benjamin Franklin became a major and afterward was prominent in local G.A.R. circles and the proprietor of little hotels in small Michigan towns. De Witt Clinton went like Grand Rapids itself into the furniture business. Only Milton and John moved from the green shores of the Grand River into American history's mainstream.

The date of Milton's departure from Michigan cannot be exactly fixed. It was after the death of his father, Alderman Littlefield, three days before Christmas in 1856, and before the last run of the *Forest Queen* on the Grand River in 1858. His reasons for moving are unavailable. His father's death may have made him realize, at twenty-six, that time was passing without his accomplishing the dazzling success he had always counted on. Apparently, however, despite his good looks, his fine singing voice, and the light which his presence constituted in Grand Rapids, he was in flight from a young man's tragedy. There are no prosaic records about it. Poetry provides little proof. But Milton pasted in his scrapbook a poem "written by my sister on the death of Annie Greene, a daughter of Henry Greene, Henderson, N. Y." That seems a stark reference to a girl in the New York village in his home North Country which he had left when he was just twenty-one. His sister Mary, five years his senior, apparently wrote many verses. But Milton pasted only two of them in the early, first pages of his scrapbook. One was about the bright girl of the little New York town who in the autumn grew silent and pale!

Then we listened so sadly—to hear her sweet song,
But vainly we listened—aye vainly and long!

The other was specifically addressed to Milton:

Brother, loved one, cease thy sorrow,
Lift thy trusting eye above!
Though 'tis dark, yet oh! tomorrow
Sure shall bring the light of love.

The Littlefields were much addicted to poetry. Milton loaded his scrapbook with verses, both grand and inane, and with instructive anecdotes from the lives of great men. But whatever part love and poetry may have had in his journeyings, more practical matters apparently were persuasive. Neither he nor anybody else in the Middle American Country was unaware of the startling panic of 1857 which coincided with growing political unrest. Not all of that unrest by any means was related to abolitionist ideas. Prohibition, adopted in 1855 in Michigan, mobilized as much moral indignation as abolition. Good causes were almost as numerous as economic difficulties. Both pushed Michigan into the Republican column and gave the state's vote to John C. Frémont, the party's first candidate for the Presidency. The swiftly developing West, the heartland of boom and bust, was full of restless, moving young men.

It was a restless, moving time. The Gold Rush of the Forty-niners had begun to spend itself, but the eagerness for wealth remained. Americans had swept to the heights of Chapultepec when Milton was a seventeen-year-old boy, but glamour attended its memory even among those who most distrusted Southern imperialistic notions. Perhaps the material which Milton left in his notebook most explanatory about himself was not about himself at all. It consisted of pages of clippings of the oratory in praise of William Hickling Prescott after his death in 1859. There were speeches by Mr. Winthrop (either Charles or Theodore), by the Honorable Josiah Quincy, Sr., by Professor George Ticknor, President James Walker of Harvard, and finally by Edward Everett. Obviously the half-blind chronicler of the conquests of Mexico and Peru was literary guide and idol of the unsatisfied young schoolteacher of Grand Rapids.

Prescott's *Mexico,* in which God and glory and gold were as intermixed as audacity and cunning, had appeared when Milton was thirteen. Perhaps he was older when a copy of it reached his hands in Onondaga County. He was seventeen when Prescott's *Peru* appeared. Perhaps, as is so often presumed, he and other young Northerners were more properly moved by Mrs. Stowe's *Uncle Tom's Cabin* when it was published about the time the Littlefields moved west. Nothing in his scrapbook indicates such a concern for her work as he held for Prescott's. The Littlefields had already made up their minds on the slavery question before Mrs. Stowe mentioned it in print. But if Prescott wrote about a long past, it was not difficult for such a young American as Milton in the 1850s to imagine himself as the handsome, amiable-appearing conquistador ready to do what was needed to get what he wanted. He could even figure himself, with a high sentimentality that Mrs. Stowe did not surpass, as the Cortés beyond the sea, the hills, the death, the plunder, the cruelty and the deceit. As one who did not have much respect for kings, and who indicated that in his scrapbook, too, Milton was of a generation which loved the story of Cortés at the last pushing his way as one discarded and neglected through a crowd to put his foot on the step of the Emperor's carriage. There Charles V, the blessed of fortune, astounded at this audacious act, demanded who he was.

"I am a man," said the conqueror of Mexico, "who has given you more provinces than your ancestors left you cities."

More provinces were not available to young Americans in the 1850s. The United States had attained its continental limits. But Prescott has been neglected as a formative force in comparison with Mrs. Stowe. Not every young man pasted everything he could find about him in a scrapbook as Milton did. But the expansive concept of God, glory and gold, inseparable and indivisible, was as real in America in the first half of the nineteenth century as in the first half of the sixteenth. Some realization of that came later as of the period when the "robber barons" grew up.

Jerseyville, Illinois, to which Milton went, did not seem to be on the road to wealth or fame. Still, though *The Grand Rapids Herald* said he had "formed business relations" in St. Louis, it was to Jerseyville that he moved. It was a small town of only 760 people off the river and the railroad, above the point where the slow-moving Illinois River pours into the Mississippi. He lived there in a hotel kept by another Eastern-born man named S. M. Titas. That, of course, did not preclude the possibility of business relations in St. Louis. In his life Milton traveled much and fast. And from Alton, twenty miles below Jerseyville, such swift steamboats as the *Golden Eagle*, the *Gossamer* and the *Kate Kearney* raced each other to St. Louis thirty miles farther downstream.

Still, Jerseyville seemed an unlikely destination for a rising young man from growing Grand Rapids. Elsewhere in Illinois railroad speculation and development proceeded at such a rate that there were some protests, like those which were heard around Milton's head later in the South, that many railroad bills "were prepared in New York and first canvassed by Wall Street men before they were sent to Springfield to secure legislative endorsement." If Jerseyville offered little to Milton's education as a railroad manipulator, it was admirably located to show him the furies of the American division over Negro slavery. Twenty years before he arrived in that vicinity, in a single month Elijah Lovejoy, the abolitionist editor, was killed by a mob in Alton, and in Griggsville just above Jerseyville a prominent citizen had to climb for safety to the steeple of the Baptist church to escape a mob after him because he had signed an anti-slavery petition. Long after Milton had been settled there, even in 1861, there were men circulating a document which proposed the division of Illinois on a line just ten miles south of Jerseyville to allow the part below to join the Confederacy.

The little town shared, too, pleasant aspects of the North and South. Even Northern settlers, like Littlefield, enjoyed the easy-going Southern pace of life on its wide, sunny Main Street. Already growing about it were the endless orchards of fruit trees which brightened its countryside in spring with the blossoms of apple and peach. It was a part of that country in which German immigrants were putting down new roots. As men who had been hunted and harried after abortive revolution in their own homeland, their feeling about the Fugitive Slave Act had about it an understandable intensity. Life was pleasant, however, even for such retired revolutionists. University graduates among them, when they settled on the Illinois land "to grow their corn and wine," were called "the

Latin farmers." Some of them raised not only grapes and grain but, as Milton was to discover, pretty daughters, too.

Milton grew no corn, nor vines nor fruit. He looked almost startlingly citified in the sprawling country town. Tall and powerfully built, his shoulders were wider than those of any of the young men who had built their muscles behind the plow. His figure tapered to a small waist and thin hips. His boots always seemed varnished, almost dustproof. Leaning as he often did against the column of the hotel porch with his hands thrust into the pockets of his fawn-colored pants, he was a dandy in Jerseyville. He was also such a man that no rustic would taunt him for the difference of his clothes from the conventionally rusty coats most men wore, when they wore any coats at all. No one treated him as if he were a fop. His clothes seemed to fit not only his figure but his deceptively easygoing personality, his evident good nature and his ready companionship. Somehow they seemed to fit also a need which before had been missing in the town. Even Democrats smiled back when Milton's lips parted in ready amiability to show his strong white teeth.

Apparently he hung out his shingle as lawyer and began practice in Jersey County's little forty-foot brick courthouse soon after he arrived. There is no evidence that he was ever licensed by the Illinois Supreme Court, but the records of his muster into the Union Army, in which he served upon occasion as Provost Marshal, listed his previous profession as attorney. Certainly around the courthouse he was deeply involved as an ardent young Republican in the politics which provided aspiring attorneys a chance to prove their forensic powers. Milton spoke much and well. As writer also, in the political debate rising to tension in such a county as Jersey, he was at least a part-time newspaperman.

Clippings he kept show that he had many admiring friends in large and small newspaper offices in Illinois at the time. There were many such offices at a time when an editor could put himself in business for $500. The two verses sent Milton by his sister were published in the Jerseyville Republican organ, *The Prairie State.* He was never its editor. His activity as a reporter, however, marked his first recorded relationship with Abraham Lincoln. His brother John told about that, later, in describing the events which led Lincoln to take John, at Milton's request, as student into the law firm of Lincoln and Herndon.

"I became acquainted with Mr. Lincoln," John wrote years later, "through my brother, General Littlefield, who was present at one of the famous debates between Lincoln and Douglas, in 1858. At Ottawa in that State, at the conclusion of Lincoln's speech, Douglas was carried by his admirers to his hotel. Then my brother, who was sitting up in a tree, acting as a reporter for one of the St. Louis papers, seeing how Douglas was carried to his hotel, dropped from the tree and, with several friends, proceeded to carry Lincoln to his hotel in true Southwestern style. Lincoln protested—'Don't, don't. This is ridiculous'; but they carried him to his lodgings."

There are some errors in John's report. Stephen A. Douglas' admirers did not carry him to his hotel but to his waiting train. Lincoln was not taken to his hotel but to the house of the Republican Mayor of the town. Also, no report of the first of the great debates signed by Milton Littlefield has been discovered in any surviving copy of a St. Louis newspaper. His place in the tree separated him from the press table beside the plain, plank speaker's platform around which "an army of young reporters" swarmed, according to Horace White, one of the ablest and youngest of the lot.

The essence of John's report is accurate, however. Such a group of strong-shouldered supporters as John said his brother led, did rush to Lincoln after the cheers which "reverberated across the prairie" had seemed to give the decision in the first debate to the elegant and assured Douglas. And apparently there was some justification for Lincoln's fear that he might be made to seem ridiculous. Democratic reporters undertook to prove that he was. They wrote jubilantly that Douglas had scored in his effort to prove that Lincoln had one position about slavery for northern Illinois and another for the southern, so-called Egyptian counties, settled largely from the Slave States.

One Eastern correspondent declared that Lincoln was "the worst used up man in the United States." And the Philadelphia *Press* ridiculed his ride on the shoulders of his stalwarts. He made, that paper said, "a grotesque figure, holding frantically to the heads of his supporters, and his pantaloons pulled up so as to expose his underwear almost to his knees."

Evidently Mr. Lincoln did not long, if ever, resent the attention of his bearers, particularly as regards Milton Littlefield. Milton himself never appeared ridiculous even when dropping down from a tree. His attire on that and every other occasion was more like that of the dapper Douglas than the drooping Lincoln. It was characteristic of him throughout his career to disregard catcalls and move directly to his purposes. More than one subsequent event proved that Lincoln had regard for his "ability and energy." John Littlefield afterward reported the results of Milton's attachment of himself to Lincoln—or the attachment of Lincoln to his broad shoulders in the crowd on the Ottawa public square.

"In this way," John wrote, "my brother made the acquaintance of Mr. Lincoln. One day he said to him: 'I have a brother (myself) in Grand Rapids, Michigan, studying law. I would like to have him read law with you.'

" 'Send him along,' said Mr. Lincoln, 'we will try to do what we can for him.'

"So after some correspondence in February 1859, I entered the law office of Lincoln and Herndon, and remained there until Mr. Lincoln was elected to the Presidency."

Young John justified Milton's recommendation. He was never so debonair as his brother, but he was an earnest young man when he arrived in the untidy offices of Lincoln and Herndon on the second story of a brick building on the public square in Springfield. Mr. Lincoln regarded the newcomer solemnly.

"I hope," he said, "you will not become so enthusiastic in your studies of Blackstone and Kent as two young men we had here."

Lincoln pointed with his long arm at a large black spot on the wall.

"Do you see that spot? Well, one of these young men got so enthusiastic in his pursuit of legal lore that he fired an inkstand at the other's head and that is the mark he made."

John made an even more startling mark on the office. He "immediately" began to clean it up. He could not remove the inkspot. There was plenty to do, however. He described the situation.

"There were two windows which looked into the back yard. In one corner was an old-fashioned secretary with pigeonholes and a drawer, and here Mr. Lincoln and his partner kept their law papers.

There was also a bookcase containing about 200 volumes of law as well as miscellaneous books. . . . Mr. Lincoln had been in Congress and had the usual amount of seeds to distribute to the farmers. These were sent out with Free Soil and Republican documents. In my efforts to clean up, I found that some of the seeds had sprouted in the dirt that had collected in his office."

Such a description, if it did not surround Lincoln with dignity, was a tribute to the germinal powers of Congressional seed. It had been ten years since Mr. Lincoln was a one-term Whig Congressman. John's description was read and verified by Lincoln's partner, William H. Herndon. The transformation of the office astounded a professional neighbor, Milton Hay, in whose office next door, young John Hay, who was to be one of Lincoln's private secretaries, was studying law and writing poems to pretty girls. John Hay, who was to be more important in Milton Littlefield's story even than his industrious brother, was neither then nor later one to clean up an office. Springfield itself seemed slovenly to John Hay. With some of the contempt for the countrified West which he had acquired at Brown University in Rhode Island, he described the Illinois capital as "a city combining the meanness of the North with the barbarism of the South." Nevertheless, the change John Littlefield wrought in the office, to which so many strangers would soon be coming as political pilgrims from the whole country, was dramatic.

"What's happened here?" the elder Hay demanded.

Lincoln seemed surprised. "Oh, nothing," he said. Then he pointed casually at Littlefield. "Only this young man has been cleaning up a little."

To Lincoln, a man whose own tall hat served as an adequate place for the filing of important papers, neatness seemed unimportant. He was more impressed when John was helpful in other ways. The tall politician had a way of suddenly seeking—and receiving—information from anyone at hand.

"Billy," he suddenly asked Herndon one day, "what's the meaning of antithesis?"

Herndon gave a definition and John ventured an answer, too.

"Mr. Lincoln, if you'll allow me, I will give you an example."

"All right, John, go ahead."

"Phillips says in his essay on Napoleon, 'A pretended patriot, he impoverished his country; a professed Catholic, he imprisoned the Pope.'"

John was not quoting the famous abolitionist Wendell Phillips but Charles Phillips, a notorious English lawyer and orator who had just died.

Lincoln regarded the young man with a good deal more surprise than when he had cleaned the room. Here was a young man who could express himself with something more than inkstands. And Lincoln responded to the discovery by talking with his student about more things than Blackstone and Kent. In a discussion of Hamlet, John remembered, Lincoln expressed his feeling that "the great beauty of Shakespeare was in the power and majesty of the lines" and that "even an indifferent actor could hold an audience by the power of the text itself."

There were many even in Illinois that year who thought that Lincoln as an actor was indifferent and unequal to any leading part in the American drama then unfolding. And as the Lincoln legend later grew there were to be more who felt that John's brother Milton became a sort of antithesis to the monumental figure of the martyred President. But in Illinois, in 1859, Milton was working even more directly than John with the forces which were to nominate Lincoln at Chicago the following summer. Around Springfield they did not get off to a very good start.

On September 27, 1859, Milton came to Springfield as a delegate from Jersey County to the Sixth Congressional District Republican Convention. John G. Nicolay, who like Hay was to be Lincoln's private secretary, "secretive, dependable, often carrying messages not to be written but whispered," was secretary of the convention. Milton was a member of the resolutions committee. The business of the convention was to select a nominee for the Congressional seat vacated by the death of the Democrat who had held Lincoln's old seat in the House. His death left the Illinois delegation evenly divided—four Democrats and four Republicans. The election of a Republican would show a rising Republican tide in Lincoln's own district. In the year before his nomination for the Presidency, however, that was not a prospect Republicans could confidently expect.

Milton joined in nominating his future Colonel, John M. Palmer, for the seat. That seemed a good choice in that time of political unrest and realignment. Palmer had been a well-known Democrat before opposition to the Kansas-Nebraska Bill placed him among those who played an important part in the formation of the Republican Party in Illinois. He was not optimistic when he undertook to make the race. Nevertheless, two weeks later he was on the stump, speaking in Milton's Jerseyville. Republicans hopefully believed he was making progress against his Democratic opponent, John A. McClernand, who supported Douglas' doctrine of popular sovereignty under which, Palmer insisted, "slavery would be introduced into all the territories." A growing number of Illinois people, old Democrats as well as old Whigs, opposed that. Then on October 17, five days after Palmer spoke in Jerseyville, violent news came over the telegraph from Harpers Ferry, Virginia.

Many Illinois people did not want slavery extended, but they had no taste whatever for settlement of the slavery issue with pikes and carbines, by bloodshed and violence. Old John Brown in Virginia was making the somber poetry to which, set to music, the North would soon march, but in Illinois that autumn, his raid, Palmer believed, "reversed the vote of the district." In swift revulsion the voters of the Sixth District turned against the Republicans, who seemed closer than the Democrats to abolitionist ardors and aberrations. Lincoln's candidate in his home district was beaten by four thousand votes. The Republicans did not carry a single county. Littlefield's Jersey went Democratic 725 to 452.

As one Jersey County Republican, Milton had too much company to be personally chagrined by the defeat. Furthermore, all friends of Lincoln were discovering that while John Brown had hurt them in the Sixth District of Illinois, he had seriously—as it proved fatally—wounded the candidacy of William H. Seward of New York, who had seemed far ahead in the race for the Republican Presidential nomination. A startled country, shocked by the news from Harpers Ferry, stiffened against Seward's prophecy of an "irrepressible conflict."

Hardly noticing the Republican defeat at Lincoln's own door, more people began to turn toward the Illinoisan who commended John Brown's courage and unselfishness but rebuked his resort to violence. Steadily around Lincoln then were growing those elements which he described as "strange and discordant, gathered from the four winds" which made the strength of the Republican Party and made him its leader. They called Lincoln far to speak; they came from far off to the office with the inkspot on the wall. For war and politics such diverse groups were creating the irrepressible combination of idealists and industrialists, cranks and crusaders, passionate young men and tough practical politicians.

The Littlefield brothers were only minor figures in that swelling company. John left a record of his composition, under Lincoln's direction, of a speech which he delivered "over fifty times" in the campaigning which carried his mentor to the Presidency. ("That's a good point, John. . . . That's very good, indeed.") It seems highly probable that Milton was in Decatur on May 9, 1860, when John Hanks brought in the fence rails, tied with flags and streamers, and Old Abe (he was fifty-one then and had not begun to grow his familiar beard) was formally launched as Illinois' Rail Splitter candidate for the Republican nomination. Serious young John was with Lincoln on May 18, when the candidate walked from his home to his office, then to the telegraph office and finally to the editorial rooms of the friendly Illinois *State Journal* where the news of his nomination in the Wigwam at Chicago was received.

That was a hot summer. Days on end contained the "torrid fervors" which had displeased John Hay the summer before despite the fact that the farmers whom he called "the Aborigines" praised them as pushing up the corn and the wheat. In 1860, even Hay paid more attention to politics of increasing temperature than to the sun which baked the prairies. The days passed like the procession of prominent strangers to the office, provided for the grave Presidential candidate in the State Capitol, which had no ink spot on its walls. And if once Hay had thought that there is "no land so sad as this," he had opportunity to change his mind in the tumult and the hurrahs which brought the campaign to crescendo in Springfield in the great rally of August 8. Springfield was a tumultuous sea of people then, but its sources were a thousand great and little towns and the countryside of farms and fields around them where the corn and the wheat were left lonely with the sun.

The crowd grew from such places as little Jerseyville where, with

Milton Littlefield as Captain, the Jersey County Wide Awakes assembled on the evening before. The Wide Awakes, as the organizations of young, high-spirited Republicans were called, were organized all over the North that summer. Their drills, lit by their own torches in night parades, were a part of every Republican demonstration. One contemporary estimate put their number at four hundred thousand. Their activity led Seward to speak of the Republicans, who had preferred Lincoln's leadership to his, as "a party chiefly of young men." And in the mounting national tension there were charges from below the Ohio that these marching young men constituted a corps ready, with the election of Lincoln, to coerce the South.

Captain Littlefield's Jerseyville Company of Wide Awakes spent all the hot night getting ready. In their stiff-crowned caps and oilcloth capes they moved in last-minute practice drills. They tested their torches. They made good-natured tumult in the streets of Jerseyville all night long. And in the moonlight they rode in two-horse wagons through the orchards and the corn twenty miles to the nearest railroad at Shipman in Macoupin County. There they woke up another town while they waited in the dawn for the long special train to take them to Springfield.

A blast from a brass cannon on the rear car announced the approach of the train which had been made up in Alton. Other Wide Awakes, already on board, shouted welcome and the Jersey County boys hurried aboard. The train was composed chiefly of flat cars, forty-eight in all, on which temporary seats had been placed under makeshift frameworks covered with green brush to give at least a semblance of protection from sun, storm or cinders. The sides were open to the prairies and, though not all the Wide Awakes got seats, none fell off the train. From the open sides of the train they shouted, till the dust caked their throats, at the people and places they passed.

As they approached Springfield the dust thickened on the roads from the movement of other people going by buggy, in wagons, on horseback, in anything that would haul in the same direction. Whole families rolled toward the capital. Rural fife-and-drum corps marched beside them. There were carryalls full of young women wearing bright-colored sashes and liberty caps. The Daughters of

Abraham were as enthusiastic if a little less noisy than the Wide Awakes. They added prettiness and color to the multitude of fifty thousand people which converged upon the city of Candidate Lincoln—a town which on quieter days counted only 9,320 inhabitants. The Wide Awakes contributed a disciplined, marching irrepressible fervor.

Captain Littlefield's Jerseyville Company was, of course, only one in the parading in Springfield. Among the hundreds of other companies in Springfield that day, however, it had a unique experience. Furthermore, the event had an historian. In a speech before the Jersey County Historical Society in 1916, H. W. Pogue, of Jerseyville, who had become an elderly and respected judge, recalled that incandescent day of his youth.

"We arrived at Springfield about 11 o'clock," he said, "where we found the streets filled with a moving procession of those who had arrived earlier. An opening was at once made for our company to join the parade, keeping with us our torches. After thus marching for about two hours, we came to a point previously arranged for us to drop out and leave our torches, with instructions to meet there in time to join the evening parade."

Though the loud night and the hot train journey were behind them and the great day half over, there was no recollection of fatigue in Judge Pogue's story.

"After this," he recalled, "for a while, it was every fellow for himself. I first satisfied my hunger, which was readily done, as lunch stands were to be found at every street corner. I learned that speaking was going on at the Fair Grounds, near the outskirts of the city, and headed that way to investigate. Arriving at the Fair Grounds, I found there were thousands of people, covering acres of ground. Speaking from half a dozen stands, located at different places on the grounds, was in progress. Prominent speakers were there from various states. At some stands there were two speakers, speaking at the same time, one to the crowds on the east and another to those on the west."

Young Pogue pushed through the crowds, sampled the speeches and then made his way back to the agreed place of meeting at the State House from which "led by Captain Littlefield we marched to Lincoln's residence. . . . Mr. Lincoln appeared in the front yard when, passing by him in single file, Captain Littlefield introduced us, one by one, when Mr. Lincoln gave us each a cordial shake of the hand, the radiant smile never leaving his face."

Pogue was pleased and surprised by the event. And he was still impressed half a century later.

"There were many companies of 'Wide Awakes' in Springfield that day," he said, "but so far as I know, ours was the only one to meet Mr. Lincoln by appointment. I afterward learned that Captain Littlefield had a brother in Mr. Lincoln's law office and it was through him that we were thus favored."

Pogue, on that day crowded with vehicles and livestock as well as men, may have put the cart before the horse. John was in the law offices of Lincoln and Herndon because Captain Littlefield asked Lincoln to receive him there. And on the day of the rally there was another incident which indicates that Milton could approach Lincoln without benefit of brother John. It put together the political and the sentimental, a combination from which neither Abraham Lincoln nor Milton Littlefield ever escaped.

Five days after the great rally Lincoln sent a note to a Mrs. Snedeker in Jerseyville.

"My dear madam," he wrote.

> Your kind note of the 8th, presenting a box of fine peaches, with the compliments of the "Daughters of Abraham," was duly received; and for all which, on behalf of yourself and them, please accept my grateful acknowledgments.
>
> Yours very truly,
> A. LINCOLN

Milton clipped the letter from *The Prairie State* and pasted it in his scrapbook. Beside the letter he wrote a note about his sweetheart: "This basket of fruit was carried by Miss Anna E. Shull and by her delivered to Mr. Lincoln in person."

So blond young Anna received Mr. Lincoln's personal smiling thanks before he sent the stilted, formal note to the undoubtedly more formidable Mrs. Snedeker. And Anna and the peaches and Mr. Lincoln were all important to Milton that year. He not only marched with his Wide Awakes. He drove Anna in a buggy on happy days from peach bloom to beyond peach harvest. Also, he marched into his thirties in a month in which Milton's recent candidate, John Palmer, a politician not given to poetry, said the waving golden wheat was the most beautiful sight he had ever seen in his life. It must have seemed less important to Milton that it was 1860 than that he was thirty years old—and thirty in little Jerseyville away from the rivers and twenty miles from the railroad.

When the hazes of autumn came in Illinois with Republican victory, Southern warnings that war would follow seemed no more worthy of attention than the honking of the wild geese headed south again. If cotton was king, the corn had its lieges, too. Even in bigger Springfield, when the dust of all campaigning had settled, the *State Journal* said that the town was "as quiet as a young lady who has just found out that she is in love." And lovers in Illinois were not thinking of war. Not even Lincoln, who had then a disturbing dream about himself as a man with two faces, could look forward to the second face of war called Reconstruction.

CHAPTER III

March to Shiloh

LESS THAN A YEAR after the great Springfield rally Milton marched again out of Jerseyville at the head of another company. Some of the volunteers who followed him in that May of 1861 were the same young men who had worn the regalia of the Wide Awakes the previous August. Their spirits were almost as gay. The blooming of the Jersey County orchards added a special, festival touch to their departure for a war which was not expected to last much longer than a political campaign. Among the Wide Awakes the march seemed part of a determination to enforce the victory they had won the November before.

That victory still seemed precarious. Before the President they had elected slipped into Washington amid threats that he would never live to be inaugurated, one of his militant friends had proposed the secret mobilization of the Wide Awakes in Washington to confound Southern conspirators in the capital.

"Would it not be well," wrote Major David Hunter, West Point graduate and earnest Republican, "to have a hundred thousand Wide Awakes wend their way quietly to Washington, during the first three days of March; taking with them their capes and caps? By a *coup-de-main* we could arm them in Washington."

Lincoln had rejected the radical proposal, but he had taken Hunter with him on his train. Unfortunately, the determined Major, without Wide Awakes to help him, had had his collar bone dislocated in Buffalo while trying to stem the surge of loyal crowds about the President-elect. The crowds had seemed sinister in their silence only after Lincoln reached New York City. From Pennsylvania Pinkerton detectives helped guard him on the rest of the journey. So no Wide Awakes were required, but in hundreds of towns Wide Awakes were ready. And when on April 15, after the firing on Fort Sumter, Lincoln called for troops, the response came first from these ardent young men. Within less than a month, on May 9, Littlefield led his company out of Jerseyville, though at almost thirty-one he might, without criticism, have stayed at home. Many younger men, particularly Democrats, stayed behind.

"Nearly the entire population of the place turned out to see them off, and bid them God-speed," said *The Prairie State*. The near-by *Alton Telegraph* added: "The Captain is a brave and noble fellow, and Illinois will furnish but few men who have energy and capacity for accomplishing more for their country than he. Jerseyville has reason to be proud of this company and of its whole-souled Commander."

Beyond the applause and the farewells of Jerseyville, Littlefield's company was mustered in at Jacksonville, as Company F, 14th Illinois Infantry, under the command of Colonel John M. Palmer, whom Milton had unsuccessfully tried to elect to Congress two years before. Undoubtedly the regiment needed the brief training it got there, though some of its officers and men had served in the German and the British armies. Undoubtedly, too, its men enjoyed the ceremonial occasions in which they took part: the celebration of the Fourth of July, which seemed more than ever important in a divided Union, and the impressive funeral given Stephen A. Douglas, who had died in the midst of his last great campaign to hold the Union and particularly Illinois strong and united behind his old adversary Lincoln.

There were lesser such occasions. Milton was chosen by the ladies of Tallula, Menard County—as ladies so often did choose him—to present a flag to their Company E, captained by a former English soldier who in service was also often in his cups. Such a presentation was an emotional ceremony, many times and in many places enthusiastically duplicated that spring and summer, North and South. The ladies were very serious in very gay clothes. Their hats sat perkily above moist eyes. And Milton, whose new blue uniform seemed specially designed to emphasize the grace of his tapering figure, clicked his heels together and bowed like an impresario. He spoke the kind of oratory the ladies and soldiers required. He could scarcely find in the English vocabulary, he said, words for the occasion, but he turned neatly to the Latin fable of the Gracchi for the mothers of Menard who, he declared, had each come to say to the Union, "These are my jewels."

"Fellow soldiers, can we give up America?" he demanded, and the soldiers and their mothers, sisters, sweethearts cried back in chorus, "No, no, no!"

"Can that dear old flag be torn from us with impunity?" he asked again, and this time answered, too: "No, fellow soldiers, no. Let us meet the traitor, and swear that he shall meet the traitor's doom."

In Missouri, to which the 14th Illinois was dispatched and where it was sometimes difficult to tell the Gracchi from the traitors, the regiment's experience was hardly heroic. A careful diarist in the organization recorded the rout which ensued when a "green German" bayoneted a skunk. A deer was felled for a feast. A lonely soldier wrote home while his comrades caroused around a fire made from beer barrels from the sutler's quarters. But soldiers, singing "Nellie Monroe" and other catchy songs, lifted occasionally, in a combination of homesickness and patriotism, the song of home:

> Bear to the prairies of the west
> The echoes of our joys,
> The prayers that spring from every breast,
> God bless you, Illinois.

Littlefield's baritone always added much to such song. His good nature served the morale of his comrades. The time was for him, however, also one in which he improved relationships which were valuable in terms of his future service. At Tipton, where after the war the one-time Confederate guerrilla, Jesse James, kept a livery stable, Milton met David Hunter, who, in the little more than half a year since he had proposed his *coup-de-main* with the Wide

Awakes in Washington, had become a general. Despite Hunter's dislocated collar bone he had been able to write on Lincoln's undisturbed inauguration day asking for such a promotion—and on the grounds that even in the army Republicans should get the first chance at such commissions. Hunter waited for his answer in the White House itself where he slept on the floor of the East Room as commander of a motley, loyal Presidential guard. Lincoln liked him. He put Hunter on his "list of officers I wish to remember, when I make appointments for officers of the regular Army." In May he made the faithful Hunter a brigadier general of volunteers. As such he fought and was badly wounded at Bull Run. Then he was sent to relieve the blustering and beleaguered John C. Frémont in Missouri.

Apparently Littlefield had met Hunter before. Certainly he was on close terms with him before Hunter, on November 2, officially relieved Frémont in the border state bog of disloyalty, politics and frustration. The Captain and the General seemed to have little in common then except their ardent Republicanism and their feeling that they were both men in the inner corps of loyalty to Lincoln. Littlefield then, was dark-haired, ready with jest and song. He looked, sometimes impatiently, to the future. Hunter, at fifty-eight, when Littlefield met him at Tipton had a dyed mustache and wore a dark brown wig. He was also, as Secretary of the Navy Gideon Welles later described him, a "violently earnest" man.

In the light of Lincoln's, Hunter's and Littlefield's later views, it was strange that one factor in Frémont's fate had been the furore he aroused by an order that slaves taken as the property of secessionists should be free. Lincoln promptly canceled that order, though the abolitionists loved Frémont for it. Hunter, too, was to become such a headlong abolitionist that his soldiers called him Black Dave. Lincoln had to slow him down, too, but did so with a gentler hand. That came later on the South Atlantic shore where the President sent Littlefield to Hunter as an agent and symbol of altering Presidential ideas about the Negro and the war.

Littlefield was involved in no such problems in Missouri in 1861. He was too far below the high feuding to have taken any significant part in it. Two weeks before Hunter formally relieved the furious Frémont, however, Milton was serving ostensibly as

Hunter's emissary, but he was also engaged on an important errand of his own. Movement even through Union lines was not easy at the time. Frémont had his pickets out not only to watch for Confederates but also to keep away any messengers who might bring the orders for his dismissal from Washington. Milton always kept the pass he received at that time from Hunter:

> Tipton, Missouri,
> October 18, 1861
> Pass Captain Littlefield of the 14th Illinois Reg. to Saint Louis, and back to this place, on public service
> D. Hunter
> Maj General

As always, Milton moved with dispatch. He had a gift for finding good horses. He liked to get into the cab and encourage railroad engineers to faster speeds. Next day he was in St. Louis. He knew the city well. He had friends there among the Wide Awakes who had been armed the previous May to prevent the seizure of the government arsenal by Secessionist militia. Those Wide Awakes, formed into so-called Home Guards, had done their job almost too well. By coincidence the men who had to make an army out of a mob had observed them. W. T. Sherman, then running a street car company, and U. S. Grant, back in a rumpled blue uniform, were spectators when those Home Guards, many of them Germans, fired into street crowds killing twenty-eight men, women and children. St. Louis was safe for the Union but resentful in it. Division was almost as sharp between Frémont's friends and his enemies clustered about the bar of the Planter's Hotel as between Union and Confederate forces in the field. Milton did not linger among them.

In Jerseyville, two days after he left Tipton, he took as his "amiable bride" the same Anna Shull who by his arrangement had presented the peaches to Lincoln. Indeed, the story of the mission on which Hunter sent him is contained not in collected military records but in the report of his wedding in *The Prairie State.*

He had been sent, that nuptial item said, "to procure new and improved arms for his regiment (the 14th) which had long been promised them." However, "finding that he would be obliged to remain in the city a day or two, he took the opportunity to come up here and provide himself with arms of a still different character from those ordered for his regiment. He was married on Sunday evening and returned to St. Louis with his bride on Monday. She has since returned to remain with friends in this place, while her husband is away fighting the enemies of our beloved country. That he may be spared and permitted to return to his young wife at the close of the war, covered with honors for gallant and meritorious conduct, is our earnest wish."

The gallant Captain's bride was amiable but not so young. She was twenty-six when he came to carry her off to that brief honeymoon in St. Louis. But she was extremely pretty. In a photograph taken about that time she wore a brown taffeta dress, trimmed with bands of velvet on its full sleeves, which emphasized her slender waist and full bosom. A lace collar framed her throat beneath a strong chin and a mouth both sensitive and firm. Her straight nose seemed shaped for ready sniffing in disdain or suspicion. But her shy blue eyes were arched with wide thin brows. Her long light brown hair was parted in the middle and pulled back into heavy braids which half covered her ears.

She looked both amiable and a little frightened, capable of taking care of herself but as if she had suffered—and might suffer again—from a wounded pride or a hurt of the spirit. Obviously she was a woman who would be both fiercely and silently loyal. She could be quickly passionate and easily injured, tart-spoken and withdrawn. In the modest photograph with the flowing taffeta dress covering and suggesting her figure, it is easy, a hundred years later, to realize what a delight Anna must have been in the lace and frills of a bride. Yet, the picture gives the feeling, too, that she would never dispense with the gold chain she wore at her thin waist like one on which a lady might keep her own keys.

She was a native of Illinois. On her mother's side her people, like Milton's, had been in America a long time. The family of her mother, Harriett Matilda McGill, was descended from a Thomas Lowery, a younger son of a Lord Shane, who had come to America from Ireland in 1737. Harriett McGill's father was Dr. William McGill, of Hunterdon County, New Jersey, "a popular physician, a large portly person of dignified and gentlemanly deportment." Less is known about the bride's father, Alfred Shull (a name which apparently had progressed from Schultz to Schull to Shull). He was a native of New York but was of the same stock as the grape-growing Germans in Illinois.

The Shulls had moved west before Anna was born and Shull died not long after. Anna's mother married again and apparently moved back east. Anna was brought up with a well-loved half-sister, Matilda Harbert, whose home in Philadelphia was often later to be a refuge while Milton was off at war, or later still on the more frequent errands of Reconstruction and speculation. Other relatives remained in Jerseyville, and it was with them that Anna was staying when she met the eligible Littlefield living alone, though seldom lonely, at the hotel.

In her quietness she seemed in many ways when she came back from St. Louis a strange bride for the outgoing, easy-giving Captain. Apparently then and later she had a gift for waiting in serenity. And she seems always to have been the sort of woman for whom such a man would wish to make a rich, secure world though he often left her insecure while he sought it. He was seldom hesitant about the things he sought, and always sought with high hope and in high spirits, sometimes with a very high hand. Without lamenting, she accepted that. Also, without lamenting, she accepted what she had noticed in St. Louis and had known before, that wherever her Captain went other women's eyes followed his figure across a street or across a room.

He stood on the dock watching as her boat moved upstream from St. Louis, but he did not return to his regiment in central Missouri on any such solemn note as the "earnest wishes" *The Prairie State* sounded for him and his amiable bride. He was incapable of loneliness. Indeed, less than a month later in the village of Buffalo, just off the strategic road from St. Louis to Springfield, he showed himself in the mood for merriment even at the expense of his Colonel. Probably he did not write Anna about it, but the incident was recorded in shocked terms by another and different ex-schoolteacher, Lieutenant William Camm, of Company K, whose diary provides a day-by-day story of the regiment. Camm was a gentle Englishman, a punctilious soldier, faithful to the sweetheart he had left behind: "I'll take a peep at Kitty's picture and then mend my pants before taps." He painted in oils, kept flowers in his tent, and in later life became an ardent advocate of the single tax. In the South he caught and kept glittering lizards as pets in his tent. Also, he was an able soldier with some past experience as a drill master.

"We are camped just south of Buffalo," Camm wrote. "At dusk quite a lot of women came to visit our camp. They were all single but one. Our string band gave us some delicious music, and when the ladies got ready to leave, before tattoo, Palmer told us to show our gallantry by escorting the ladies home and got his own hat."

Colonel Palmer, who had started out as an itinerant clock salesman in rural Illinois, was a man of dignity who was to become a governor of Illinois and a candidate for President of the United States. A month after the visit of the ladies at Buffalo, he was made a brigadier general. But that night he allowed his vigilance to lapse when he went to get his hat.

"Captain Littlefield," recorded Camm, "constituted himself master of ceremonies, selected his own and our ladies and left the married woman for the colonel to escort and carry the baby. When he realized the situation he exclaimed, 'Well, young man, this is a pretty how-de-do.' But he took the baby in his arms and toted it like the good, fatherly man he is."

And Camm added for the proprieties he maintained even in his diary, "My partner was a quiet sensible girl of 18."

Colonel Palmer may have taken the incident only as a good, fatherly man. He was also a man stiffly sensitive about the dignity of his own position, who later resigned from the army in a huff because General Sherman in the midst of battle directed him to take orders from an officer who Palmer believed was subordinate to him. The how-de-do that Littlefield played on him at Buffalo may have had nothing to do with a letter which the Colonel wrote soon afterward to the hard-drinking and well-loved Governor Richard Yates of Illinois stating that Littlefield had not properly discharged his duties as Captain. Palmer's specific charges are not available. Milton, however, wrote the Governor from Camp Lamine Bridge, Missouri, on Christmas Eve that he had talked with Palmer and that when the Colonel saw the Governor again "he will make the case seem different."

Apparently Palmer did, for Littlefield kept his captaincy in the

14th Illinois and when a year later he was promoted to Lieutenant Colonel in another regiment, Governor Yates accepted his suggestion as to his successor. Also, if his behavior at Buffalo troubled Palmer, it did not prevent Milton's appointment as a deputy provost marshal of General Hunter's forces around Springfield less than a month later—an experience which may have prompted his later appointment to a similar post by General Sherman. When Littlefield wrote Yates that Colonel Palmer was appeased, the Colonel had become a general and had more concerns than seeing the ladies home, getting his hat, or the memory of that occasion. So had Littlefield. For him and others of the 14th Illinois, the camping, singing, practical-joking war came to an abrupt and bloody end along the Tennessee River in April 1862, when they moved by pink peach blossoms again to the crimson field of Shiloh.

The regiment, moving from Missouri, had arrived just too late to take part in the toughening General Grant's "unconditional surrender" investment of Fort Donelson in February. But it was part of the armada of thirty thousand men in seventy steamboats which, with flags flying, bands playing, men cheering, moved southward and upstream on the Tennessee River toward the bloody rendezvous at Shiloh. On the voyage Lew Wallace of Indiana, the General who was to become the author of *Ben Hur,* wrote of "the scurrying winds and the pearl-sky with clouds of sulphurous smoke." The rains which aided navigation stilled the cheering. The quieter fleet moved between more silent shores. The literary General described the beauty of the yellow stream, the rocky bluffs and the wooded shores. He was more impressed by the sullenly still and empty cabins and houses and towns they steamed past. "Desertion was over them all." And between the lonely shores Wallace wrote his weird feeling that "there should be somebody somewhere on the shores to enjoy the wonderful spectacle we were offering."

The silence ended soon enough. The Tennessee was still in flood when the 14th Illinois and other units climbed the slippery bluffs at Pittsburg Landing and went into muddy camp not far from Shiloh Church. And in complacent camp there they received in surprise the onset of the Confederates in the most sanguinary battle ever fought on the American continent until that time. The desperately won Union victory there is clear now, though the South long held an emotional memory in an often-sung ballad of "the vict'ry won at Shiloh." The North was better justified in its version that "the South never smiled after Shiloh."

There were to be no more Bull Runs. But General Grant came in those two bloody days to the grim conviction that no swift suppression of rebellion could be contemplated. Only "conquest" would suffice. Above all, perhaps, the battle proved that Southern contempt for Northern courage needed revision. No Southerner ever afterward suggested that a lady's thimble would hold all the blood the Yankees would spill. There was death enough and gallantry on both sides. Any one man's courage in that red tide—even Grant's leadership on crutches or Sherman's heedless bravery at the front of the fighting—was only an item. But on those two April days Milton Littlefield behaved with a gallantry which no charges of misdeeds afterward could ever erase.

Milton never directly claimed heroism for himself, though he wrote Anna a letter full of pride for the conduct of his company. Long afterward, when he made a detailed address about the fighting in the West, some of his hearers complained that he put too little about himself into the story. Soon after Shiloh, however, he was insistent that the 14th Illinois and Company F get the credit he believed they deserved. He wrote letters to editors whose reporters had assigned to other regiments the rôle the 14th Illinois had played. He was particularly disturbed by a report in *The Chicago Tribune*, reprinted in *The Missouri Democrat*, about the visit to the front after the battle by Governor Yates of Illinois. He was angered by what he declined to believe were merely reporters' "innocent blunders":

"For instance, the visit of Governor Yates to an Illinois regiment just after the fight; the presentation of their flag, pierced in some thirty places by grapeshot and bullets; the fall of their brave color bearer—Fletcher Ebey, of Winchester, Illinois; the soul-stirring speech of the Governor to this regiment, of whose number one-third of all engaged in action had been killed or wounded; the earnest cheering that followed the speech, why was all this attributed to the Illinois Twenty-seventh, when it all belonged to the Illinois Fourteenth Regiment?"

The proof was available, an erring editor was informed: "In

Frank Leslie's Illustrated News of April 26th, is a sketch of perhaps the finest charge made during the battle of Shiloh, when on Monday, April 7th, at 3 P.M., the Illinois Fourteenth and Fifteenth Regiments and the Indiana Twenty-fifth and Twenty-seventh regiments . . . were led on the double quick across an open field about a quarter of a mile in the face of a battery pouring its constant fire of grapeshot—supported by a vastly superior force of infantry to the one advancing, besides a long line of rebel cavalry whose carbines rang a terrible unison to the music of our muskets. Yet on and on our brave men went as into the open jaws of death, until the enemy wavered, fell back, fled precipitately. Battery, infantry, cavalry—all routed and driven before that charge."

Formally, Brigadier General James C. Veach of Indiana, the commander of the brigade in which the 14th fought, praised the regiment for its part in the "gallant charge on Monday evening which drove the enemy beyond our lines and closed the struggle of that memorable day." And Milton's Colonel cited him as one of those who "distinguished themselves on numerous occasions during the battle." Less formal testimony was given by Sergeant J. A. Davis of the 14th who, on leave soon after the battle, told *The Alton Telegraph* of the "undaunted courage of this whole regiment, and especially of the daring gallantry of Captain Littlefield, of Company F, who stood erect in front of his men, during the whole engagement, but escaped all injury, except having about three inches torn from the left shoulder of his coat, by a ball from the enemy."

There is no record that Sherman formed his opinion that Milton was a "good officer" while the fighting went on at Shiloh. That testimonial came later and in terms of activities which often plagued Sherman most. But for Littlefield the quieting of the guns at Shiloh marked the beginning of activities in those phases of the conflict which, more than battles, shaped the peace beyond it.

Illinois men saw the South first only after Shiloh. The voyage to the battleground had been through the closed corridor of the river valley. It was across the river that Palmer, as the General he had become, remembered first seeing a vagabond swarm of slaves looking toward the army as toward freedom. It was not the last sight Illinois men were to see of such congregations, pitiful and farcical, jubilant and forlorn. But there were other things to see and try to understand in a land which was in so many ways both familiar and strange, offensive and alluring.

Captain Littlefield wrote only of the battle in his letter to Anna. He was too concerned with justice for his men in history to keep a diary of the little things of which the history in which he participated was made. That task was accomplished by the scrupulous Camm, now a lieutenant colonel. Homesick as that precise ex-Britisher often was for his Kitty back in Scott County, Illinois, Camm found not only a confusing South but an enchantress South as well. In the same month as Shiloh, on the road to Corinth, Mississippi, he had shaken off the fevers of the region, to ride into the woods to the tent of General Palmer. It was in that tent, long before Lincoln reached any such decision, that Palmer showed Camm "a long letter" he had written to his friend, the President, "urging him to enlist Negro troops." Camm was sympathetic, but he gave much more room in his diary to the blossoming South around him.

"I had been told," he wrote, "that the flowers of the South had no scent and the birds no song, but the tent was sweetly odorous with flowers and outside the birds seemed to be trying to see which could sing loudest and sweetest."

He knew that he might be misled by beauty: "Old fields, exhausted under slave labor, are overgrown with broomsedge, and look through the dark, green woods, like ripe harvest fields in Illinois."

He did not really fear that he would be fooled. Not by birds or flowers or fields—certainly not by the Southern people. They no longer hid as they had along the shores of the Tennessee, but showed themselves in a variety almost more startling than the facts about bird song and flowers. They made no such simple population of masters and slaves as many Northern boys had been led to expect. The brick houses with Greek Revival columns, box-hedged gardens and the avenues of trees were no more typical than the cabins, even hovels, in which so many white people lived. There were saucy slatterns as well as decorous, crinolined belles. Men wore dirty shirts as well as gleaming starched ones. There was surprising, even sniveling, hospitality as well as hostility. But of one general Southern characteristic, Camm was apparently as sure as some Southerners had been about their conviction that Northerners would not fight. Camm was sadly sure that in sharpness no Rebel could be a Yankee's match.

Camm was a little sad about that. It had troubled him in Missouri when he noticed that his comrades seemed to lose any sense of the sanctity of property when its owners might possibly be an enemy. On the march to Corinth he approved General Sherman's efforts to teach his men the exact lines to follow in connection with the "delicate right" of foraging. They could appropriate hay, fodder and firewood, but to take a hen, Sherman told them, was "as much stealing as though committed in our own country." The boys heard his orders, but apparently they continued to capture such Southern hens as did not surrender voluntarily. Futhermore, they seemed to take a particular delight in stealing from the sutlers with their own troops. They took special pride in trading with enemy civilians who were stubborn in a bargain even in the midst of an occupying army.

"Some of the people here," Camm recorded sadly, "refused our treasury notes, but accept any kind of Confederate shinplasters with readiness. The result is they are badly imposed upon, for some parties in St. Louis supply our men with some imitations of Confederate scrip and bills at $1.00 on the $100.00."

(Camm was obviously unaware that such counterfeiting in the Confederacy could be based on high moral grounds. One of Littlefield's Reconstruction associates was General Byron Laflin of a papermaking family in the Berkshire Hills of Massachusetts. There, while the war waged, Federal authorities discovered that one of the paper mills was making bank-note paper watermarked "C.S.A." But it turned out—or the manufacturer claimed—that he was working with Union sympathizers who planned to destroy the value of Southern currency by flooding the rebellious region with counterfeit bills. Undoubtedly he found patriotic soldiers ready to assist in the process. His excuse was at least as plausible as in some other cases in which the law was broken for the most patriotic reasons, according to those who gave them.)

Not all Southerners were as simple as those who preferred false notes, then or later. And in East Tennessee and Mississippi many became sharper fast. Some, indeed, lost little bargains to make greater ones. There were partnerships in trade which disregarded the division in the nation. Some Union boys, like any other soldiers far from home, swapped their pay for the souvenirs of a war which even after Shiloh they hoped would be over soon. Not all the white women they met were as respectable even as those who came out at dusk to visit the camp in Buffalo, Missouri. A colored girl, who gave herself in gratitude for freedom, did not reject the gift of an army blanket she had lain on. Indeed, if the increasing swarm of Negroes, male and female, all came singing "Jubilee," many of them had fingers still sticky among their deliverers. Some even looted the Yankees in connivance with their masters. They laughed together about it.

Colonel Camm only freely took items which enriched his diary. On the zigzagging march from Corinth to Memphis he stopped at "a citizen's house" near La Grange, Tennessee, and wrote of the forest around him, of the gums, the magnolia, the catalpa, cypress and pine. The huckleberries, dewberries and blackberries were superabundant. He made a special item on June twenty-second of the first mimosa he had seen in full bloom, at Lamar on the march to Holly Springs.

Not all was beauty. There was also heat and storm: "the atmospheric phenomena of this part of the Lord's truck patch would fool the man that made the thunder." It could subdue even the army of William Tecumseh Sherman who was taking command of Memphis. The General had splendid plans for the entry of his troops. But on July 21, when General Stephen Augustus Hurlbut's division, including the 14th Illinois, marched into that city, the sun was too much even for the soldiers who had taken the fiercest heat the Confederates could give at Shiloh.

"The 14th leading straggled in, route step, down the gutter on the shady side of Main Street," Camm wrote, "and then had to stop to cool. Some citizens waited on us with water in front of their residences. One lady asked me to dismount and come in, and she gave me water, clean towels to wash and wipe my face and neck.

"Indeed, it was all a reverse of the spitefulness and insult we had been told to expect. Small British flags, or shields, were shown at some business places."

It did not occur apparently to Camm that Southerners could sing as well as birds, when necessary.

He spent a day bathing and resting in camp in shady woods on the high east bank of the Mississippi. Then he went into town and had a melainotype of himself made for Kitty. Next day he and other officers went to the theatre. Then his rest and ease were disturbed.

"The officer we always welcome most came to camp today. The paymaster," he wrote, but fell into melancholy questioning.

"Isn't it queer that those who get the highest pay quibble most about anything that seems to be against them?

"What is there in the conditions under which we live that makes some men, so many, love money more than country?"

He did not identify the men whose avarice disturbed him. He was highly conscious of his own righteousness, however, and disturbed about more things than the love of money at the time.

"It seems," he wrote, "that Captain Bryant and Littlefield had preferred some sort of charges against me, but General Hurlbut burned them while making some pointed, if not to say profane remarks. No officer here can do his duty without incurring the enmity of such men."

Camm made no record as to what the charges were. Thomas J. Bryant since the beginning of the war had been Captain of Company D, from Greene County which adjoined Littlefield's Jersey. General Hurlbut, though he became the first commander of the Grand Army of the Republic, was as soldier and, later, as Illinois politician something less than impeccable in his official and personal behavior. He undoubtedly swore as Camm said. But the better established fact is that a week later, obviously with his approval, General Sherman named Littlefield Assistant Provost Marshal of Memphis, where the love of money was as real as the fevered meeting there beside the muddy river of embargoed Southern cotton and eager Yankee gold.

CHAPTER IV

Summer in Memphis

IN THE MEMPHIS heat, when Milton marched with his company to the cooler Mississippi bluffs, traders were already established buying cotton on Federal permits for New England mill owners as eager for the bales as the Illinois troops were for the shade. In the bar of the Gayoso Hotel the biggest speculators spent money freely on luckier, higher officers of William Tecumseh Sherman's new army of occupancy. Such cool hospitality was as welcome as the paymasters always were to young soldiers getting fourteen dollars a month and ready for the chance to spend it in a night. Soon after Sherman's arrival the paymasters and the traders both turned money loose in the river town like high water after drought. Milton Littlefield had special opportunity to watch that process and its effects. General Sherman, whose incessantly flashing light gray eyes were sometimes blind to things he did not want to see, reported on one simple aspect of the torrent.

"You may have been troubled," he wrote to his superior, General Grant, whom he had succeeded in the command at Memphis, "at hearing reports of drunkenness here. There was some after payday, but generally all is as quiet and orderly here as possible. I traverse the city every day and night, and assert that Memphis is and has been as orderly a city as St. Louis, Cincinnati or New York."

Grant at Corinth, Mississippi, and everybody else in the Union armies in Mississippi and Tennessee had heard reports of a great Memphis payday brawl. That spree became a part of the folklore of the army like the Tennessee quick-step which served until after Appomattox as the name for diarrhea. But the greatest debauch was not one of young men in liquor. Its effects lasted longer even than the hangover of a whole army. Memphis provided the original scene and design for the corruption of North and South together. It became, the Confederate historian Clifford Dowdey said, with some exaggeration of an overrun town of 22,600 people, "about the most splendid of all the oases which the Union kept for its people in the South." It was, too, a place of power in a hurry, noisy with the whistles of big steamers, the bells of heavy supply trains, the knocking of dray wheels and the rattle of omnibuses over the rough streets. Also, the city on the bluffs became a capital of accepted intersectional cheating in areas where the intoxication of arbitrary power met the effective shrewdness of supposedly defenseless people. It was also an outpost where the demands of respectability in the distance seemed to justify every depravity on the scene.

In such a city Milton rode with special powers. As Sherman's Assistant Provost Marshal, he often traversed the city with the General who reported on its good order to Grant. In the seldom breaking heat and easily stirred dust, they rode from the camps of the troops and the makeshift huts of the runaway slaves on the city's weed-grown margins to the magnificent spectacle of the Mississippi River before the Gayoso Hotel on Front Street. The streets were "navel deep in dust," reported William Howard Russell of the *London Times*.

Littlefield left no record of his impressions of his rides with Sherman through the dust to the river. But to the General with whom he rode, the Mississippi, stretching wide to the brown and green sandbar of the Arkansas shore, was the symbol of the nation's inescapable union. "The spinal column of America," Sherman called it. The metaphor was appealing but a little too erect. The stream could float a corpse or cotton—often both. And, as officers like Littlefield learned, not all that came down the river represented the idealism of the North, nor was mixed only with the chivalry of the South. The muddy, miasmic stream was also the great gut of the continent, carrying the poisons of intersectional hungers and twisting in all its peristaltic coils.

Sherman confronted the river town as commander—even, as his biographer Lloyd Lewis suggested, as prophet. Littlefield, with the dust on his face emphasizing the strong, white teeth of his smile, had a junior officer's view of it. Its encamped and idle soldiers outnumbered the sullenly defiant or deviously compliant citizens. Sometimes the natives were less disturbing than the Northern civilians who had joined them. Russell saw in the crowds a "strange kaleidoscope of negroes and whites of the extremes of civilization." There was, he said, "a nomad drift into and out of the place, which abounds in haunts for Bohemians, drinking, dancing saloons, and gaming rooms." Rowdies remained who had riotously ruled between effective Confederate and Union control. The decorated vices of the cotton-rich, good-time river town were compounded by the poverty, idleness and pilfering of the swarm of Negroes who had hurried from the plantations to plague their deliverers.

Shields McIlwaine in *Memphis Down in Dixie* wrote that before the war "racehorses, gamecocks, cards, dice, liquor and 'easy ladies' —whatever any man required—could be had in the planter capital." No austerity to vice attended the town's occupation. The pale and painted girls in the "parlor houses," who had once awaited the planters, loved the boys in blue as well, particularly after payday. Such women and male panderers, too, were minor figures in the corruption of Memphis; some were involved in the lapses in his control which Sherman admitted to Grant after the payday brawl.

"It would take all my command as customs inspectors," he wrote, "to break open all the parcels and packages containing liquor."

Other parcels passed, too, not all containing liquor. The reports of a correspondent of the militantly rebellious *Memphis Appeal*, which had moved out with its presses on a flatcar following the Confederate armies, apparently were sent almost daily to the printing offices the *Appeal* established wherever it could safely stop. Both the dispatches of spies and precious drugs were slipped out under the crinolines in the secret parts of a girl's clothing or were dragged out sewed up in the bloating belly of a dead mule. Funerals moved with undue frequency to "old family graveyards" in the country. Arms and salt and quinine moved with the dead. There was some winking as well as watching among Union soldiers. Even the severe Sherman himself connived at slipping through the lines cigars, liquor, boots, and gloves to his old West Point friend, Earl Van Dorn, the Confederate cavalry leader, who lacked such comforts in his camp not far away. Other Union officers connived, too, and sometimes for less sentimental reasons.

In the confusion of disloyalty, trafficking, smuggling, speculation, and exuberant desire for frolic on the part of his own young army, Sherman designed with care a plan for the orderliness of Memphis. He was unwilling to trust any one regiment to furnish the permanent provost guard. He named a trusted officer, Colonel De Witt Clinton Anthony of the 23rd Indiana Infantry, as his permanent Provost Marshal. In addition, he informed General Grant, "Instead of furnishing a permanent provost guard I give Colonel Anthony two good officers to assist him and change the regiment weekly."

Littlefield, of course, was one of those two "good officers." The other was Major Fisher, of the 54th Ohio Volunteers. And Sherman gave them broad powers. Since officers and men had abused their privileges, the provost marshals were ordered to enforce a virtual curfew at tattoo every night. In his impatience with "riots and nuisances," Sherman ordered them to seize the contents of any house in which noise, drunkenness, and fighting occurred and, if that did not suffice, "the house will be burned or pulled down according to its position." The provost marshals were to suppress riots by "blows, the bayonet, or firing when necessary." Furthermore, he made it clear to Anthony, Littlefield and Fisher that "of course, the military are not bound by the licenses issued by the city authorities, as licenses are designed for revenue and not to sanction or encourage crimes and nuisances." Even the most orderly businesses needed the approval of the provost marshals to open and keep open their doors.

Those were sweeping powers. They involved much discretion on the part of the provost marshals, and supposed a monumental morality in them, too. Sherman's order that all who would not take the loyalty oath must leave created, wrote McIlwaine, a traffic in false certificates of allegiance, which relieved Confederates of the necessity for swearing, at "from $10 to $500—or whatever the traffic would bear." There is no evidence that Milton was involved in such traffic. Indeed, this Memphis historian says that it was after his time that General Hurlbut, who succeeded Sherman in command of the city, "seemed determined to undermine the whole efficient system of Sherman and turn it into a paradise for thieves."

What Sherman demanded was order and loyalty. He had no desire to make his provost marshals the nurses of his army or the reformers of a town. As a matter of military necessity Sherman was sterner with disloyalty than vice. In his own person the General had risen from his pew in Calvary Church to make it clear that its minister would keep "the President of the United States" in his prayers or not pray at all. Before Sherman arrived Grant issued an order through his Provost Marshal that "no newspaper will be permitted within this district unless the editors and proprietors thereof take an oath of allegiance." But some of those who most disturbed Sherman and Grant, too, were harder to catch or curb. They were both Northerners and Southerners who proved the indissoluble union of Americans meeting with a profit motive even in war—or especially then.

That motive was seldom more apparent than in Memphis in 1862. Its name was cotton, often called king and sometimes devil. The Confederacy had embargoed cotton, though it provided the South's only tangible resource in purchasing arms abroad. Mr. Jefferson Davis thought that for lack of it England would intervene. England, of course, did not, but as cotton piled up on the plantations, its price soared in the outside world, in New York as well as in Liverpool. The year before Sherman's occupation of Memphis, on the rim of the cotton kingdom, cotton was selling in New York for 31.2 cents. While Littlefield was Assistant Provost Marshal in Memphis, it was rising toward 67.21 cents. And dollar cotton (price paradise!) was to become a reality in the following year. Such a rising price, said Hodding Carter in his story of the *Lower Mississippi*, "was enough to make thieves of the most honest, traitors of the most devoted, business associates of the bitterest enemies. And it did."

There is no evidence that Littlefield in his strategic position as a provost marshal was involved in the cotton traffic either. He was certainly in the midst of it. Indeed, four days after Milton led Company F of the 14th Illinois Infantry into Memphis in the blistering heat and three weeks before he became Assistant Provost Marshal, the traffic which enriched the enemy and was attended by the leakage of military information seemed to General Grant to be getting out of hand. Grant that July used almost the same words about the speculators which the conscientious Camm had written in his diary about some of his comrades in arms on payday. The General spoke of those "whose love of gain is greater than their love of country." But the gentry operating from the Gayoso had friends in Willard's Hotel in Washington close to commanding power. Grant was told to stick to his fighting and leave the cotton dealers alone. Under orders from Washington he withdrew an order prohibiting the payment of Union gold for Confederate cotton. The General's indignation was not canceled with his order.

The trade continued and the corruption which attended it. Charles A. Dana, assistant to Secretary of War Stanton, described the situation as it developed. "The mania for sudden fortune out of cotton, raging in a vast population of Jews and Yankees scattered throughout the country, has to a large extent corrupted and demoralized the army. . . . Every colonel, captain, and quartermaster is in secret partnership with some operator in cotton, while every soldier dreams of adding a bale of cotton to his monthly pay."

Dana did not go as far as Grant in putting the whole blame on the "Jews, as a class" who, the General said, "come in with their carpet-sacks in spite of all that can be done to prevent it." Grant's irritation with "the Israelites" may have been more furious because, as an unfriendly correspondent reported, his own father, Jesse Grant, had appeared at his headquarters as the front for some Jewish speculators from Cincinnati.

Dana knew better than to limit the blame to the Jews. He himself had originally planned to buy cotton in the area in partnership with so elegant an American as Senator Roscoe Conkling of New York, later famous for his "haughty disdain, his grandiloquent swell, his majestic, super-eminent, overpowering, turkey-gobbler strut." Conkling became the political leader of many of Littlefield's old friends and relatives in upstate New York and also a chief castigator in that area of war profiteers—"a myriad of sharks following the ship." Later while praising the brave, he was even rougher than Dana about others.

"But with them came knaves," he said, "titled and even shoulder-strapped, a darkening cloud of vampires, gorging themselves upon the heart's blood of their country. Shoddy contractors, bounty gamblers and base adventurers found their way even into the army. . . ."

There were others in the cotton speculations whose old New England Yankeeism was as authentic as that of any of the abolitionists. Indeed, Boston was the capital of textiles as well as transcendentalism. In the dubious enterprise around Memphis the fat, brassy Jim Fisk, epitome of the Yankee Peddler, who later helped Jay Gould raid the Erie and corner gold, became wealthy enough to go into big scale postwar operations for himself. The operations of men like Fisk from the Gayoso Hotel made trivial by contrast the traffic of Jews who, as Grant said, landed with their carpet-sacks "at any woodyard on the river and make their way through the country." And Fisk, whose activities after the war in New York made the contemporary activities of carpetbaggers in the South trivial, too, was operating around Memphis for such eminently respectable firms and persons as Jordan & Marsh and Francis Skinner & Company of Boston.

It seems highly likely that Milton met Fisk, certainly speculators like him, in the Gayoso Hotel that summer. He was undoubtedly often there on errands of both business and pleasure. The hotel was as ornate as the impeccable steamboats which long had brought fastidious as well as frolicsome people to it. Ladies were to be seen there. Ellen Sherman visited in Memphis that year. General John A. McClernand, who had beaten Milton's condidate for Congress in 1860 and hoped as a Democratic soldier-politician to supplant Grant, came to Memphis not only with his bride but also much of his bridal party. The wives and sweethearts of junior officers, even privates, came down the river to see their men. It is highly probable that the slim Anna visited Milton there in that first summer after their marriage. Certainly the military bands gave concerts for the ladies. Musicians played for dances. Even below Memphis General Grant watched Mrs. McClernand swinging through a waltz with her handsome husband, and a pretty young Rebel from a riverside plantation teasing Grant's stern aide, General Rawlings. Not only generals danced. There was music for all.

The Gayoso was the central spring of the splendid oasis. General Hurlbut, to whose division Milton was still attached, had his headquarters in the Gayoso. Milton, as a man whose fondness for the best hotels was to mark him as long as he lived, was naturally a familiar and popular figure in such a place. Though he never drank to excess, he liked the associations of cool bars. He certainly participated in some of the many "lavish goings on" in Memphis mentioned with as much envy as indignation in Southern histories. At such parties, for which opulent visiting civilians often gladly paid the bills, Milton was always welcome for his good looks, his ready baritone and his authoritarian position in the policing of the city.

One piece of documentary evidence of Milton's popularity, provided by an item in *The Memphis Bulletin* at the time, throws as much light on the paper as on the Assistant Provost Marshal. When the *Appeal* retreated in honor from Memphis with the Confederate troops, another paper, *The Avalanche,* remained. It had been an extreme advocate of secession, a fire-eating defender of the South. Apparently, however, its operators had little taste for the hardships and heroism of itinerant independence demonstrated by the *Appeal.*

Before Sherman arrived and Milton succeeded to such duties, Grant's provost marshals undertook to police the press. Then *The Avalanche* shifted its proprietors, its sentiments—and its name. Some years before it had absorbed another paper, called *The Memphis Morning Bulletin,* which had been too moderate to survive in the excited prewar middle South. But the *Bulletin*'s almost-forgotten name was just the one required by the avuncular *Avalanche* and Grant's and then Sherman's provost marshals. It was exhumed in haste. Even so, the new *Bulletin* was edited with clammy subserviency. In an article headed by his name, the *Bulletin* said of Milton:

"This officer has been for some weeks past detailed as assistant Provost Marshal of Memphis, and in that position has made hosts of friends, who will be pained to learn that he leaves this afternoon to join his command in Hurlbut's division. Captain Littlefield is the oldest volunteer captain in the U. S. Army, and has seen hard service in Missouri, at Donelson and at Shiloh. He has had higher positions assigned him in the new levies, but he prefers to remain with the men with whom he has seen hard service. He has fine abilities as a provost, having had extensive experience, and cannot fail to wear well in any position that may be assigned to him. The kindest wishes of hosts of friends will follow Captain Littlefield wherever fortune may cast him."

The fact, claim or lament that he was the oldest volunteer Captain in the whole army obviously came from Milton. If true, the Captain at thirty-two emphasized the youth of the Union Army. Its officers were young, Hurlbut forty-six, Sherman forty-two, Grant only forty. Even more significant and painful to Littlefield, the critical diarist Camm had been pushed above him as Lieutenant Colonel of the 14th Illinois Infantry—and Camm was only twenty-five. Milton was acutely aware of his rank at his age, despite the special prominence which his post in Memphis gave him and the opportunities it provided for him to make so many friends—and perhaps a few enemies.

The new levies were important in Milton's career. Before he was made Assistant Provost Marshal, it was clear that Lincoln's second call on August 4, 1862 for three hundred thousand more troops, to fight a war that was going far from well, would necessitate new officers, too. Certainly in such an expanded army higher rank might be expected by a veteran volunteer, even if the call, which necessitated a draft, was to be painful to many who had no desire to volunteer at all. It was not particularly important to Milton then that a widespread reluctance to the draft was to stimulate a trade in finding substitutes—individually and en masse—in the North and also among the runaway slaves in the South. That search for substitutes was later to make Negroes in the South almost as desirable as Southern cotton to men and communities in states like Massachusetts and New York, and Illinois—particularly to cotton mill operators in New England who, almost as much as they wanted cotton, wanted to keep their hands at home. Milton's problem in 1862, however, was not with Negroes as soldiers, which was to concern him later, but was a personal matter in connection with his official duties.

The *Bulletin* statement that he had been offered promotion "in the new levies" appeared in September but the promotion itself was delayed. Obviously, something more than his preference to remain with the men "with whom he had seen hard service" intervened. It is, of course, possible that General Sherman insisted that he could not spare Milton then from his post as Provost Marshal. No explanation is available in the official records. But Milton himself saved documents which, while attesting to his virtue, suggest that at the end of the hot, crowded Memphis summer there was some question about his accounts as Assistant Provost Marshal. He carefully saved a receipt written in Colonel Anthony's own handwriting:

Office of the Provost Marshal
Memphis, Tenn., Nov. 7, 1862

Received of Capt. Littlefield, Six hundred and seventy-two dollars, in full settlement of his accounts as Assistant Provost Marshal of City of Memphis.

D. C. ANTHONY
Provost Marshal
Memphis

The sum was not significant. The receipt might have been routine. Perhaps the letter which Sherman wrote ten days later to General Hurlbut was routine, too.

"It affords me pleasure," Sherman told the General who afterward was to head the Grand Army of the Republic, "to inform you that Capt. Littlefield has reported to me at Memphis and has satisfactorily settled and explained his account. Col. Anthony has receipted to him in full."

Milton's accounts had not only been settled but "explained" and the result afforded Sherman "pleasure." Evidencing his delight, on the same day, General Sherman issued an order in which the "Captain Littlefield" of his letter to Hurlbut was referred to in the rank of lieutenant colonel of a new 14th Illinois Cavalry with headquarters at Peoria, Illinois.

The miasmas at Memphis on the Mississippi left no mark on Milton. But the muddy river seemed almost to make one last effort to pull him down. With the emblems of his new rank on his shoulders, he was one of those aboard the "ill-fated steamer *Eugene*." That vessel had seen much service as a packet on the river. Not long before Milton sailed on her, the *Eugene* had been fired on by guerrillas on the shore above Memphis and Sherman had ordered the destruction of a whole village on the shore to let the people know that "all such acts of cowardly firing upon boats filled with women and children and merchandise must be severely punished." No guerrillas lay in wait when Milton sailed, but near the head of Plum Point bend, which Mark Twain later described as "famous and formidable," the *Eugene* suddenly collided with the sunken wreck of the steamer *Neptune*.

Milton was standing near the table in the main salon, undoubtedly contributing as much to the pleasure of his fellow passengers as he always did on such trips, when the collision occurrred and the force of the blow threw him and the other passengers to the floor.

"In an instant," he told a reporter soon afterward, "a terrible scene of confusion and panic took place. The screams of the women and the shouts of the men, the crushing of timbers and the sharp orders of the officers were all mingled in a tumult of sounds. . . . Simultaneously with the first shock of striking, the boat commenced to sink. Before she could be cleared from the wreck, and headed towards the shore, her bow was sunk so deep that the stove in the cabin fell over and set on fire the carpet and the floor. The flames caught the dress of a lady nearby and blazed up in an instant. This added horror seemed completely to destroy the returning senses of most of the passengers. A few gentlemen exerted themselves to extinguish the burning dress of the lady and the flames in the cabin. Fortunately they succeeded without her receiving any serious injury."

"Colonel Littlefield," the reporter said, "exerted himself to restore order and calmness." He was not entirely successful.

"Many of the passengers continued to rush wildly about," the news account continued. "Colonel Littlefield had gone forward to see how far the boat was from shore, and was leaning over the railing, when he was knocked overboard by a sudden rush of passengers.

"He fell into the water, arose and caught a dry goods box, but slipped off again and then caught hold of a stage plank which had floated from the boat. On this he floated down the river. As he floated he distinctly heard the voices and saw not less than seven or eight persons clinging to planks, boxes, etc., and crying for help.

One by one they dropped off, and Col. Littlefield thinks not one of these was saved.

"He himself floated some twelve miles down the river, to Fort Pillow, where he succeeded in making himself heard by the sentinel, and a party of soldiers came out in a skiff and rescued him from his perilous position."

Fort Pillow was only a place of rescue to Milton then. It was to be a year and a half before a Northern story of an alleged massacre there by Nathan Bedford Forrest's men of such Negro troops as Milton was to lead seemed evidence of Southern fury over the arming of the blacks. In the fall of 1862 it was important to Milton only as the place where, with some difficulty, he got the steamer *Tigress* to go pick up the survivors of the *Eugene* and where the *Platte Valley* took them aboard for Memphis.

The accident only gave Milton more to tell when he finally got back to Anna in Jerseyville. He had come home, as *The Prairie State* of that town had wished, sufficiently "covered with honors for gallant and meritorious conduct." No item in that paper telling of his return survives. But he had clearly grown in stature when he returned to the little town. It may have seemed to him to have shrunk in his absence. He came back wearing not only the insignia of his new rank but the dark brown beard which appears in all the pictures of him taken later. Carefully tended and close-cropped below a clean shaven upper lip, it emphasized his easy smile and gave him a new impressiveness.

Like other soldiers he had grown the beard following the masculine American fashion to which Lincoln had given his approval on his own chin not long before he became President and which more and more soldiers were following in the camps. Beards marked the varying character of men. Women apparently liked them and often mentioned them in describing their loves and heroes. Ellen Sherman, when she visited Memphis soon after Littlefield had left it, wrote her father that the war was changing her General. Sherman's red beard was already grizzled, she said. Memphis had made its mark on him. There was not then—or long after—a fleck of gray in Milton Littlefield's trim whiskers. They made him impressive but no less debonair.

Obviously, not everything about the Jerseyville to which Milton returned was congenial. The little town seemed to embody the Republican excuse for political reverses that year that all good Republicans had gone to war for their country while Democrats had remained at home to be elected to its offices. In the elections that autumn Anthony L. Knapp, one of two brothers who kept the Democrats strong there, had been chosen for Congress from Lincoln's district in a delegation from Lincoln's home state in which Democrats predominated nearly two to one. Anthony Knapp was just two years older than Milton; his brother Robert, a year younger. Both, like Milton, were natives of New York. Neither of them had been to Shiloh or Memphis, but they held power in Jerseyville.

Much of the applause for the returning Colonel was elsewhere. *The Union Herald* of Springfield spoke enthusiastically about him and his new regiment, the 14th Illinois Cavalry, which it said was "the first regiment authorized under the late call." Those who wanted to "join a crack regiment," that paper said, should enlist forthwith. And it added: "As an inducement to join this regiment, we would say that Lieut. Col. Littlefield is a brave soldier, a courteous gentleman and a glorious good fellow." Milton's old newspaper friends in Alton recommended him as as brave and good a man as Illinois affords. And his friends on *The Grand Rapids Eagle*, when Milton went back to visit his family in Michigan, were "agreeably surprised" by a call from him. "Milton is looking and appearing first rate," the *Eagle* reported, "and his numerous friends in this city will be pleased to see and congratulate him on his proud position in Uncle Sam's Army."

Despite the dominance of his political opponents in Jerseyville, his position was a proud one. He was certainly no longer the oldest officer for his rank among the volunteers. His visits about Illinois, to Michigan, constituted almost a procession to the music of kind words. He was prepared as a gentleman, bright-eyed and dark-bearded, to go back to war in the saddle. Yet, according to the records, he was honorably mustered out of service on November 26, 1862, less than a month after his promotion and long before the 14th Illinois Cavalry even got the horses on which to ride to war. He did not go south with the regiment to the Mississippi bluffs where the men with whom he had first set out to war were engaged in the long siege of Vicksburg. Apparently, he never saw Memphis again. It had taught him all it could. And that seemed much in other southern towns in Reconstruction, when a reviving Memphis was stricken by yellow fever, and death governed its dusty streets. That was when the stricken city made a saint out of a harlot who turned the girls in her parlor house into nurses and brought the dying to the beds which had only served pleasure before. Good and evil are much mixed up in history. Memphis for Milton was an instructive interlude. He had more to learn. When at last the cavalry regiment started for the front, Milton was already in Washington about to assume at a higher rank new and very different duties to which he was sent from the White House itself.

CHAPTER V

The Enchanted Islands

AT THE END of the three-day voyage from chill, damp New York, Colonel Littlefield's ship swung in by the blockading fleet. He was close enough, under the yellow sun, to see the South Carolina shore to which President Lincoln had sent him. Sometimes, the Colonel was told, the *Arapo* and other vessels on that regular run moved close enough shoreward to see the steeples of the "hated little rebel city" of Charleston. His ship stayed out beyond the fleet and at such distance, on that day in early April 1863, the shore was only a low, flat line far off. Then, nearer and greener, Edisto was passed, and other islands. And Littlefield first saw Hilton Head, where his headquarters were to be, as a long, low, sandy point running out into the sea with no visible dwellings upon it except the white tents of the soldiers. Even in the sparkling sun, it looked like a very desolate place.

That desolate appearance from the sea was only the first of that shore's deceptions. As the ship approached the landing, Hilton Head was clearly a lively place. The wharf was crowded. On it was a varied assemblage of officers and soldiers—some of them, Littlefield noted particularly, black soldiers in blue coats and scarlet trousers. Mingled with them stood a great motley crowd of "contrabands" as the former slaves of Rebel masters were known. Milton gave them a special, concerned scrutiny as men involved in his mission. After Memphis, their appearance was not strange to him, but now he regarded them in terms of Lincoln's hopes, too.

They were the same tattered, suspiciously silent or loudly laughing men whom Charlotte Forten, the best chronicler of that time on the islands, had stared at in surprise at the end of a similar voyage. That pretty mulatto schoolteacher from Philadelphia and Salem, Massachusetts, had come south as a protégée of the poet John Greenleaf Whittier. She had a poet's eye for the islands, too, though she added to it a sharpness which sometimes pointed her piety, and a realism even about her own race to which her modicum of Negro blood tenaciously bound her. When she first saw the Negroes on the dock they were, she wrote, "the most dismal specimens I ever saw." She came later to the conclusion, happier for her, that that was deception, too.

Perhaps Charlotte, like Littlefield and some others, came south expecting too much. Unlike the punctilious Captain Camm after Shiloh, they had not anticipated a South of flowers without scent and birds without song. Abolitionists were often more romantic than aristocrats in residence. Charlotte wrote in first, swift disillusion: "The palmettoes disappoint me much. Most of them have a very jagged appearance, and are yet stiff and ungraceful. . . . The cotton fields disappoint me, too. They have a straggling look, and the pods are small, not at all the great snowballs that I had imagined. . . ."

That was first, possibly homesick, impression after the neat North. There was nothing dismal about the green islands behind Hilton Head. In the decade before the war Frederick Law Olmsted on his famous journey in indictment of slavery was almost seduced by the climate and the country. In a bright February he faced the warm world outside his window on a rice plantation where the camellia-japonica were blooming, the buds were swelling on a jessamine vine, and a mockingbird was whistling loudly. "Nowhere in the world," he wrote, "could a man with a sound body and a quiet conscience live more pleasantly."

Certainly, when Mr. Lincoln, at last aroused to a desperate eagerness to stir the slaves, sent Littlefield to that green coast, the tall, ruddy Colonel was obviously sound of body and gave every sign that his conscience was easy. The last was not unusual there then. Indeed, hardly any people anywhere were ever so confident in their consciences as those who composed the company Littlefield joined. Seldom has there been such a congregation of Puritans in Paradise. The green and golden Sea Islands, since their occupation in 1861, had become strategically important as a depot of supplies for the South Atlantic blockading fleet. They were strategic, too, in the earnest effort to demonstrate the abolitionist faith in the Negro as man and soldier to which President Lincoln was a belated convert.

If Memphis was a Union oasis, the Sea Islands constituted an abolitionist Eden. Moreover it was an Eden from which evil had been expelled—or, as personified by the slave masters, had run away. (There was some difference of opinion, of course, about the terminology. President Jefferson Davis applied the name Eden to the once-idyllic South of happy slaves, "Before the tempter came, like the serpent in Eden, and decoyed them with the magic word of 'freedom.'") In Memphis, the speculation Milton observed had been in cotton. On Hilton Head, Edisto, St. Helena, Port Royal, Paris, Folly and other islands the grand speculation in which he participated was in the possibilities as soldiers and citizens of the black people, some of whom had been born in Africa.

In Memphis communication even between Yankee and Rebel had been almost monetarily simple. On the South Carolina shores many of the agents of salvation, intent upon their own messages, listened to the spiritual singing of the Negroes and disregarded, when they could, the incomprehensible island-to-island communication of the black men's drums. They were not, however, the first white men who were not always able to comprehend Negroes on that shore. Their Gullah dialect—a "jungle tongue" some Union soldiers called it—often seemed an incomprehensible jargon. By the 1860s the Southerners had lost their clear early understanding that men who came from Africa varied in breed and character as much as Europeans. Indeed, few Europeans were so different as submissive Pawpaws and majestic Coromantees. Those who regarded Negroes as children and those who wanted to count them as chattels were equally removed from an early English evaluation that "noe man deserved a Coromante that would not treat him like a friend rather than a slave." Yankees and Rebels expected the responses they sought. Both were surprised when they failed to get them.

Even in such a garden of hopes, Littlefield moved in direct, business-like fashion. From the ship he went straight to the headquarters of his old Missouri commander with the dark wig and dyed moustaches, General David Hunter, then ending his services as commander of the Department of the South. He presented the letter, signed by Lincoln's chief secretary, given him at the White House. Hunter read:

Executive Mansion
Washington, March 31, 1863

Dear Sir:

Lt. Col. M. S. Littlefield, who bears this, comes to you to offer his service in assisting to organize Negro troops. Both the President, and Secretary of War have great confidence in his ability and energy and would be glad to see him at the head of a regiment. The Secretary of War this morning told me that either you or Gen. Saxton had authority to give him such duty as he might be needed or fitted for. I specially commend him to you.

Your obt servt
John G. Nicolay

Maj. Gen. Hunter

General Hunter was not surprised. In the same week he received another letter from the President about a first, feeble expedition of Negro soldiers to the country around Jacksonville, Florida.

"I see the enemy are driving at them fiercely," Lincoln wrote, "as is to be expected. It is important to the enemy that such a force shall not take shape and grow and thrive in the South, and in precisely the same proportion it is important to us that it shall."

The letters gave Hunter, as a man of occasional dour humor as well as a wig, some amused satisfaction. His friend, Mr. Lincoln, a year before had countermanded Hunter's order liberating the slaves left in, and crowding into, the shore he occupied. Lincoln had let die on the vine Hunter's efforts to enlist Negro soldiers, though the General had cockily denied that he was organizing "fugitive slaves." Instead he told a laughing Congress he was making "a fine regiment of persons whose late masters are fugitive rebels." He could, he said, organize fifty thousand more before the end of the year.

Hunter was expansive then; Lincoln was the tortoise the abolitionists called him, hardly hoping that in his attitude toward the Negro he would outrace any hare. Now his mind had changed and Littlefield came as his man. It is doubtful, however, that Hunter or anybody else then saw Littlefield's mission in the terms Littlefield's officers described it at its completion three years later.

"General!" they saluted Littlefield by the brevet rank he had then been given for his work. And beyond the exclamation point their final evaluation of his work proceeded in part: "Foremost among those who combatted the shortsighted policy [of rejecting Negroes as soldiers] which marked the first year and a half of the war, you, General, were to be found. It was no easy task you imposed upon yourself. We all know what scorn and contumely were showered upon the heads of those who first suggested the employment of colored troops. But humiliating reverses in the field and the doubts of final success engendered thereby, taught the nation and the Government the wisdom and necessity of adopting the views of yourself and your coadjutors."

Then: "You finally succeeded in securing the necessary authority from the President to enlist colored men; and hastening to the Department of the South, you began those labors, which have been unremitting for three long years in filling the depleted ranks of the Army."

Those statements may have been as exaggerated when they were made, obviously with Milton's approval, as they have been forgotten in history. No place has been preserved for Littlefield in the legend of the Liberator. His name is not even mentioned in the work on *The Negro in the Civil War* by the Negro historian Benjamin Quarles. There is no record that Milton, during his early service in Tennessee and Mississippi, showed any special interest in the mobilization of black men. He was nevertheless a special item in the plans, diabolical-seeming in the South, which Lincoln pressed in the dark winter and spring between Union military disasters at Fredericksburg and Chancellorsville.

When Littlefield had come from Illinois to Washington in the winter of 1862-63 Lincoln's unpopularity in a bogged war effort had aroused even murmurs of impeachment. His renomination for a second term seemed seriously in doubt. And Lincoln himself had become increasingly critical of his generals—particularly the West Pointers. One evening when Milton's younger brother John, the faithful law clerk, dropped in casually to call, and found the President with a "raging tooth," the tall, aching Lincoln made a parable of frustration about pigs trying to get into a pasture in connection with the Yazoo River strategy of Sherman and Grant above Vicksburg. Lincoln was humorous but he hurt.

The White House was as accessible to the Littlefields as the office of Lincoln and Herndon had been in Illinois. From such a vantage point, John was watching Washington then with the eyes of the painter and lecturer he was to become rather than with those of the lawyer Mr. Lincoln had trained him to be. Later, advertising his pictures and public addresses, he said without contradiction that he "had the entree of the White House during the whole of Mr. Lincoln's administration." Milton never published any such claim; it applied to him as much as to John. Young John, an obvious office seeker at that time, got a safe sinecure as a clerk in the Treasury with Lincoln's endorsement. Milton already had his post as a glamorous lieutenant colonel of cavalry. His new assignment was less a plum than a part in the President's plans to use the slaves to strike the South. That was not an assignment which would serve Milton's popularity in Illinois where 2,001 deserters had been arrested in six months, including many who protested that they had enlisted to save the Union, "not to free the niggers."

Mr. Lincoln had, as he said before he issued it, been moved by "pressures" toward his Emancipation Proclamation, finally promulgated as the year began. Southerners charged that his new enthusiasm for Negro soldiers had as its purpose the incitement of servile insurrections—the South's old, worst fear. Actually the enlistment of Negroes as soldiers had been begun by Southerners on the very Sea Islands to which Littlefield was dispatched. There, according to Ulrich B. Phillips in *American Negro Slavery,* the first slave code had been modeled after that of Barbados from which many of the masters and slaves first came, "with the striking exception that in this period of danger from Spanish invasion most of the slave men were required by law to be trained in the use of arms and listed as auxiliary militia." But times and adversaries had changed in 1863.

What had been a precaution had become a crime in the South's eyes. White officers of Negro soldiers, Jefferson Davis let it be known, would, if captured, be treated not as soldiers but as capital criminals. It was such duty and hazard which Milton accepted in the same last days of March in which Lincoln dispatched Adjutant General Lorenzo Thomas to the Mississippi area to organize black regiments and in which he wrote Andrew Johnson, then Military Governor of Tennessee, urging him to enlist and arm the Negroes there. In apparent desperation, turning to men he trusted, what the President proposed at that moment was terror.

"The bare sight of fifty thousand armed and sullen black soldiers on the banks of the Mississippi," Lincoln told Johnson, "would end the rebellion at once."

A week after the President wrote that, Milton was on his way south. He seemed hardly a man for a sullen command. And John Hay, who sailed south close behind Littlefield, was equally strange as one engaged in arming slaves or reconstructing rebellious states. Hay, then only twenty-five, combined an almost fatal sense of his own importance with a gay poet's playfulness in the most serious times. Later he wrote that "when the President had any delicate matter to handle at a distance from Washington, he very rarely wrote, but sent Nicolay or me."

This time Hay followed Lincoln letters. His trip may have been, as he suggested, a holiday. He undoubtedly looked forward to seeing his soldier brother who was ill in the South. But the trip was no impromptu excursion. It had been planned for two weeks—the weeks in which the President concerned himself much with his new hopes in Negro soldiers. On the day after he arrived at Hilton Head, Hay reported promptly to Nicolay that he had talked with General Hunter about Milton.

"Littlefield is still at Hilton Head," he wrote, "but the General is glad to receive him & will put him in position immediately. He directs me to say to you this, and to convey his kindest remembrances."

Then in the same paragraph, he explained part of the enchantment of the occupied Eden: "I wish you could be down here. You would enjoy it beyond measure. The air is like June at noon & like May at morning and evening. The scenery is tropical. The sunsets unlike anything I ever saw before. They are not gorgeous like ours but singularly quiet and solemn. The sun goes down over the pines through a sky like ashes-of-roses and hangs for an instant on the horizon like a bubble of blood. Then there is twilight, such as you dream about."

There was more than a bubble of blood on the horizon. Hay and Littlefield arrived just before a naval attack on Charleston up the shore resulted in the worst defeat the Union Navy suffered in the war. And as Hay prepared to sail home, Rebel pickets near Folly Island were shouting across the lines, "Joe Hooker's licked," in gleeful announcement of the new disaster at Chancellorsville. On the idyllic islands so crowded with earnest white men and suddenly freed Negroes, there were few signs of the speedy ending of the insurrection which Lincoln had told Johnson armed and sullen black men would assure.

Hunter, as he promised, put Littlefield promptly into place. Milton was a latecomer compared to other leading officers dealing with the Negroes. A firstcomer among them, who was to stay longest, was General Rufus Saxton, mentioned in Nicolay's letter, who fathered the whole Negro flock, soldiers and refugees. Other officers already in command of black regiments were Thomas Wentworth Higginson, a former radical Unitarian minister from Massachusetts, and James Montgomery, onetime Jayhawker in Bloody Kansas, both of whom had been associates of John Brown and personally embodied the marching on of his soul. And though he arrived a little earlier, Milton was overshadowed by the twenty-five-year-old Colonel Robert Gould Shaw, who brought from Massachusetts a regiment of Northern Negroes formed in exultation there "by a zeal for the welfare of the colored man" . . . "in addition to wishing to fill the Massachusetts quota" in the draft. Rich, well-born, almost girlishly beautiful, Shaw came as a white knight leading black men to freedom. Six weeks later he fell at Fort Wagner in Charleston Harbor as the martyr in that cause. Popular fury made him almost a crucified god when word was sent north that Southerners answering a request for his body had said, "We buried him under a layer of niggers."

Without fury or fanfare Littlefield then took over the temporary command of Shaw's men as well as his own, while the regiment's Lieutenant Colonel, another wealthy young man, Edward N. Hallowell, of Philadelphia, recovered from the wounds he had received when Shaw died. Milton marched as no legendary figure. But he marched; so did his men. Both received special praise in a newspaper report of a review in honor of General Quincy Adams Gillmore, Hunter's successor, who in August, to the pleasure of the President, announced the capture of Fort Wagner and the practical demolition of symbolic Fort Sumter.

This was the first review, the correspondent said, in which a brigade of Negro soldiers had marched with the remainder of the column. They handled their muskets and obeyed the marching and step orders, he wrote, in a manner which reflected credit upon themselves and their officers. To Colonel Littlefield, he added, "who has labored assiduously to produce this wished-for result, and who has on several occasions given evidence of his patriotism and fidelity, a full share of praise should be accorded."

The handsome Colonel noted in his scrapbook that the correspondent who praised the marching of his brigade was a friend of his named Will. Apparently he received General Gillmore's confidence and friendship as well. The General needed counsel, and Littlefield, as everyone on the Sea Islands understood, had been sent there by the President himself. Despite the parade in his honor Gillmore was not an entirely happy man that fall. He had been brought south as a great artillerist to take Charleston which had withstood the ironclads. And despite the fall of the forts and the islands about it, the city still withstood his siege and his great "Swamp Angel" guns. Furthermore, sometimes the General felt almost as harassed on the islands he commanded as he was frustrated by the city which defied his shells. Visitors, refugees, reporters and reformers made his command not only a military operation but a confusing governmental and social enterprise as well.

At thirty-eight, Quincy Gillmore, who had graduated first in his class at West Point and established a world reputation as an engineer for his famous work on *Hydraulic Limes, Cements and Mortars,* was an artillerist with few peers. However, Secretary of the Navy Gideon Welles, whose forces on that seacoast had to work closely with Gillmore, appraised him as a man of scientific brilliance but less gifted in the management of men. He was a man who blushed easily, "a fine, wholesome-looking, solid six-footer, with big head, broad good-humored face, and a high forehead, faintly elongated by a suspicion of baldness, curly brown hair and beard, and a frank, open face." On the Sea Islands Gillmore was a mathematician in Eden with the management of a diverse assortment of men and women of two races on his hands.

A friendly historian of the missionary migration from the North indulged in understatement when he wrote that some of those who came "hoping the climate would be good for their health, or from a spirit of romance, or to see a tropical country with its peculiar production, or in a spirit of sectarian zeal" did more harm than good. There are some evidences that they nearly drove General Gillmore crazy.

Certainly many of the missionary migrants were more trouble as individuals than the mass of ten thousand Negroes around him—slaves left by their hastily departing masters and more who had come in by the singing group or half-starving boatload, escaping from plantations still within the enemy lines. They included the old and the young, lively pickaninnies, the hobbling and the blind. There were the ardent, too, gleaming black young men and lean young women who on dress occasions matched the bright uniforms of soldiers with gay head handkerchiefs and starched white aprons.

Not as many of the men as Lincoln—or Littlefield—had hoped joined the troops. But the males and females encompassed the scale of color and quality all the way from creatures who looked as if they had just emerged from the jungle to the delicate Charlotte Forten. As one of those who had come to serve the freedmen and often worry General Gillmore in the process, she taught pupils whose little faces ran all the way from chalk to chocolate. More than their elders they represented a new unity in an old variety when they sang a song Whittier, at Charlotte's request, had written for them:

O, none in all the world before
Were ever so glad as we!
We're free on Carolina's shore
We're all at home and free.

Not everything seemed to General Gillmore to constitute such shrill innocence. Some things rattled against the General's peace of mind like the hard seed in the dried gourds the Negroes shook for their dancing. Most such troublesome matters should have been the exclusive business of Gillmore's less brilliant classmate at West Point, General Rufus Saxton, who had been Military Governor even before Gillmore arrived. Saxton, "a handsome man with luxurious English whiskers and moustache," had been passed over in his wish for a command in the field, but had labored earnestly at his assignment. He "certainly adorns the pulpit," Whitelaw Reid wrote of him at a Negro church celebration at the close of the war, but added that he looked, "to judge of his intellect by his face—narrow but intense; not very profound in seeing the right, but energetic in doing it when seen." Less analytically, Colonel Higginson described him as a "simple, manly" officer much loved by his colored subjects. But in 1863 Saxton was "quite radiant," Charlotte Forten reported, after his marriage in the little Episcopal church in Beaufort to a Miss Thompson, one of the teachers who had come from Philadelphia. And Charlotte added cryptically, "A strange marriage, it seems to me."

Apparently, General Saxton ("Saxby" his colored people called him) remained in a romantic daze. He had not only a bride, but in Beaufort, next door to the erstwhile establishment of Barnwell Rhett, the extreme and departed Secessionist, a "fine, airy, large-windowed, many-porched Southern residence" which he had acquired at a confiscation sale for two thousand dollars. Unfortunately, it had been stripped of its furniture by a Treasury agent who had sold that, too, as abandoned property. Sufficiently refurnished, the house was the scene of many parties given by General Saxton and his bride. They loved to play charades in which they were sometimes joined by Jean Margaret Davenport Lander, the popular Shakespearean actress.

Dramatic on and off the stage, at the beginning of the Lincoln administration Mrs. Lander had gone to the White House to tell of a plan to assassinate the President which had been confided to her by handsome young Virginians. Then as a young war widow, still in her early thirties, she had offered her services as a nurse. She had been rejected by the superintendent of women nurses, Dorothea Dix, who had stipulated that her aides be not only over thirty, but also "plain looking." Kindly General Saxton, with no such prejudice, was glad to have her help on the Sea Islands. She was then "a small, beautifully formed lady, with a sweet, expressive face, and a voice as clear as a silver bell."

Not all the women on the semi-tropical islands of South Carolina, Georgia and Florida were so lovely. The stalwart Mrs. Frances Dana Barker Gage, reformer and journalist, was there. So was Harriet Tubman, the famous black zealot who had served John Brown. But if Mrs. Lander was the famous beauty on the golden islands, there were other pretty nurses, schoolteachers, missionaries, whose names entered like dainty items the stories of journalists as well as official reports: Miss Towne, Miss Harris, Miss Smith and Miss Foote. Also, there was Chloe Merrick. She was the young teacher about whom Littlefield preserved mention in his scrapbook.

Perhaps Milton was interested in Chloe Merrick only because on a trip north she bought for the colored women of Fernandina, Florida, a flag blazoning the word "Liberty," which they presented to Littlefield's first Florida troops. Milton had a way, however, of picking the girls who presented the peaches to a President or flags to soldiers. And Chloe Merrick was a young teacher who attracted attention. John Hay, at Fernandina in the same spring Milton came south, noticed her particularly, as one of those in charge of the high school in the little Florida town, leading light mulatto and white children together in a song about the wings of the morning.

Moving up and down the southern coast, Milton was often at Fernandina. He did not see Chloe only at flag presentations. Officers and teachers rode and sailed together. It seems highly probable that Milton and Miss Merrick made the sight-seeing trip so many others made across the mouth of the St. Mary's River to the Dungeness estate on the southern end of Cumberland Island. John Hay found the wide gardens and the great ruined house there grounds for wonder "at the luxuriance of nature & the evident shiftlessness & idleness that had characterized the owners."

Milton saw Dungeness with different eyes. One of the early owners of the place was a member of his family, Catharine Littlefield, who married General Nathanael Greene in 1774. In the South in which Milton was to seem so alien, it was odd that his distant cousin, Catharine Littlefield, had been the lady who had inspired the Yankee schoolteacher, Eli Whitney, to invent the cotton gin which in so many ways made inevitable the war in which Milton was engaged. Also, though that seemed significant only later, it was strange that, in the South which was to resent Yankee confiscation of plantations, much of General Greene's property had been presented to him by Georgia which had taken it by confiscation from a Tory.

Young men like Milton and girls like Chloe Merrick were not concerned then about such things. There is a possibility that Chloe was more concerned with her mission than with men. She had been sent south by the Freedmen's Aid Society in Syracuse—the nearest city in Milton's boyhood. She set up schools in Fernandina and St. Augustine in Florida and later at Columbia, South Carolina, and finally at Wilmington, North Carolina. Also she had attracted the attention of an older beau who was destined to be very important to Milton. She could not have been unaware of the romantic shore.

The ruined gardens at Dungeness were still magnificent. Bamboo, banana, fig and pomegranate grew wild around them. And behind the house, in which Union soldiers had scribbled inscriptions on the walls, a road ran for miles through a cool forest of moss-draped live oaks. Charlotte Forten wrote in her journal of a ride with an officer companion through such a wood: "The air was soft, Italian." There was the low, faint murmur of the sea. The ground was carpeted with green fern, large purple sand violets, and a white flower tinged with lilac. And when they emerged from the wood into the shell road, Charlotte wrote, "it was like leaving Paradise."

Sometimes even in such a southern Eden, containing "Liberty" on banners, liberty itself tested the patience of General Gillmore and threatened the preservation of the proprieties which seemed to him important. No behavior of Littlefield's ever troubled Gillmore. But before Gillmore—or Littlefield—arrived on the scene, even Charlotte Forten was piqued when Colonel Higginson sent her word that he thought it best that she "not join the regiment just now." Charlotte went on: "He fears scandal. There have been of late very scandalous reports of the ladies down here, so of course as usual, *all* must suffer to some extent." Later, after Gillmore had assumed command, she wrote of a "very inhospitable reception" on her return from a visit to the North. She and another returning woman "were told that an order had been issued by General Gillmore forbidding any lady to land unless provided with a pass from himself or the Secretary of War." She had to spend the night on the boat "watched closely meanwhile by no less than three lynx-eyed guards."

General Gillmore himself watched other matters with less satisfaction than he sometimes expressed. On December 14, he wrote to General Henry W. Halleck, then Lincoln's general-in-chief, about the policy of organizing Negro troops in which he gave Littlefield more and more authority. That policy had had, he said, "a fair trial and a successful issue under my own eyes." Prejudice and ill-feeling which had existed between white and colored troops in his command had "disappeared under the excitements of an active campaign, of which the labors and the dangers were shared alike." On the same day on the same subject, however, he wrote to Secretary Stanton a less encouraging report. Though there were "nominally five regiments of South Carolina colored troops" only one had ever reached the minimum number of men required by law. And the "present rate of recruitment furnishes no ground for expecting," he said, "that they will be filled within a reasonable time." He and Saxton, he said, believed that the best thing to do was to add the fragments to Littlefield's command.

General Gillmore was not merely dealing with details of troop organization. At that time he was shaping—or falling into—a grand design involving not only Negro troops but also, long before the word became the name of an angry later period, plans for reconstruction of states in rebellion. Gillmore's frustration as artillerist before the battered but holding walls of Charleston may have persuaded him to the rôle he assumed. Undoubtedly inactivity added to his irritations as the commander of the missionary as well as military Department of the South. Sufficient Negro troops did not seem to be available on the South Carolina coast or the thin coastal footholds in Florida to meet the hopes Lincoln had expressed in the spring.

The President was apparently not discouraged. He used impressive statistics about black troops in his message to Congress on

December 8, 1863. Then Lincoln, in announcing his Proclamation of Amnesty and Reconstruction, said that "full one hundred thousand are now in the United States military service, about one-half of which number actually bear arms in the ranks, thus giving the double advantage of taking so much labor from the insurgent cause, and supplying the places which otherwise must be filled with so many white men."

As a consequence or coincidence, just a week after Lincoln announced his program, General Gillmore officially suggested to General-in-Chief Halleck that troops be sent into Florida to recover and reconstruct that state. There, his proposal indicated, was a soft wall in the defenses of the Confederacy and beyond it wide regions in which Negro recruits could be secured. At practically the same instant Gillmore made his suggestion to Halleck and dispatched Littlefield to Washington.

The ostensible purpose of Milton's trip was to urge, with the backing of Gillmore and Saxton, equal pay for Negro soldiers. That was an increasingly popular cause. In addition to the men of the martyr Shaw, Negroes had died fighting heroically at Milliken's Bend above Vicksburg. Also, though in the North prejudice against Negro soldiers still existed, there was an increasing interest in crediting Negro soldiers to the draft quotas of Northern States which the Negroes had never seen. The same New England textile men who had been so eager for cotton at Memphis already had, when Milton arrived, a lobby in Washington working to secure legislation to increase Negro enlistments in order to reduce the draft of their employees. And many Northerners, subject to the draft, approved the views of a Private Miles O'Reilly expressed in newspaper poetry:

Some say it is a burning shame
To make the naygurs fight,
An' that the thrade o' bein' kilt
Belongs but to the white;

But as for me, "upon me sowl"
So liberal are we here,
I'll let Sambo be murthered in place o' meself
On every day in the year.

Manufacturers, malingerers and idealists all felt that equal pay and increasing bounties might speed up the slow rate of Negro enlistments about which Gillmore had lamented to Stanton. And in Florida a source of recruits might be found which had not been available before. In one of the letters which Milton carried north for Gillmore, that General told Halleck, "If you desire he will converse with you upon the Florida project."

Milton did. There is, indeed, good reason for believing that the "Florida project" was the first—or at least the equal—reason for Milton's mission. As a practical man even on a fantastic shore, he had been aware from their inception of the already months-old plans to "reconstruct" Florida long before Lincoln's plan of amnesty and reconstruction had been invented or at least announced. Evidently Milton was one of the supporters of the project, which if it did not provide the design for the plan the President announced to Congress on December 8, was, with the President's participation, a quick test of it. The operation brought him into questionable company—but in companionship with Lincoln, Hay and Gillmore. Also it brought him early into relationships with men and factions he was to confront again in Florida after the war.

One of the men most active in urging a Florida invasion as a basis for early Florida Reconstruction was Lyman D. Stickney, one of the Treasury agents appointed by Secretary of the Treasury Chase to handle the seizure and sale of such rebel-abandoned property as General Saxton's house in Beaufort and the Sea Island plantations on which Saxton supervised the farming of refugees. As a Chase man at a time when the Secretary of the Treasury seemed Lincoln's chief opponent for renomination, Stickney was a strange adviser of Lincoln and such Lincoln men as Hay and Littlefield.

Stickney was, said his fellow tax commissioner, a conniving crook. That associate was Harrison Reed, who was to be Milton's great friend later as Governor of Florida. Reed was then over fifty but still ardent enough to be taking a serious interest in Chloe Merrick. He had been born in Massachusetts where his father kept a hotel and had himself been printer, storekeeper, farmer and newspaperman. In his twenties he had moved west to Wisconsin where one of his achievements had been, he reported, the organization of the first Sunday School in Milwaukee. Also, he failed in business there, but later served as editor of *The Milwaukee Sentinel*. After that he edited the Madison organ of Governor James Duane Doty, who notoriously mixed private speculations with public service in that territory.

As Doty's friend, Reed acquired abandoned lands upon which the government had built gristmills, a dam on the Fox River and dwellings for the Menominee Indians. There he built the town of Neenah. He had troubles with his partners, however, moved back to Madison and then to Washington, D. C., where in 1861 he was apparently happy to be appointed by Secretary Chase as one of his Southern tax commissioners. He hated Stickney, who neglected his duties and labored at his political schemes. Reed damned him as widely as he could as speculator and grafter, but President Lincoln left a written estimate of Stickney as a "worthy gentleman."

Actually, Reed was undoubtedly right in his insistence that his associate was far from that. In the *Florida Historical Journal*, Ovid L. Futch has shown that Stickney, while a forceful personality and a man of disarming demeanor, was an adventurer and scoundrel. Originally a Vermont lawyer, before he was appointed by Chase, Stickney had been in Florida at the outset of the war as the partner of a Virginian "who, it was rumored, had moved to Florida to set up a base for receiving African slaves." The name for that illegal traffic was blackbirding. In addition to an interest in the slaves which he secured in that partnership, Stickney got an old sloop in which he "began operating between Key West and the mainland, trading with Confederates on the mainland and U. S. government officials at Key West." When Federal authorities embargoed the sloop, Stickney took up residence in the principal hotel in Key West and began to agitate for an election to send a delegate to Congress —obviously himself.

Then he disappeared, leaving unpaid a hotel till of $144. He turned up in Washington in June 1861, and received from Chase, who thought he was an old Florida resident, the job as tax collector. He spent most of his time, however, away from his post, often making patriotic speeches to freedmen on the Sea Islands and ingratiating himself with such officers as Gillmore, Saxton and Littlefield at Hilton Head. Colonel Higginson mentioned him at an emancipation celebration where the Massachusetts preacher-soldier said he "added something." Certainly Stickney added strangeness to crusade.

Lincoln undoubtedly knew his relationship with Chase when Stickney went to Washington in September 1863, to present the Florida project. Stickney carried with him a petition to Lincoln, in the name of the "loyal citizens of Florida," to send a large military force there for the purpose of relieving the people of "Confederate rule and the reestablishment of a loyal state." Such a state would send representatives to Congress and, as some critics emphasized later, delegates to the Republican National Convention. A careful Florida historian says that Stickney was "popularly reported to have talked with the President" about the plan then. Certainly he saw his friend and patron, Chase, who wrote in his diary on September 6:

"In the afternoon Mr. Stickney called. He had just arrived from Florida, and lastly from Morris Island. He says that it is easy now to take possession of Florida; that five thousand men can accomplish it. General Saxton desires the command, and General Gillmore approves the expedition, and is willing to spare one or two regiments to aid it. If the business can be promptly taken hold of, and pushed vigorously, Mr. Stickney is confident that Florida can be restored as a Free State by the first of December."

When Littlefield arrived it was clear that Stickney's schedule had been optimistic. Milton saw Secretary of War Stanton, however, and talked specifically to him about giving to Gillmore for the Florida expedition other regiments of Negro soldiers recruited in the North. There is no documentary evidence that he saw Lincoln or even Nicolay or Hay about the matter. The overwhelming probability is that he did. He was in the North several times that fall and winter. He was with Anna that fall, presumably in Philadelphia. In Washington he saw his brother John who so often visited the White House and who that winter moved from the Bureau of Internal Revenue to the office of the Register of the Treasury. Milton found crowded Washington still much like Springfield. Access to Lincoln was almost country easy. His presence in Washington in

December coincided with the time when the President was drafting the details about the application of his plan of reconstruction in general and the Florida foray in particular.

The President's basic plan provided that when citizens numbering a tenth of the population in 1860 took a prescribed oath of loyalty, the government set up by them in any rebellious state would be recognized and protected. Though Hay wrote that the plan was well received when announced to the Congress, not everybody in the North liked it. The South regarded it as an "insulting and brutal proposition" by the "Yankee monster of inhumanity and falsehood." Even Union soldiers, with some skeptisicm about the kind of "ten per cent" citizens Mr. Lincoln might get, caught a rattlesnake, ceremoniously administered the oath to it, and turned it loose. Around the White House apparently the preferred view was that expressed by General Nathaniel Banks, who was to have his troubles in Louisiana, that a free state could be made there in sixty days "with as little trouble as it would take to execute a dog law in Massachusetts."

Florida seemed as simple. Obviously Lincoln did not first consider it after Littlefield had brought Gillmore's letter to Halleck in mid-December. But the President was so secretive about the whole matter that Secretary of War Stanton was not fully informed as to the purpose of the undertaking. Secretary of the Navy Welles whose ships were necessary to the expedition was kept entirely in the dark about it. The President, he said afterward, was "trying a game himself." Stanton in a report later to the Joint Committee on the Conduct of the War declared that "the military operations projected by General Gillmore, being communicated to the President, they presented in his judgment a favorable occasion for carrying into effect the measures of amnesty declared in his annual message."

It was a Sea Island and White House project and lively young John Hay left records of the administration's great interest in it. No other subject, except the still-doubtful renomination of Lincoln, to which hostile critics later tried to relate the expedition, received so much attention in his diary at this time. And it is clear that, if no personal political consideration moved Lincoln, John Hay was prepared to let the occupation and Reconstruction of Florida put him in the Congress of the United States.

Lincoln spent Christmas Day on his Reconstruction plans. He liked the idea when three days later Hay received letters from the disarming Stickney and others asking Hay "to come down to Florida and be their representative in Congress." Lincoln told Hay to go try the amnesty idea first on Southerners in the military prison at Point Lookout, Virginia. Then Hay wrote, "he will appoint me a commissioner to go to Florida and engineer the business there." Lincoln did more than that. He provided Candidate and Reconstructionist Hay with a commission as Major. (At twenty-five Hay was subjected to some criticism because he was not in uniform.) Hay himself bought an orange grove in Florida to make it his residence, if necessary, for Congressional purposes. Sworn in as soldier, and ready to set out as politician, Hay told the President good-bye on January 13.

"Great good luck and God's blessings go with you, John," said the President.

Lincoln put his blessings on Hay's errand on the same day in a letter to Gillmore. He understood, he said, as if he had only vaguely heard about it, that "an effort is being made by some worthy gentlemen to reconstruct a loyal state in Florida." He had sent Hay, who would explain the President's views on the subject, to aid in the Reconstruction. Gillmore was to be "master" in the matter, but the President asked his co-operation in carrying out the plan "in the most speedy way possible, so that when done it will be within the range of the late proclamation of the subject."

Two days later Gillmore named Littlefield to enroll recruits in Florida while Hay was enrolling reconstructed citizens. Littlefield was appointed General Superintendent of the recruiting service for colored regiments in the Department of the South, president of a board to select officers for new regiments, and was charged with the payment of all bounties to new black soldiers. Furthermore, a correspondent of *The New York Tribune* reported, Gillmore assigned to Milton as assistant an officer who had been the General's own "popular and efficient assistant adjutant general."

Milton went to work preparing a placard of his own, urging the enlistment of "loyal men of Florida" to be posted beside placards, prepared by Lincoln, which Hay had brought to invite citizens to attest their loyalty to the Union. Milton's appeal did not seem quite as sanguine as the hopes Hay brought south with him. His recruitment of Florida volunteers, he said, had been authorized by the President of the United States and he, as Superintendent of Recruitment for colored soldiers, had been authorized to pay bounties to each recruit from both the United States and "the State where he will be accredited." Those to whom he appealed, his placard noted, had been called upon frequently before to enlist under the old flag to put down this wicked rebellion. Some had served well but "there has, as yet, been no united action on your part.

"Now we call upon you again."

Some other officers were less confident about the expedition. When he arrived at Hilton Head, John Hay met a major from the Florida coast who was, Hay thought, "rather severe on the measures initiated by our friends the tax collectors to reconstruct the State." Harrison Reed would not have cared to be so lumped with Stickney in that or any other enterprise. Even General Gillmore, when Hay first arrived, seemed a little perplexed about the project of which he was supposed to be the author and instigator, dwelling on the deficiencies of transportation for land attack. He seemed reassured when Hay saw him the next day, however. Then the General told that young Major-for-the-moment to "say to the President that he would cordially co-operate in carrying out the President's wishes." Hay was reassured, too. Gillmore, he wrote in his diary, "seems frankly and sincerely anxious that the President's intentions shall be fully carried out." The General apparently had no more doubts. And he understood clearly his military objective.

"I hope we will get enough votes out of the territory already in our hands in Florida," he told Hay. "If not, we will occupy some more territory."

It seemed as simple as that. A parade atmosphere attended the expedition. In a review of the force "which is to invade Florida, 6,000 men, black and white, artillery & mounted infantry," Littlefield's colored men marched as smartly as in the special review for Gillmore in the fall before. The white and Negro women of the island watched them go. The February sun was as warm, the islands as green, as Olmsted had reported them a decade earlier. On Hilton Head sound bodies moved and consciences were clear.

The women raised their voices to join the marching men in the farewells of a crusade:

> "Sound the loud timbrel o'er Egypt's dark sea,
> Jehovah has triumph'd,—his people are free."

The transports and gunboats slipped off toward Florida leaving the waving women behind. There is no record of their reaction to the systematic General Gillmore's instructions to the commander of the expedition that "you will see that no females accompany your command, and will give strict orders that none shall follow except regularly appointed laundresses, who will be allowed to accompany the baggage of your respective commands." No long separation was expected. Florida did not seem far off and foreboding.

The voyage was brief over a sun-flecked sea. There was little resistance at first landing on February 7. Stickney exuded confidence like a balm. And Hay and Littlefield, and the main body of white and colored men, artillery and mounted infantry arrived a little later to find Jacksonville "gay with flags and busy with shipping." The two young Lincoln men from Illinois both put up their posters in the Florida town.

CHAPTER VI

Gallows in the Sun

HAY HAD TIME for both loafing and literature in Florida. While he stayed at the camp of instruction near Jacksonville, which Littlefield commanded, he wrote *"Lèse-Amour"* which his biographer thought was one of his best lyrics. Also, he put into his diary a picture of Littlefield, as a directing off-stage presence, which contrasts sharply with subsequent ideas of him as the easy commander of undisciplined Negro troops. Hay wrote that he was taking things easy in the evening, after a day of offering amnesty for oaths to some dirty Confederate prisoners, when he heard the dead march playing and went out to record the grim evidence of Littlefield's justice.

Milton had been ordered by General Truman Seymour, the expedition's field commander, to preside over a military commission to sit "without regard to hours" on the trial of some Negro soldiers of the 55th Massachusetts Volunteers charged with raping a Florida white woman. Hay, whose eyes erred only where women were concerned, had described in his diary such a woman in the frightened and sparsely settled territory as might have been their unknown victim: "a lady, well-bred and refined, dressed worse than a bound girl, with a dirty ragged gown that did not hide her trim ankles and fine legs."

There was no doubt about the identity of the 55th Massachusetts. That regiment, the second recruited in the Bay State, shared with the 54th, which young Colonel Shaw led south, the enthusiasm of Boston Unionists. One of its white officers was a son of William Lloyd Garrison. Though all were credited to Massachusetts' draft quota, its men had been recruited from twenty-five states, the District of Columbia, Canada and Africa. Only a third of them had ever been slaves. They marched as a symbol of freedom. But Littlefield's court met only one day before showing its justice to John Hay.

He heard, Lincoln's young secretary-in-uniform said, "the dead march sounding and a regiment marching by." Hay and his companions went out and entered the square made by the Negro troops: "It was light enough to define the gallows clearly against the sky. A cart drove in & after pulling & hauling & swearing was backed under the gallows: The poor devil stood upright apparently engrossed by the trivial details: wanted more rope &c. His sentence was read, the noose adjusted, he said a few words to the crowd & the cart beginning to move he jumped up & tried to break his neck but failed & gasped & jerked & struggled dreadfully. His stentorian breathing could have been heard over the square. A man jumped up on his shoulders & hung on him swinging. No effect. Another man got on: he still gasped. At last they raised him up & jerked him down hard: & he ceased struggling & after a while the crowd dispersed."

Hay wrote of his own part in the dispersal, "We foraged for supper." But the scene fascinated him. Next morning he went by the gallows again "& saw the poor devil still fluttering his rags in the wind—his head horribly oblique, his eyes staring wide, his mouth open & his blackened tongue protruding. A curious crowd of negroes, boys and crackers lingered around him, some who had been there last night taking a permanent station near him & detailing with intense relish to those less favored the hideous show of the night before."

From Littlefield's gallows Hay went to examine his loyalty enrollment books again and, he said, "found a large number of citizens had signed, some of position and influence." Actually, however, he knew that even among the dirty prisoners most Floridians were like "the leading man of the town, Judge Burritt" who hung in indecision between the Union and Confederacy as represented by its generals, Gillmore and Joseph Finegan; "Between the Gillmore who is here & the Finegan that may return he knows not how to choose. If he is true to Gillmore he may get cotton. If he is false to Finegan he may stretch hemp."

The gallows and the appurtenances seemed to be on John Hay's mind. He wrote no discouragement in his diary but already the question, which Whitelaw Reid raised in Florida soon after the war, must have been clear to him. Reid then traveling with Chief Justice Chase, but not always speaking for him, could not figure the sense in remarking a state out of Florida with hardly a third of the population of Cincinnati "scattered over a peninsula of swamps and everglades and outlying barren islands" in which ex-Rebel whites were determined to rule. Giving such a place and people senators and representatives, the journalist thought, would be giving a ridiculous reward to traitors who deserved punishment. Furthermore, not even the captured Confederates given by Hay a choice of pardon or prison were ready to buy that bargain. Though Hay mentioned no misgivings as to his mission, the swinging corpse was somehow a portent in the February sunshine. He sailed on the steamer *Alice Price* back to South Carolina for respite. The other enroller, Littlefield, of course, remained with his men in Florida.

The news of the expedition's fate in northern Florida—up the rotting railroads, below the damp margins of the dismal Okefinokee Swamp, on its interrupted way to the Suwannee River—came late and dramatically to Hay at Beaufort. There the young secretary, Gillmore and Saxton received the news in a manner which has always pleased the poets and saddened their readers. There was no untrodden snow in Beaufort. The February night would have been warm but for the chill breeze from the river. But the sun was low, gone through a sunset in which once again it had hung upon the horizon like a bubble of blood. And this time not Hay but the other literary man in the Sea Islands country, Colonel Higginson of the black 1st South Carolina Regiment, invoked the aid of Lord Byron in telling how the news came.

"There was a sound of revelry by night at a ball in Beaufort," Higginson wrote of a party given by the young officers celebrating the birthday of George Washington. Then "suddenly in the midst of the 'Lancers,' there came a perfect hush, the music ceasing . . . and as we all stood wondering we were 'ware of General Saxton, who strode hastily down the hall, his pale face very resolute, and looking almost sick with anxiety. He had just been on board the steamer; there were two hundred and fifty wounded men just arrived, and the ball must end."

The ball did end instantly, Higginson said, "though with some murmurings and some longings of appetite, on the part of some, toward the wasted supper." John Hay had already gone to the hospital ship *Cosmopolitan* when Saxton strode like a "mighty shadow" through the flag-hung ballroom. Shouts from the ship had given the bald facts of disaster before the first ropes had been flung ashore. There was wailing tumult along the docks. Then black and white soldiers broke lanes through the crowd. The ambulances which had brought the ladies to the ball moved to the ship. And aboard her the young Presidential secretary watched the dying men, particularly a young colonel who picked at the bedclothes and murmured about military rank. Then Saxton came back from the ball he had terminated, glowing, Hay remembered, with the triumph of a generous action performed.

Saxton "asked us up to his room, where we drank champagne and whiskey, and ate cake," the President's agent noted. Not all the supper was wasted.

Littlefield, of course, learned of the disastrous Battle of Olustee, much more quickly and in less romantic fashion. In that engagement near the Suwannee River. Union forces suffered more casualties in proportion to the men engaged than in any other battle in the Civil War. Littlefield had not been in action, but he and his men had plenty to do when the routed Federals, white and black, came pouring back toward his camp along the railroads they had confidently followed in their advance from Jacksonville ten days before. Milton had no time to lament the evident ending of the first purpose of the expedition to find more Negro troops. Reconstruction was no longer anyone's concern. There were wounded men to help, great stores of supplies to burn or save. Working to help restore order in the retreat, Littlefield's men made up the rear of the battered army as it retreated into Jacksonville.

Some little satisfaction was saved for Colonel Littlefield in the behavior of the men he was training at the camp and those he had helped train who had been engaged in the battle. General Seymour attested to that later: "The colored troops behaved creditably—the 54th Massachusetts and the 1st North Carolina like veterans. It was not in their conduct that can be found the chief cause of failure, but in the unanticipated yielding of a white regiment from which there was every reason to expect noble service, and at a moment when everything depended upon its firmness. The misfortune arose, doubtless, from this regiment having lately been filled with conscripts and substitutes, of a very inferior class."

That white regiment, which failed at the crucial moment, was the 7th New Hampshire, commanded by Colonel Joseph C. Abbott, graduate of Phillips Academy at Andover, lawyer, newspaper editor, who after the war as a United States senator was to be one of Littlefield's closest associates in railroad manipulations and other aspects of Reconstruction in North Carolina and Florida. No fault was attached to him at Olustee for the cowardice of his inferior substitutes. And not even the inferior substitutes were blamed so indignantly for the failure as was John Hay's principal, President Lincoln.

In Lincoln's own Cabinet, Secretary of the Navy Welles first learned of the reverse, he wrote, "in a whisper" from Secretary Seward before it had been mentioned in the papers. Welles' first reaction was that "this suppressing a plump and plain fact, already accomplished, because unfortunate, is not wise." But he added that the Florida expedition had "been one of the secret movements that have been projected, I know not by whom, but suspect the President has been trying a game himself." Welles may have been wrong in his conclusions, certainly he was about the publicity. The day after he spoke of suppression of the story, a chagrined if not chastened John Hay read the journalistic explosion about it in Northern papers which the regular-running *Arapo* had brought to Hilton Head.

James Gordon Bennett's *Herald*, which called Florida the "smallest tadpole in the dirty pool of Secession," led the attack. It charged that the sole purpose of the Florida expedition had been to trump up a state organization to send Lincoln delegates to the approaching Republican Convention, and to send Hay to Congress. While Horace Greeley's *Tribune* said that "it is quite possible that the Administration may desire the return of a loyal state to the Union without reference to the next Presidential election," other papers were less charitable.

"Of course, no military purpose took an army into Florida," said *The New York World,* "as the conquest of Florida would do no more to put down the rebellion than would the occupation of Yucatan or Coney Island. The object is political. Florida has been marked out as one of the rotten borough states which are to help make Mr. Lincoln President."

Hay fumed at the "lies" but his efforts then—and afterward—to relieve himself and Lincoln of responsibility for the expedition have not convinced historians. Hay's own careful biographer, Tyler Dennett, described the Florida invasion as "premature, perhaps ill-advised." He did not think the journalistic clamor could be lightly dismissed: "It is quite probable that, if the conditions in Florida had turned out to be as the President had expected, there would have been Florida delegates at Baltimore, and that they would have been instructed for Lincoln. There is also some plausibility to the inference that under such conditions Hay, who, while in Florida, invested $500 in land, might have been the first carpetbagger Congressman."

Littlefield's failure to secure the troops he hoped to enlist on the Florida expedition was a matter of much less public concern. Somehow in the months after Olustee, he did find other colored recruits he sought and for which there was increasing demand. If he was depressed by the Florida fiasco, he showed no sign of it. Furthermore, he had seen the railroads along which the Union forces had advanced and retreated. They were badly rundown then. General Seymour expressed the exasperated opinion that "the Union cause would have been far more benefited by Jeff Davis having removed this railroad to Virginia" than by any Union victory along it. The railroad was sagging and rusting when Seymour's forces retreated but Littlefield kept the memory of the line in his mind for later operations. However unstrategic it may have seemed to Seymour, it was to be highly strategic in Milton's later career. For him, Florida in 1864 was both a fiasco and a foundation. He did not linger over failure.

His prestige was high in the Department of the South. Indeed, the most impressive description of the handsome Colonel ever written was one sent north for publication at that time. It was written by the Reverend E. W. Jones, chaplain of the 21st U. S. Colored Troops, of which Milton remained the Colonel in addition to his other duties on the staff of the General commanding the Department of the South. The Reverend Mr. Jones came from Jefferson County on the shores of Lake Ontario in the upstate New York country in which Milton was born. His letter to newspapers there reintroduced Milton to old neighbors and new associates.

"His exterior is 'beautiful to behold,'" the chaplain wrote. "A finer-looking officer is not to be found once in a thousand years. Tall, straight, full chest, high forehead, dark hair, and a countenance commanding at once your love and admiration. But the real beauty of our colonel is not in a fair exterior, but in a true nobleness of soul, and magnanimity of spirit. In him the rigid officer and the benign friend, the stern commander and the social companion, are most happily and sweetly blended. Among his fellow officers and equals in rank he is always a center of attraction; and among his superiors his opinions are always treated with profound respect. He is a personal friend of President Lincoln, who always greets him with cordiality. The Colonel is yet a young man, and that unflinching perseverance, united with that perfect moral integrity that have so far elevated him, will soon raise him to higher dignities and honors."

Chaplain Jones sent his regards to his "brethren, the members of the Black River Conference" and added the news for such homefolks that his Colonel Littlefield was "a cousin of my esteemed fellow townsman, Colonel Calvin Littlefield." Such a letter from his chaplain was undoubtedly appreciated by Milton at Hilton Head and interesting to his old neighbors in New York.

Apparently Milton's chaplain's letter brought the Littlefield cousins into communication again and put together, too, the war fortunes of boys in cool, green upstate New York and Negro soldiers on the hot, crowded southern Sea Islands. That process also began an association for Milton with the New York men which was to shape the pattern of his return to the South after the war was over and Reconstruction begun. No such prospect was involved, however, in the arrangement for the benefit of Jefferson County in which the Littlefield cousins and others were engaged in 1864.

That transaction could not have been a secret at the time, and the facts became a charge only afterward in the local politics of Jefferson County. What happened seemed in 1864 not a crime but a public contribution to the people of Jefferson County. Indeed, in the laudatory biography of Colonel Calvin Littlefield in the *Genealogical and Family History of Jefferson County,* it was stated that he "rendered very material aid in recruiting the quota in the town of Ellisburgh [Milton's birthplace] and of Jefferson County, and through his services the county's quota was filled without resort to the draft."

The story was told in less laudatory fashion later in a political handbill circulated in the county. It was specifically directed at Norris Winslow, a "leading citizen" of Watertown, when he ran for the State Senate in 1869 as the candidate of the "Customs House machine." That political organization was headed in the area by Congressman Addison H. Laflin, whose brother also was to be one of Milton's associates in Reconstruction speculations. Also involved with Winslow were Calvin Littlefield and John B. Clarke, described as Milton's brother-in-law. They were charged with profiteering in bounties, amounting to $195,300 ($700 per recruit) from Jefferson County for 279 Negroes assigned to the county draft quota by Milton at Hilton Head. The handbill, signed "One Thousand Republicans" but sounding very indignantly Democratic, went on:

"Gen. Littlefield certified to the mustering in of a large number of colored men; in fact, we believe all the certificates came through him but whether he ever obtained a single man, of course, cannot now be ascertained. We believe it is claimed that the colored recruits cost $300 each, but no one except Winslow & Co., knows that they ever cost a dime. In truth, there is good reason for believing —not only that they did not—but that they were never furnished. In other words the only existence they ever had was upon paper. Had the men cost anything would Winslow and associates have been elevated from men in moderate circumstances to those of affluence? The probability is, that the whole $195,300 was pretty much all profit, and Winslow's share was perhaps $100,000.—Will he have the kindness to inform the people, whose suffrage he is now soliciting for Senator, what the precise sum was?—We dare him to do it!

"We assume that he made 'a pile.' He must have done it; for the store was given up at once. He becomes a banker—not a regular one, with Government stocks as capital—he had enough of his own. He buys a banking house; he buys a dwelling, and furnishes it luxuriously; he buys an expensive turn-out, and is driven by a servant in livery! All this shows that he made a 'big thing' in furnishing colored troops. ONE HUNDRED and NINETY-FIVE THOUSAND THREE HUNDRED DOLLARS, in the space of three or four months. All other business men of Watertown did not make much more in the same time—possibly not as much.

"The reasons for doubting that the men were obtained, are: First —That few, if any, colored recruits were secured from the Rebel States at that time. Among the scores of agents who went into those States from our State, in the winter of 1865, in pursuit of this class of soldiers, it is well known that they returned without securing any men. Second— Such soldiers could not have been obtained without money, and it must be apparent to everyone that very little money was used; for, had the expenditures been large, the parties would not have been made immensely rich, as they were, by the speculation. Third— The war closed about the time the mustering certificates came on from General Littlefield; *the men were not wanted*; there was general rejoicing over the suppression of the rebellion, in the midst of which, the certificates were presented to the proper authorities, and, being all right upon their face, they were paid, without particular inquiry as to whether the recruits had or had not been received. Had the war continued, and the men been wanted, the people would have known whether General Littlefield's certificates represented human beings or straw men. As the case stands, they can never know; but may they not be pardoned for guessing what the facts were. . . .

"P.S. The members of the War Committee know that Winslow was paid in County Bonds at 95 cents on the dollar—the large portion of it in advance—so that he was at no risk by the advancement of County money."

Milton Littlefield was never troubled or followed by this burst of political indignation in Jefferson County. In the North, in 1864, the bottom of the barrel had been scraped of such "substitutes of a very inferior class" as had broken and run in the 7th New Hampshire at the Battle of Olustee. And certainly there was nothing new or strange about the desire for Negro troops for the draft quotas which white men did not want to fill.

The handbill was not disregarded. It came, said the indignant *Daily Reformer* of Watertown, which was energetically supporting Winslow, from the printshop of a weekly paper called *The Re-Union. The Daily Reformer,* in an editorial headed, "Patriotism Distorted Into A Vice," sharply replied. Its answer, however, both condemned the charge and acknowledged the facts at the same time. The blast against its Winslow, that staunchly Republican paper said, was chiefly composed of "rigmarole and lies." It was an "allusion of the smuttiest kind" and one coming from "a vulgar and brutal Copperhead." However, as to the profits of Winslow (and associates) in the process, the *Reformer* admitted: "Well, he ought to have made some, for he took great risks—risks that nobody else could be found to be willing to take to the extent he did." The Littlefields, the paper went on, "patriotically gave their time and hazarded their lives in the warm climate of the South to get the soldiers requisite to fill our quota." They got "acclimated, brave and efficient soldiers." And the result of their labors was to "save our young men at home, whose services in their various industrial pursuits were very much needed and desired."

Such young men were very much "needed and desired" at home in other northern communities, too. At the time Jefferson County got credit for its colored men in the distance, John Hay called the procedure "the Massachusetts idea" in a talk about it with Sherman and Grant, neither of whom liked it. Sherman, indeed, had defied an act of Congress, passed on July 4, 1864, authorizing Northern governors to send agents into the South to recruit Negroes "who shall be credited to the State which may procure the enlistment." When some such agents had asked Sherman where they might begin to receive their colored men, he had named eight cities all in Confederate territory far from any Union troops. The idea was not limited to Massachusetts though it had been a part of that state's motivation.

Undoubtedly, the idea had been a part of the Massachusetts purpose in the forming of the 54th Massachusetts Regiment, which the doomed young Shaw led off to war to the applause of abolitionists and poets in Boston, and the 55th which furnished the man hanged in Jacksonville. President Lincoln, in the message in which he announced the Amnesty and Reconstruction Proclamation which preceded the ill-fated expedition to Olustee, mentioned as one of the advantages of enlisting Negro soldiers that of "supplying the places which otherwise must be filled with so many white men."

Nothing could be more clear than Littlefield's statement in his appeal for enlistments on the Florida expedition calling attention to the Federal bounty each recruit would receive and another bounty "from the State where he will be accredited." (There was a gap between the $300 he promised and the $700 which Jefferson County paid.) Perhaps as the officer "charged with the payment of all bounties to colored recruits" in the Department of the South, he was partial to Jefferson County. Also it is possible that some of the bounty money stuck to his hands or those of his cousin, friends and associates there. The process in which he took part, however, was not a rare deal but a plan publicly blessed by local taxpayers and high public officials. During the war the Northern States paid nearly $300,000,000 in bounties for recruits.

The only odd thing about the matter, as indignantly stated in the handbill, is that Littlefield's Negroes were credited to New York, not his own Illinois. In Illinois on September 22, 1864, a few days after the draft was instituted there, the Illinois *State Register* stated: "A new feature . . . We noted the sale of three likely able-bodied men yesterday—color not stated, as it is immaterial to Uncle Abe—at $400, $450, and $600 respectively, average a little less than $500 each. They were bought to fill a Woodford County order." Three days later the same paper noted that "the demand for substitutes seems to be on the increase. Yesterday their par value averaged from $700 to $900. About a dozen, most of them Negroes, were picked up and are already in the service of Father Abraham."

An item in the Illinois *State Register* carried an official's report that such recruits were "shipped from one point of the United States to another as cattle are shipped and sold." In one Congressional district in Illinois the average county bounty was $1,055.76 which was at least in competitive proximity to a similar figure in New York of $1,060. Whoever got the money, Jefferson County at $700 seems to have got a bargain. (Also, the transaction may have been a blessing for Abraham Lincoln in New York, which he carried that fall by only 6,749 votes out of 700,000 cast.)

Milton's concern in Illinois that autumn was not recruits but Lincoln's re-election. His friend, the President, then did not underestimate his danger even in his own bailiwick, though, in the growth of the Lincoln legend since, many Americans seem to be unaware how precarious even the possibility of that legend was in 1864. Emancipation was far from universally popular in the North. Grant's casualty lists were endless and heartbreaking. The draft was hated most as victory seemed most certain. The draft dragnet for the insatiable-seeming demands of the generals caused fears among Lincoln's friends in many states. "Leading Republicans all over the country," Nicolay and Hay wrote in remembrance, "fearing the effects of the draft upon the elections, begged the President to withdraw the call or suspend operations under it."

Lincoln, in statesmanship and probably good political sense, too, declined the clamor of the politicians about the draft. Its suspension for the obvious purpose of his re-election would probably have done more harm than good. In other details, however, as Charles A. Dana, then serving as Assistant Secretary of War wrote, "All the power and influence of the War Department . . . was employed to secure the re-election of Mr. Lincoln." Major General John A. Logan, who had raised a regiment at the beginning of the war in the southern counties of Illinois, said later that when he came home that fall to campaign for Lincoln, he did it "at the special and private request of the President." General Logan was only one of many who received such requests. In all, said Don C. Seitz in his study of Lincoln as politician, "something like two hundred thousand soldiers were furloughed to go home and vote." Milton Littlefield was one of them.

Such campaigners in uniform were needed. Lincoln's electoral vote obscures the great popular vote of McClellan in the whole country. Even Illinois was a battleground. Lincoln lost his home county of Sangamon—and every county surrounding it. That was Littlefield's as well as Lincoln's country. And Milton's Jersey County, in the midst of war, voted even more Democratic than it had before he went to war. Jersey went for McClellan in an even greater majority than Sangamon did—1,546 to 817. Such a home vote stiffened Milton's Republicanism, and slackened his ties to the county and town. He took what satisfaction he could out of the replacement of his home-town Democratic neighbor, Anthony Knapp, in the Congress by his and Lincoln's friend, Shelby M. Cullom. Cullom, Milton told celebrating Republicans in Springfield, would stand by the government and the army.

There was triumph to celebrate but grudge to remember. Milton called upon the "patriots" of Illinois, *The Springfield Journal* said, to continue to take care of the "traitors at home." He referred briefly, the *Journal* said, "to the shooting of three Union men by bushwhackers at Fidelity, Jersey County, while attempting to arrest a deserter; and the refusal of sundry citizens to go in pursuit of the murderers." Some of the same sort of people, he said, had threatened to shoot him for coming home to discharge the "solemn duty of voting for Abraham Lincoln."

"I have done that," the *Journal* quoted him as saying, "and now I am ready for the field again."

There was plenty for him to do in the field. Sherman's telegram to the President, on September 3, that "Atlanta is ours and fairly won," not only began the turn of the political tide to Lincoln. It also meant, as Sherman approached the sea along which his old Assistant Provost Marshal served, a swarming to the route of his army by thousands of Negroes. They emerged, one observer said, as if a man had pushed a walking stick into an anthill. Black preachers and "yaller gals," field hands and house servants lined the roads. They reminded Brigadier General John W. Fuller of blackbirds on a fence. They followed the Sherman column as a heaven-sent cloud of dust by day and pillar of fire by night. Handsome Negresses were stowed away in the baggage wagons and young exhausted mothers drove along with switches little swarms of wide-eyed black children as though they were little black sheep. The Negroes charmed, amused and served Sherman's men. Six months after Lincoln's Florida fiasco Northern newspapers were predicting that Sherman would bring out of Georgia "two able-bodied Negroes for every white soldier in his ranks." Actually as many as twenty-five thousand Negroes joined Sherman's columns as they moved along. Many turned back. Still nearly seven thousand followed in the march to the sea—to blue Ossabaw Sound below Savannah, but only a short sailing distance from the white tents and black soldiers of Hilton Head.

Among those waiting on the shore, Littlefield was no longer the Captain, elderly for his rank, who had served Sherman in Memphis. Before the blue Western host with which Milton had begun his service had reached the shore, he had been promoted to the rank of brevet Brigadier General. And the crowded year was marked, too, with another event equally important which emphasized how busy Milton had been.

On August 21, 1864, his lonely Anna was delivered of a son, born prematurely, in New York. With her baby she went to Philadelphia to live with her half-sister, Mattie Harbert. And it was three months afterward before Milton saw Anna or the tiny son who bore his name. Even then the boy was so small that his tall father could cradle him on his forearm and hand. Undoubtedly he sang to the child and his unfamiliar beard and baritone caused the boy to cry in a way that made Milton and the large-eyed Anna laugh together. So many things seemed coming together. He saw Anna and his boy, became a general, and began to plan a home worthy of them all, at the same time. He had helped re-elect the not-ungrateful Lincoln. It is possible that he had then, due to his help in the solution of Jefferson County's draft problem, more funds than he could have saved from his salary as Colonel. But Philadelphia returned-to was almost as unreal as the Sea Islands first-seen.

"The reign of shoddy," as said Milton's friend of later times there, Alexander K. McClure, was in full swing. Men who had been accustomed to beer, he wrote, required full baskets of champagne. Unknown women went into Caldwell's, bought diamond necklaces with cash, snapped them around their necks and went out wearing them. Extravagance became so common that ladies like the young wife of Thomas A. Scott, the railroad magnate, wore few jewels or none at all. Anna Littlefield did not have to so restrain herself. But Milton was aware of the dazzling prospects in Philadelphia.

He had friends in that expanding American city, in which wealthy men had been almost as much concerned with sustaining Union and freedom as with assuring new wartime programs of tariff protection, national banking laws and railroad development. The Union League, which cherished the economic changes, had been formed to "take treason by the throat." And Philadelphia had close ties with the Sea Islands. Charlotte Forten, home again and "knowing that Negroes were as capable of progress as whites," had grown to dusky grace and good works in the city. Milton's associate in the command of Negro troops, Edward N. Hallowell, the martyr Shaw's successor, belonged to a Philadelphia family of rich merchants and earnest abolitionists. Furthermore, as seemed so often the case everywhere, Milton could count on friends in the press. About the time he came to see Anna and the boy, the *Inquirer* wrote, of his promotion on November 26, that he had "for a long time been acting in the capacity of his new rank and rendering efficient service to the army in connection with the bureau for recruiting colored troops in the South."

"It is seldom we have the privilege," that strong Union paper went on, "of announcing the selection of an officer in our gallant army which bears with it equal testimony as to self-sacrifice and sterling patriotism. Aside from Colonel Littlefield's personal bravery and unflinching heroism in all the conflicts in the campaign in the Southwest, he has added to his worth to the country by the cheerfulness with which, at the first breaking out of the Rebellion, he abandoned a valuable and lucrative practice as an attorney and separated himself from all those domestic and social pleasures which can only be estimated by men of such moral and intellectual culture as his."

Back in the South Milton had a star on his shoulder, a son in Philadelphia. He was still just thirty-four years old and the war seemed almost, as Sherman had said of Atlanta, "fairly won."

The restored Union stretched back all the way from the no longer desolate point of Hilton Head to the river he had watched with Sherman—the wide muddy river which ran by Illinois, collecting all the best and the worst of America into one great stream. On the swampy southern margins of the continent, he had a right to feel that he was part of the flow to the future. And as such a man at such a time he was undoubtedly "beautiful to behold."

CHAPTER VII

High Trees at Tidewater

ON FEBRUARY 13, 1865, while Sherman's armies hammered northward, General Littlefield on Hilton Head issued an order formally establishing the Village of Mitchelville for freedmen who swarmed the area. The settlement was named for General Ormsby MacKnight Mitchel, who attained his fame as an astronomer but turned from the stars to war. In 1861, as soldier, he found himself the new master of thousands of Negroes on the South Carolina Sea Islands from which former masters had fled. Mitchel instituted the custom by which freedmen adopted the surnames of their former masters, sometimes to the chagrin of Barnwells, Ravenels and Rhetts. Any other process on his crowded islands, such an astronomer realized, would be like picking new names for the stars. Four years after Mitchel died of the fevers from which low country planters had regularly retreated long before they fled from Union forces, the problems of the freedmen were still both earthy and astronomical.

Much had happened on that shore. When Littlefield signed the Mitchelville charter, Hilton Head at the entrance to deep, wide Port Royal Sound had become a sandy boom town crowded in war and waiting confidently for peace. Beyond the wharfs on which

Littlefield, Charlotte Forten and so many others had first observed the "contrabands," were rows of roomy cottages built, one observer said, under a liberal construction of the regulations about providing officers with quarters. Behind them stood warehouses and other government buildings. Next was the street of the sutlers, those merchants who followed the flag everywhere a soldier had a dollar and a desire.

Their line of two-story buildings, "blooming out in the most extravagant display of fancy lettered signs," was sometimes ambitiously called Broadway but more often was damned and designated as Robbers Row. Near by, an immense wooden hotel was under construction to accommodate Northern visitors coming on regularly plying vessels and who, it was apparently believed, would be coming forever. A railroad was projected from Fort Royal Sound nearly due north to Branchville, South Carolina, by-passing Charleston which Sherman had by-passed, too, but connecting with "the whole railroad system of the South." And a newspaper was appearing, devoted to the thesis that a metropolis was bound to emerge from the sands.

"Everybody seemed possessed with the mania for speculation," said Whitelaw Reid. "That a great city must spring up hereabouts has been laid down as an axiom. This is the best harbor on the coast while that of Charleston is positively bad, and that of Savannah is contracted and not easy of access. Situated midway between the two, the speculators insist that it ought to fall legitimate heir to the trade of both. Besides, the Carolina sea-coast must have a seaport, and Charleston is so utterly ruined, they argue, and so odious to the nation that Northern trade and capital would discriminate against it, in favor of its younger rival."

With his headquarters there, General Littlefield was not immune to the great gamble which Reid said involved naval officers of the blockading fleet as well as the army ashore. The General had his plans for the peace but at the time he was more active than ever in the greater speculation in freedom which originally brought him to the islands. He promoted no seaport. But his order, issued from the Headquarters of the U. S. Forces on Hilton Head, St. Helena and Tybee islands, proposed a town which might be a model for freedom—and which many believed it was. Littlefield's order, formally organizing the village from the settlement which had grown by the old field in the cane and the palmettoes, began with the statement of the obvious: "One of the results of the Civil War has been the accumulation of a large Colored Population upon Hilton Head Island, S. C. Their present condition demands the sympathy and co-operation of the philanthropic and those in authority, to aid them in organizing, as far as possible, the means of self-government, by establishing schools, and police and sanitary regulations."

All the "lands set apart for the colored population, near Hilton Head" should be declared to constitute the village and "only freedmen and colored persons residing or sojourning within the territorial limits of said village, shall be deemed and considered inhabitants thereof." For them schools were to be set up, with compulsory attendance laws carrying penalties for parents whose children failed to appear. The village government, composed of a supervisor and treasurer named by the Military Commander of the District and an elective council, was instructed to provide other ordinances "to prevent and punish vagrancy, idleness and crime. To punish licentiousness, drunkenness, offenses against public decency and good order, and petty violations of the rights of persons and property. To require due observance of the Lord's Day . . ."

Such lofty proposals may have seemed pretentious so close to Robbers Row where crowds of Negro customers, cheap liquor and Cape May diamonds helped make swift fortunes for the sutlers. The Yankees who brought knickknacks, shoes and bright handkerchiefs, however, also brought the concepts of morality, small farms, free schools and universal political democracy. And as Littlefield wrote his orders, they represented an effort to deal with a situation more imperative at the moment than even the metropolis expected to grow on wide, deep Port Royal Sound.

His problem was no longer the recruitment of black soldiers. A romantic visitor wrote vivid word home about long lines of uniformed Negroes, "their glistening bayonets setting the red rays of the sinking sun to flickering in grotesque lights and shades over the shouting and dancing slaves." A far greater problem was the ebon multitude of those who neither marched nor danced. Many such had been on the islands when Mitchel and the Union forces first arrived. Others had come down the rivers and across the swamps, but Sherman, who counted by the mile the colored people who joined his march to the sea, relieved himself at Savannah by diverting thousands more to Hilton Head.

Also, there, prodded as he felt by Lincoln's suspicious and saturnine Secretary of War, Edwin M. Stanton, Sherman issued his famous Sea Island Circular. Under it, the Sea Islands from Charleston to Port Royal, rice plantations along the rivers thirty miles back from the sea, and lands bordering the St. Johns River in Florida were set aside for the settlement of the freedmen. That order seemed to provide, though Sherman denied later such an intention, the famous delusion that freedom would include forty acres and a mule. And even the semblance of such a promise produced a greater dark tide.

On Christmas Day, three days after he had taken Savannah, Sherman suddenly told Littlefield's associate, General Saxton, to plan the reception on Hilton Head of seven hundred freedmen "who would be at the wharf in an hour." They were, the earnest but overwhelmed Saxton said, "mainly women, old men and children. . . . Half of them had traveled from Macon, Atlanta and even Chattanooga. They were all utterly destitute of blankets, stockings or shoes; and among the seven hundred there were not fifty articles in the shape of pots or kettles, or other utensils for cooking, no axes, very few coverings for many heads, and children wrapped in the only article not worn in some form by the parents."

That was only a first consignment. Others were sent and more freedmen followed spontaneously in the hope of land without which they were mumbling, to every listening Northern visitor apparently, they couldn't see what good it did them to make them free: "Gib us our land and we take care of ourselves; but widout land, de ole massas can hire us or starve us, as dey please."

Land was distributed. By May General Saxton reported that forty thousand were settled in the area. And in the process Mitchelville, which Littlefield organized, became an exciting example much visited by those from the North who were most anxious to prove the possibilities of freedmen whose freedom had been their first concern in the war. General Littlefield had been busy with the village's affairs when his regiment received the surrender of Charleston. He was preoccupied with its problems even when he made a visit to that ruined place where Sumter was "now a shapeless heap of sands and mortar" to receive the flag which the town's freed folk's chosen colored girl presented to him for his 21st Regiment U. S. Colored Troops on March 3.

The 21st was "Littlefield's Infantry" from its creation in March 1863. Its Lieutenant Colonel, Augustus G. Bennett, then a captain, had been transferred to it from the 81st Volunteer New York Infantry. More young officers had been taken from that white regiment and some from other New York organizations on duty in the Sea Islands. Association with them had tightened Milton's ties with his native State. He had kept tight his ties with the regiment as his officers attested at its muster-out: "Occupied, as you were, in the perplexing duties of Superintendent of Recruiting, you might have been pardoned for indifference toward us, but contrary to this, you have always evinced the deepest interest and done everything in your power to promote the good of all."

The regiment's triumph was Charleston, and, with very different feelings that March day, Milton shared the view of young Mrs. Ravenel that old Charleston was dead. Stirring speculation and the victor's ideas of salvation were down the coast on Hilton Head. Charleston seemed a dead city marked by its cemeteries, the rubbish around Calhoun's tomb, and the rude graveyard for Union prisoners which had been made of the race track which once had been Charleston's gayest gathering place. The old town was strange to those who loved it and those who hated it, too. The varied people in and beside the parade to the Citadel pointed its paradoxes—and those of the South around it.

The slim, tawny girl who gave Littlefield the flag was, one of the Northern correspondents who quickly crowded the region wrote, "understood to be a granddaughter of one of the greatest soldiers America ever produced; a General whose brilliant military record (of which every history book of our country makes very prominent mention) has been fitly closed, and made doubly dear to us by unswerving fidelity to the Union." And he added in inadequate explanation, "Of Southern birth and Southern social habits, in his early manhood he had a daughter born in Charleston; and the child of this lady herself a woman grown, was selected to be the standard bearer on this occasion." She could have been Frémont's granddaughter but was probably not. General Winfield Scott, "Old Fuss and Feathers," who had retired early in the war with the eulogy of Lincoln, was Virginia born. Though not "in his early manhood" he had been in Charleston, a six-foot-four major general in his forties in 1832 watching the Nullificationists for Andrew Jackson. In the sociology of miscegenation, thirty-three years would easily have sufficed to produce a granddaughter with the flag.

Among the other dusky girls in that ceremony on the grounds of the Citadel, the patrician Mrs. Porcher mentioned sarcastically "Miss Middleton and Miss Alston, young ladies of colour"—both undoubtedly taking their names under the Mitchel system of nomenclature. Some such young Negro women, Whitelaw Reid noticed a few weeks later, wore "bonnets of last year's styles, with absolutely a few of the coquettish little triangular bits of lace and flowers which the New York milliners have this year decreed." Others wore handkerchiefs which Reid referred to as turbans. There was much bright evidence, however, that before Sumter gaily fell there were more Negro seamstresses and mantua-makers than white ones.

Few of the Negro men were like Robert B. Elliott, later Congressman, who was educated in England at High Hollow Academy and Eton College. No more, were men equal in ability to Robert Smalls, who was to be known as "the Gullah Statesman" in Congress because he spoke that dialect there. There was the greatest diversity among the colored people who before the war had outnumbered the whites in Charleston. The proportion of slaves in its population exceeded that of any other southern city. Among them were 3,500 free persons of color and 5,000 domestic servants trained to staff the noted hospitality of the city. Its grace was not staffed by apes. Some, indeed, dark and erect, made not too fantastic the abolitionist's concept of the Negro as "God's image in ebony."

The census before the war had shown more Negroes than whites among the craftsmen of Charleston. Not all the white people were patricians. Before the war more than a hundred white women were listed as domestic servants. And there were white hucksters and draymen, fishermen, bakers, butchers, brickmasons, other craftsmen and many unskilled laborers. After Union occupation a hundred of the 274 laborers on the city's bushy streets were whites and the officer in charge reported that a lower percentage of the whites than the Negroes among them could read and write.

Little remembered is the fact that the first fair employments practices legislation began in the prewar South as laws designed to protect white craftsmen from the competition of slave artisans. Slave owners, between crop seasons, sometimes offered slave labor on construction projects at rates which undercut the whites. It seems, also, almost completely forgotten that five million white Southerners owned no slaves. Some of them, as "po' whites," shared and sometimes deserved the contempt of the slaves and slave owners together. Still the familiar picture of the freedmen as loosed apes in the white man's South was not drawn from imagination merely. Even the sympathetic Reid recalled those with the black faces and woolly heads, so familiar on the Sea Islands, and the thick lips and the "mouths now and then broadening into a grin or breaking out into that low, oily chuckling gobble of a laugh which no white man can ever imitate."

Neither black nor white was simple. Patrician as well as plebeian whites were eager—if not always grateful—for Union rations. Charleston was home to all kinds of both. The battered town was not only the city of Mrs. Ravenel and Mrs. Porcher, but the native place also of the Grimké sisters, Sarah and Angelina, who had long insisted that slavery was a system of "oppression and cruelty, licentiousness and wrong." After the war they recognized the sons of a wanton brother by a handsome slave girl and one of those boys later gave the old Grimké name to Charlotte Forten as his bride.

James L. Petigru, whose stubborn Unionism had been respected even by his hot-headed neighbors, was dead. But very much alive was Franklin J. Moses, Jr., who had torn down the American flag from Fort Sumter, trodden it underfoot and hoisted the Secession ensign in its place. He had not then begun the course which was to make him the Reconstruction "Robber Governor" of South Carolina. Some others, who had hastened away before Littlefield's men arrived, were significant. Dr. John Bachman, the Northern-born

Lutheran minister and collaborator of Audubon, took the last train out, while Confederates were setting fires, for fear of special unpleasant attentions which might be paid him because he had opened with prayer the Secession Convention in 1860. In escape—frying pan to fire—he found himself on the route of Sherman's bummers on the Cash plantation near Cheraw and became Jefferson Davis' principal witness of barbarities which attended the fall of the Confederacy. (Incidentally and perhaps irrelevantly, the master of that plantation was Colonel Ellerbe Boggan Crawford Cash, whose later lethal defense of his "honor" against an innocuous neighbor made South Carolina determine that his duel should be its last.)

Littlefield was back at Hilton Head when the Northern personages, assembled for Lincoln's elaborately planned ceremonial of retribution, came there before going to Charleston. It was significant that they visited first Milton's new Village of Mitchelville. The *Arapo* brought them from New York to Hilton Head on April 12. And on the following day William Lloyd Garrison, Theodore Tilton, editor of *The Independent*, George Thompson, the famous English reformer, and Judge William D. Kelley "took a trip to the self-governing Negro settlement of Mitchelville, a mile and a half away." Judge Kelley, then and long after a Congressman from Philadelphia, was probably more symbolic of the past and future than the others present. A founder of the Republican Party, abolitionist, advocate of the use of Negro troops, he was to become famous in history as "Pig Iron" Kelley because of his equally earnest advocacy of high tariffs on iron and steel, which the Republican Party had won along with the war.

Others accompanied them. Members of Henry Ward Beecher's congregation in Brooklyn had chartered a ship to accompany the *Arapo* south. For both the whites and blacks it was a highly emotional occasion: "from the hysterical contraband to the dispassionate judge there was no reserve or restraint in the general flow of tears." General Littlefield's emotions on the occasion are not of record. But as a leader in the labors there and a lover of great poetry he must have been moved by Garrison's reading, as he opened his speech, of Moses' triumphant song in Exodus about the arrival of the Lord's children in the Promised Land.

Milton himself was called upon often as an orator that spring.

He spoke on occasions of rejoicing and of great sorrow. Between Appomattox and the death of Lincoln, he outlined his views about Reconstruction in a speech at Savannah. That occasion was one in honor of General Gillmore who, after absence on other duty, had returned to the command of the Department of the South. The big, bald, easily blushing Gillmore said his thanks and spoke of the "glorious news" from Raleigh where Sherman was arranging cessation of hostilities with General Joseph E. Johnston for the surrender of the last great Southern army. Then, reported *The Savannah Daily Herald,* he offered a toast, "Universal Peace, based upon Universal Freedom." Obviously, Gillmore had brought his friend, General Littlefield, along for any more extended speaking. Milton followed Gillmore in an address in which he undertook to express his views about the peace in prospect. He was not abashed. His courteous manner did not conceal something close to contempt for the conquered. His magnanimity was almost that which he might have shown to mistaken children.

On the shore of Georgia, he mentioned proudly his recent enthusiastic visitor to Mitchelville, William Lloyd Garrison, on whose head Georgia thirty-five years before had put a price. Milton tied himself and his fellow Yankees to Garrison's state where that "Christian band of patriots," the Pilgrims, had planted their feet and the tree of liberty on the rocky shore. Such Yankees, he said, sought liberty, not gold.

"In crossing the old Atlantic," he told the Southerners who had gathered in subserviency, "they were led by no such allurements as guided De Soto and his followers."

It had been 350 years since the Spaniard had visited Savannah greedy for any treasure. Little gold was apparent there in 1865. Milton emphasized the differing quests, liberty above allurements.

"This principle is what had given New England her fame, the Yankee a name," he went on in cool instruction, "and this was what the people of the South contended so strongly against, Free Labor. We have fought for this, and will fight for it still. We know that the Yankee side of the question is Industry and the opposite is Idleness; the contest is over at last, and the question has been decided on the side of self-government and universal liberty."

Having almost repeated Gillmore's brief toast, he went on slowly in a voice which seemed full of leashed power.

"The people of South Carolina, Georgia and all the Southern States, can have peace if they wish it, by simply complying with the laws and showing themselves unconditionally loyal. The United States Government can afford to be generous; she will be so when those in rebellion repent of the errors of their ways, become good peaceable citizens, and prove it by their actions. All that you people want is to go to work; your state is rich in natural products. Develop the resources of your state, and improve the soil, you will in a few years far exceed the wealth of former times.

"If instead of standing upon a sentiment, mourning for lost aristocracy, you will go at once, like a good business man, to restore harmony among your people, industry with all classes, there will be no questions of your rights or wrongs."

Then he paused. In his tall figure there seemed almost a lazy, latent, dangerous power. What he had stated in his own language was his understanding of the Lincoln plan which he had followed the year before into Florida. But a choice for the South was involved in that plan. Milton's beard, close-clipped, did not conceal his firm jaw. He and all the other men in the army and navy wanted to go home, he said.

"But"—he lingered over the word almost as if he held it in utter assurance. His lips twisted above his dark beard in a slight smile which contained the shadow of contempt. "But you cannot set yourselves at work in a day. Should you want help to put yourselves in order, why, we will send down some of our Yankees in blue, to put you in running shape. If you cannot do this, do not be at all disappointed if you should find, one of these fine mornings, some of these Yankees filling your places. You have now but a short time to consider. The world moves, and so does the Yankee nation."

No clear record of the Georgia reaction to those remarks remains. Resentment then wore a very ragged coat. But evidence of Littlefield's reputation as a speaker lies in the fact that he had hardly returned to Hilton Head before he was called back to Savannah again to deliver the address on an occasion in an occupied city in which Union anger and mourning were combined with new Southern fears.

On that Saturday afternoon, the body of Lincoln, seven days dead, lay in Independence Hall in Philadelphia on a first stop of a seventeen-hundred-mile funeral procession following much the same route he had followed in coming from Springfield four years before. It is possible that Anna joined the three-mile-long line of mourners. There were children in the exhausting procession no older than little Milton.

Savannah seemed far off, suspect and strange to the mourning nation, but on that afternoon the largest assemblage of human beings ever seen in the Georgia city, a local paper said, gathered in Johnson's Square. The paper put the number present at between four and five thousand. The official report of the proceedings, published later, estimated eight and ten thousand persons. Certainly those who "appeared in obedience to the call . . . to make suitable demonstrations of the sincerity of our citizens in exhibition of their sympathy with the nation in its late melancholy bereavement" overflowed the square and spread in packed masses along Bull and Bryan and Congress streets.

Great black banners bearing legends of sorrow had been prepared. The Honorable C. P. Leslie called the meeting to order but he presented as its authoritarian president the Federal Provost Marshal of Savannah. There were forty nine vice presidents and a couple of dozen secretaries, including both soldiers and citizens. Prayers were said; hymns sung. A long resolution was adopted laying "the foul crime at the door of those inglorious authors of treason, secession and rebellion." The unanimity with which it was passed was absolute. Then: "The 14th Maine Brass Band, who had taken their position near the Speaker's stand, played an appropriate air, after which General Littlefield, who had just arrived from Hilton Head, ascended the stand and was introduced to the meeting."

The General advanced to the front of the platform like a man ready in anger to march again. He swung about, bowed to the officers and dignitaries who shared the platform, then slowly surveyed the great crowd before him with eyes which almost seemed to be seeking conspirators among those assembled. Slowly his bold eyes softened and he began to speak, in a voice almost too low to reach the restless fringes of the crowd, of the dead President. He spoke of Lincoln, he said, as one who had the good fortune "to share the friendship and mingle with him." His voice rose as he placed Lincoln in a history colored by much indignation rather than in the record of a personal friendship. And his words took on the dimensions of demand when he enjoined all present "to swear before God and High Heaven to mete out to our unrepenting traitors death, and to the assassin the assassin's doom." He was angry and sad by turns. But at its end the speech was essentially, as he had described it when he began, "an humble tribute of respect to the memory of the purest patriot and noblest man of modern times."

Humility never seemed to be one of Milton's special gifts. He laughed more easily than he wept. But he had lost much in Lincoln's death. He spoke, however, with more zeal than show of emotion. Shaken as others were by the appalling news from Washington, he had carefully written his speech; he had sailed from Hilton Head to Savannah; he had held the attention of the crowd which spread from the square into adjoining streets. And, of course, as speaker he had been dramatic, immaculate, and erect.

Afterward, much praised for what he had said, he walked back to the river, climbed down the stairs to the cobblestone landing where the slow river crawled by the wharfs toward the marshes and the ocean. The river in the April twilight was no longer red with the soils of Georgia and Carolina. Bells and voices sounded. Ropes were thrown. General Littlefield walked forward to face the breeze from the sea. The wind whipped his cape around his tall lean figure. There were no stars in the sky. The familiar shore and its often-passed landmarks were imperceptible in the dark. As his boat turned north beyond the river entrance by Bloody Point and Old Woman's Folly he was suddenly very much alone.

There was no room for loneliness at Hilton Head. More dignitaries came south. Secretary of the Navy Welles sailed on a trip on which Lincoln had planned to accompany him and met in the southern waters many, including the Chief Justice of the Court of Claims, who, he said, had come south for speculation. Chief Justice Chase arrived on the trip upon which he brought along the observant Whitelaw Reid. Reid recorded not only the presence of Northern speculators but also the possibility of economic development based on flourishing freedmen on their own land. At Hilton Head, where hopes of a new metropolitan port were highest, Reid contemplated with a romanticism not rare at the time the possibilities of a black boom on the old shore.

"The Sea Island soil produces the best cotton in the world," he wrote, "and the negroes already have it in a state of more thorough cultivation than was ever before known. The increased wants of the freedmen will stimulate trade, and small farmers will not be able, as the planters were in old times, to go to Savannah or Charleston and buy supplies wholesale. Whatever the fortunes of South Carolina, the Sea Islands must henceforth be flourishing. Whether negroes will not, by and by, prefer to trade with persons of their own color, remains to be seen. Real estate ventures must be further complicated also, with the possibilities that the whole sea coast of South Carolina (if not the entire state), will speedily become one vast negro colony. Already, the only inhabitants on the Sea Islands are negroes, and the same race is in the majority for many miles inland. Compulsory colonization has always been a failure; but is it not probable that there will be a natural tendency of negroes to places where flourishing negro communities are already established and the local government is mainly in their own hands?"

Perhaps Reid when he talked to Saxton, Littlefield and others should have had more doubts about the future. He discounted some of the talk of the speculators about metropolitan prospects. But he only noted as an improbable item, when he was entertained by General Saxton and his charming missionary-teacher wife in the mansion they had bought at Beaufort, their "worrying doubt about the security of the title" to the house in which they had had so many happy times, like the party at Christmas in 1863 when the lovely Mrs. Lander and Charlotte Forten joined them in charades. Apparently Reid did not associate Saxton's doubts about his house with the rights of the thousands of Negroes settled on the plantations about it. He wrote only of Saxton's problem.

"Rebels, who have abandoned their houses," he said, "may, some of these days, return, get pardon, and propose to take possession."

"Suppose he should profess repentance, for the sake of getting back his property, precisely what is there to prevent this fervently-loyal Major-General from having the prince of all the fire-eaters for a neighbor?"

The prospect seemed incredible to Reid, but he added, "In Beaufort, as at Hilton Head, there are wonderful efforts to create a flame of speculation; but capital is timid, and looks sharply to the guarantee of title deeds."

All possession of such property by generals and freedmen alike seemed suddenly much more precarious late that same month when President Andrew Johnson issued on May 29 his amnesty proclamation. With some exceptions, it granted "to all persons who have directly or indirectly participated in the existing rebellion," amnesty and pardon, "with the restoration of all rights of property," except as to slaves and lands involved in legal confiscation proceedings already in court. And on the same day by proclamation he set up the first provisional civilian government in North Carolina on terms which denied suffrage to the newly created black citizens and enfranchised many recent participants in armed secession.

This North Carolina proclamation, said George Fort Milton in *The Age of Hate,* was "a signal to the prostrate South that Johnson would walk in Lincoln's footsteps." The proclamation did, indeed, follow the lines of Lincoln's program, which Milton Littlefield had followed in Florida. And in South Carolina, after Sherman passed through, there was no such reluctance about swearing oaths and resuming rights as John Hay had found. The first Secessionist Governor, Francis W. Pickens, ex-Confederate Senator James L. Orr, and Samuel McGowan, Major General in the Confederate Army, sat in the state convention Johnson recognized. So did twelve gentlemen who had been members of the Secession Convention. Three-fourths of the delegates, said the watching Sidney Andrews, itinerant correspondent of *The Boston Advertiser* and *The Chicago Tribune,* had titles, most of them secured in the Confederate Army. There were, of course, no Negroes in the convention.

Perhaps that was Lincoln's plan, too, and perhaps had he lived it would have been his still. It certainly did not satisfy those who had succeeded in pushing Lincoln. In Boston, Wendell Phillips declared that it would have been "better, far better, for Grant to have surrendered to Lee than President Johnson to North Carolina." In South Carolina, Littlefield was a loyal Lincoln man still but along with his associate and superior, General Saxton, he was confused in his work with black men.

It was John Littlefield in Washington who promptly associated himself with the Lincoln legend, already mightily growing. Though he was not among those at the bedside when Lincoln died, he painted a much-admired picture of the scene. Indeed, when John spoke later at Tremont Temple in Boston a reporter said that the picture had given him "world-wide fame." Also John painted a portrait of Lincoln which, engraved for general sale, pleased many. Robert T. Lincoln was quoted in one of John's advertisements as saying that "the picture is in all respects more pleasing to me than any I have." And Lincoln's old law partner Herndon, then about the business of collecting materials concerning Lincoln as a man, politician, lover, small-town lawyer, wrote John from Springfield: "I have shown this portrait to many of our old citizens here and they all unanimously give it as their opinion that it is the very best. —You have followed closely the original, and there is where so many err—being too ideal."

Such praise prepared John to give up his clerkship and set himself up as an artist, then as a lecturer on Lincoln, too. He had written Herndon before the engraving of his portrait was prepared: "If you desire to have a faithful likeness engraved of Mr. Lincoln, I may be of some service. I am now painting General Grant in oil and expect to publish this picture in pure line engraving, the head of which will be six inches long. I expect also to paint a life-size head of Mr. Lincoln which I will have engraved if I can bring it about. It is quite doubtful if there is a living artist that has such varied and serviceable remembrances of the good man as your humble servant."

In South Carolina, where Milton remained, the Lincoln image was not so clear. Indeed, the pattern of peace in his image, as proclaimed by President Johnson, seemed in its effects startling to many on the Sea Islands who felt that they had most loyally followed Lincoln. The amiable General Saxton, who had been peremptorily handed the problem of settling Sherman's refugees on Christmas Day, expressed the view that "a large majority, probably nine-tenths, of the people of South Carolina," are opposed to the Federal government. Certainly more than Mr. Lincoln's tenth, however, were coming forward, taking the oaths, and coming home to claim the properties they had abandoned in the Sea Islands. Some such lands had been sold to satisfy delinquencies in a direct tax Congress had levied upon the property of the nation. Congress had authorized the seizure of other property when "the lawful owner thereof shall be voluntarily absent therefrom, and engaged . . . in aiding or encouraging the rebellion." Such lands involved not only Saxton's house, but the thousands of acres on which Saxton had put under "possessory" titles (which sounded all right to colored folks) thousands of Negroes. Also such lands involved property in which Littlefield was interested, too.

Some pitiful patricians, accustomed to coaches and footmen, were coming home to Beaufort in mule-drawn wagons to confront the "squatters." Their plight has been so ardently remembered that even Saxton in their story has seemed a villain. Indeed, their return, in recollection usually in the guise of ladies in distress, is much better remembered than the twelve thousand Union dead in the Beaufort cemetery alone, denied any home-going by the fevers and the war. Undoubtedly some of the Union people in Beaufort in 1865 (sutlers and speculators, visitors south on swift errands in hope of quick profits, politicians looking for material to sustain the Radical furies) were the rascals they have been portrayed. Not all the natives who came back, however, were innocent penitents.

Even South Carolinians have long recalled the story of the Sea Island gentleman from Edisto Island who out-Charlestoned Charleston in defiance of the Union. At the Secession Convention in 1860, he rose to announce that, regardless of what South Carolina did, Edisto was going to secede. After Secession and surrender, Edisto was also the island which, according to Southern historians of the period in the state, demonstrated most clearly the difficulties sometimes met "in effecting the restoration of lands" to their former owners. On Edisto, stubborn Negroes in possession held their land, saying, "Gov'ment drap we here. We can't go till Gov'ment take we off." They suggested that the planters go to Charleston and shuck oysters. Also, after Secession and surrender, Edisto, the island of the extremist even in South Carolina, was the scene on which Littlefield made his plans for something more than forty acres and a mule.

If unfriendly postwar testimony about General Littlefield can be believed, he put his faith in the rich resources of a South, resurgent with the aid of some Yankees in blue, in lands on that island. While others dreamed of a great city at Hilton Head, Milton was interested in "great timbered possessions on the Edisto" which would furnish lumber to expanding Philadelphia. Lumber was a new enterprise for him though he had spent the years of his youth beside the great woods of Michigan. He was not, however, the first Yankee who realized the riches in the tall trees near deep water on the South Carolina shore. Governor Duncan Clinch Heyward, whose people owned many plantations and thousands of slaves in the area, said, in his charming book about the rice islands, *Seed From Madagascar,* that the greatest mistake the old rice planters made was not taking timber into account in the value of their lands. Others recognized it. Up the shore at Georgetown a man from New Jersey, David Risley, had built the largest lumber concern in the South before the war. Then, wisely, Risley had spent the war in neither New Jersey nor South Carolina but traveling in South America and the West Indies. He came back to build an even greater fortune. There seemed in 1865 an equal possibility for Littlefield—certainly one equal to the metropolitan hopes of many fellow officers on Hilton Head.

By late summer, however, the capital which had been timid in the spring about the titles to a great seaport for a black metropolis had become more timid still. And even General Saxton in his Beaufort headquarters as officer of the new Freedmen's Bureau and as soldier seemed increasingly more like a refugee himself. General Saxton had been content, doing his job well as he saw it and others reported it, in spite of the fact that he was in wartime "under all manner of slights and obloquy from other officers who thought his work unworthy of West Point." In the peace, however, it was increasingly evident that he was no match for Southerners who had lost a war but had no intention whatever of losing their land.

General Saxton's feelings were undoubtedly sharpened by the item that in Washington the effective agent of the South Carolina government President Johnson had recognized was a Sea Island neighbor, too. That agent, William Henry Trescott, was no "prince of fire-eaters." But his wife had inherited large plantations, then under Saxton's supervision, on Barnwell Island near Beaufort. Trescott was a diminutive, persuasive man who knew his way around Washington where he had served as Assistant Secretary of State under Buchanan. Washington somehow seemed farther and farther away from Saxton. And half a year after William Lloyd Garrison had read Moses' triumphant song in Exodus to listening Negroes, to Littlefield, Congressman "Pig Iron" Kelley and others at Mitchelville, the tiny Trescott triumphed over the big, whiskered, faithful Saxton. At a "very harmonious conference" with the President, Trescott secured assurances that Saxton would be required to issue a circular correcting the "false impression" that the government intended the Negroes to have land. Saxton followed his orders.

The Negroes who loved General "Saxby," as they never ceased to call him, would not believe him. Indeed, his directed disavowal came at a time of a new march to the sea, this time composed of Negroes alone. Some said such Negro soldiers as Littlefield led were responsible for the rumors which created the widespread delusion that lands in the low country would be divided among Negroes at Christmastime. Such may have been the case. Certainly Littlefield, as the organizer of many of those troops, had not come to his work like Saxton, who told Reid that he would have preferred other duty but "I was ordered to do this thing, and I have tried to do it faithfully, till the government gave me something else to do. I was educated in its school and for its service, and I thought it my business to do whatever it required." Littlefield had been educated in no such school. He recognized a difference between discipline and docility. He was a man who wanted what he went after. He would not have remained immobile in "worrying doubts."

Undoubtedly the Negro troops he led were, as such, an affront to the white people in the towns they garrisoned after the white soldiers had hurried home. However, no greater outrages in 1865 were charged against them than those laid by Dr. Bachman of Charleston and others at the door of Sherman's tall Westerners. But the last soldier in Sherman's army had been paid off by August 1, 1865. The blue host which had crossed South Carolina in the spring left only 7,500 officers and men, white and Negro, in the state at the end of the year.

A leading South Carolina authority on the period wrote that "the discipline of some of these Negro troops was effective and satisfactory." But their white officers, he said, even those whose only purpose in leading Negroes had been to "fight for the flag" as officers, "resented the aversion which they and all others in like relations naturally excited in the white people, and were thus tempted to condone conduct on the part of their soldiers which should have been repressed." That may well have been the case. Undoubtedly aversion was resented and returned. And the man who had set up Michelville might have resented—where Saxton was only hurt—the rejection of the refugees on the broken-promise land to which he had helped lead them on the shore where Lincoln had sent him. Littlefield who was to be charged with looting states was not incapable of loosing rumors in a state through men he had taught to be soldiers, too.

In late summer Johnson's provisional Governor Benjamin F. Perry wrote Secretary of State Seward: "The complaints are general throughout the State, that the Colored Troops are a great nuisance & they do infinite mischief with the Freedmen by misrepresenting the purposes and intentions of the Government. They tell them that the lands are to be divided, that they are not to work for their employers, & that the white race is to be driven out of the country or exterminated. There is great apprehension of danger in the lower part of the state and there have been serious disturbances with the Freedmen."

There were some ugly incidents though nothing compared to the charges against Sherman's men. Apparently, however, the chief basis of white complaint was, as stated by Perry's biographer, that "with utter disregard for their obligations, they left growing crops and trekked in hordes toward the seacoast, where they expected to receive lands from the government."

However the rumors started, they did create a great black pilgrimage on the roads, through the woods, on the bypaths, of Negroes toward the shore. They moved almost as instinctively as lemmings and to the equal death of their hopes. On a bright moonlight night in early fall, Sidney Andrews, the journalist, saw crowds of them moving between Columbia and Orangeburg plodding to the east. They were, he said, "trudging along with their whole earthly possessions in a bundle on the head. . . . They had but few words; 'Goin' to Charleston,' was often their only reply. Whether talkative or taciturn, there was a firm foot and an unruffled voice for the coast. . . . There had recently been some robberies of travelers on that road, and guerrillas suggested themselves with every outline seen in the sheeny darkness. Yet it was only the exodus of the Negroes, going out ignorantly and mistakenly, yet seeking nothing less noble and worthy than freedom."

Such movement, as planters pointed out, deprived them of hands. The travelers to the sea got no Christmas gift of lands. Indeed, E. Merton Coulter in *The South During Reconstruction* says, "Transcontinental railroads received from the Federal Government about 200,000,000 acres, yet after the war not one free acre did the negro receive except through the ineffective homestead system." What the Negroes got that Christmas in South Carolina was the Black Code which provided for different, sterner regulations of the freedmen than the laws governing the whites.

Perhaps such regulations seemed only natural to the all-white legislature. It seemed like a surreptitious return to slavery to many suspicious abolitionists in the North. At a time when Northern Radical angers were rising in Congress against Johnson's program, such special laws helped to bring on the Congressional Reconstruction which followed. Among other provisions, the South Carolina code made it illegal for any Negro to follow any calling other than farming without securing a license from the judge of the district courts. Negroes had to pay high licenses to follow trades for which no licenses were required of white men. So the year of Union victory ended with the denial of land to the freedmen and the enactment by white South Carolinians of laws which bound freedmen to the land. There were those who followed Lincoln who somehow did not feel that that was the program which he would have made of peace and freedom.

Their views at the moment seemed irrelevant in South Carolina. Saxton was dismissed from his position though later the army gave him other duty elsewhere as a quartermaster. And "Littlefield's Infantry," the 21st U. S. Colored Troops, was mustered out of service as the first year after surrender began. Some ceremonies marked that event at Hilton Head where the sands had blown high about the porches of the officers' quarters and many sutlers had shut up their shops on Robbers Row. Mitchelville, a mile and a half away, was no longer the symbol of anything but houses half hidden by the brush. For a last time Littlefield's black soldiers in blue coats and red trousers moved on the parade ground where little pines and palmettoes were beginning to encroach along the edges. His officers composed their farewell statement to their organizer and commander.

"General!" they saluted him. They traced his whole record in the recruitment of Negro troops.

"By your efforts," they told him, "thousands of colored men have been lifted out of the slough of slavery and dependence into the dignity of soldiers and free men."

They concluded:

"Be assured, General, your invaluable kindness, your generous encouragements and amiable official bearing toward us all under all circumstances will long be remembered; and, in taking leave of you, perhaps forever, believe us we shall always cherish for you the kindliest feelings of regard and affection; and it is our sincere wish that your future may be brightened and blessed with all that is desirable of wordly honors, prosperity and happiness."

It was an emotional occasion. But it had been nearly a year since Littlefield in Savannah had said that "we of the army and navy wish to go home." There seemed at the last less pertinence in his declaration, then, that "but if you will not accept the terms . . . we are willing to remain for life to accomplish it." The last parade had marched on the hobnail-ringing streets of northern cities. No bands awaited Milton's arrival in Philadelphia. He had made plans for himself and Anna and the boy, in terms of his faith that a South accepting the principles of Industry and Free Labor might "far exceed the wealth of former times." They were, however, as uncertain early in 1866 as the land tenure of freedmen, or General Saxton's title to his house next door to Barnwell Rhett's, or Milton's own timber at Tidewater.

Undoubtedly he had made arrangements before the last farewells. Still it was not until May that he opened his business as lumber merchant at 319 Walnut Street, Philadelphia. His hazard in that enterprise was not made clear until two years later when the righteous and unreconstructed *Journal* of Wilmington, North Carolina, directed a question to the equally ferociously Southern Raleigh *Daily Sentinel* about Milton who was then in the South again: Is this, it asked, "the same General Littlefield who figured so largely in the Philadelphia lumber market in 1866-67, making large contracts for the furnishing of lumber on the faith of mills and great timbered possessions on the Edisto, or somewhere else South, and who utterly failed to deliver any at all?"

Such insinuation about him was not new then. Before he got home, the marches of war were over and the charges and countercharges of Reconstruction had begun. The carpetbagger was created before the soldier took off his blue.

CHAPTER VIII

No More Parades

WHEN MILTON CAME home in the late spring of 1866, the great blue host seemed as gone as if it had never existed. The Grand Army's camps of instruction and demobilization had become almost as ghostly as the graveyards it had left behind in the South. There were no more parades and in Philadelphia the noise of tramping feet, ringing with hobnails on the pavements, had been succeeded by the sounds of hammer and saw, changing mightily William Penn's once "greene country towne."

The new Chestnut Street bridge opened the west bank of the Schuylkill to development. Politicians and builders were already planning in the growing metropolis the new city hall which, as James Bryce wrote later as a man not uncritical of what went on within it, would far overtop the Cologne Cathedral, the Pyramid of Cyclops or St. Peter's at Rome. Industry was expanding behind the protective tariffs which, as much as freedom, the war had produced. The plutocratic Union League Club, which had been organized to "take treason by the throat," faced the future with approximately the same purpose as to the economic and political life of the country. And rising was the Huge Wigwam which that summer held more than ten thousand people at each of two noisy conventions in which the great American debate over Reconstruction of the South took place.

Littlefield came home late. By autumn only 11,043 Union veterans would still be in uniform. Not all the more than a million men who came home found adjustment easy. The quest for jobs had assumed the dimensions of a flood. There were even, months after demobilization, veterans "seen in dingy blue uniform begging on ferryboats and steam cars, or straggling through the streets with hurdy-gurdies." There were, of course, always opportunities for generals. All kinds of companies, as Ida Tarbell found in her study of the oil industry (then only seven years successively booming and busting since the digging of the first well), understood that in the sale of stock and other things, too, "the name of a general was the most popular and persuasive argument in the country." There were, however, many generals. Most of them came home before Milton. There seemed, however, ample opportunity in the city for him when he opened his office on Walnut Street for the sale of lumber from the South. Certainly the General, proffering the "tall and stately pines" (of which Philadelphia's Charlotte Forten had written) to eager Philadelphia builders, made Edisto sound like El Dorado.

On Walnut Street, as one of his critics said of him later, he was always "amicably accessible" and operated with an air of "rollicking munificence" but as civilian in the style of the times, North and South, he was accustomed to being addressed by his military title. Already the recollection of service was beginning to bind men together in the Grand Army of the Republic which was founded that year with Milton's old commander, General Hurlbut (who was to face increasing charges of public drunkenness and official corruption) as its chief. Many veterans who oratorically rejoiced over peace had a secret homesickness for war—even an angry unspent passion for the South. Like others, Milton felt a little strange in his civilian clothes though he wore them with the flair he had given to his blue tunic with the stars on the shoulders. He wore, a Southern editor recorded, "a pair of lead-colored pants with black stripes down the legs, black coat, beaver hat, white shirt with a linen bosum and cotton-tail and a 'killing cravat,' also a large gold ring on the little finger of the left hand."

The reference to the cotton-tail of his shirt was undoubted slander. His worst enemies attested to his elegance. Like other gentlemen's of the time his pants were fawn-colored, of shepherd's plaid or checked. His waistcoats were bright and some embroidered with flowers. He was never, however, uniquely garish. Indeed, a historian of the Union League clubs, which were putting Northern conservatism to work for Southern radicalism, noted that gentlemen "were dressing less soberly in the 1860's." Unlike Littlefield, he said, many gentlemen were beginning to abandon long black coats for plaid and checks and "every gentleman wore diamond studs and rings. Only when his diamonds were off color or too large and numerous did he rate thereby as vulgar." Milton's diamonds were neither many nor big on Walnut Street. But he was adequately debonair and if he had any "worrying doubts" about his prospects or his property, like those General Saxton had admitted the year before, nothing in his appearance ever showed it.

He strode like a soldier on Walnut Street, and on Sansom and Chestnut, Broad and Market, too, where the carts rumbled over the cobbles, and carriages stood at the curbs. And he strolled in peace on the shady sidewalks of Germantown where he had settled at last with Anna and their two-year-old son. In both places men and women turned to look at his broad shoulders and high head. There was nothing ostentatious about his and Anna's little house in Germantown on Shoemaker Lane (later called Rubicam Street). Near the house ran the tracks of the Reading Railroad. Also, near by—already an antique—was a tunnel reputed to have served as a passage in the Underground Railroad, though other old passages like it in the ancient community had been built in colonial times only to connect the house with the barn.

An atmosphere of good American history marked Shoemaker Lane. William Penn's chief associates and George Washington and his officers had moved under Germantown's trees. Littlefield's cousin, Catharine, may have been in that vicinity as a bride of three years when her husband General Greene was delayed by the bad roads and the darkness in bringing up the left column to Washington's aid in the Battle of Germantown. In such a green suburb the war from which Littlefield returned was not yet history but only last year's news. The future there with young Anna and their boy seemed in promise almost as full of happy endings as the past.

Anna was not quite thirty, thin and large-eyed, energetic and gay. She kept her floors as clean as her tables. She was a good cook. She sang—some lively songs but gentle ones, too. She had many favorite hymns. She put a sound of homesickness, not merely for heaven, in "Shall We Gather at the River?" But she wore her light brown hair high in a saucy pompadour. In her presence, any worries Milton had about a business based on long planning in the Sea Islands were both lulled and sharpened by turns. And it can only be conjectured that he realized—as others did earlier—that his titles to timberlands which he had acquired in South Carolina were becoming increasingly uncertain.

It was hot in Philadelphia that summer, steamier than on the Sea Islands where even in August the breeze rattled through the palmettos. A white feather fan which Milton had sent Anna from South Carolina was more decorative than effective. Milton missed the tall windows which in the South had seemed to let in more breeze. He felt a stuffiness away from the sea which had so long been so near. And he was hotter still in his black coat that month, only a short time after he had opened his lumber business, when South Carolina gentlemen arrived in Philadelphia.

He knew many of them. They were the same consciously righteous politicians who had been so active and successful in efforts to restore all lands to old owners regardless of the extent of their participation in what Milton, among others, still commonly called "rebellion"—even "treason." But if pardons had been freely granted to them and, at their request, to others in South Carolina, beyond that in Philadelphia the late Rebels were feted and embraced. There were bands and parades, much oratory and great exultation when they arrived on August 14 at the National Union Convention organized by President Johnson's earnest friends and supporters.

Governor Perry, who a year before had told President Johnson that Littlefield's "black troops are a great nuisance & do great mischief," his successor, Governor James L. Orr, and others came to Philadelphia by Washington. There they were given cordial conference by the President. From the capital they proceeded to the convention in "cars crowded to suffocation with delegates" most of them from the South. And in Philadelphia, former Governor Perry particularly showed himself in no mood of penitence in the peace. He even considered it an "outrage," his biographer wrote, to suggest that C. L. Vallandigham, the convicted Copperhead who had denounced the war and "King Lincoln's" leadership in it, not be allowed to sit as a delegate in the convention. Perry publicly proclaimed his feeling that to exclude Vallandigham would be an "unmanly, impolitic and ungrateful" course toward a man who had made great sacrifices for the South. He would sooner, he said, see the convention break up and go to hell.

Others, including Littlefield, regarded that as its proper destination. It was perhaps doomed before it convened, as a historian of the Republican Party wrote, "by the senseless and reactionary legislation passed by the newly established state governments in the South, which so alarmed the radicals in the Congress." Horace Greeley in the *Tribune* was declaring that the convention was "composed of ninety percent Rebels and Copperheads." The gathering seemed almost designed to dramatize his exaggeration. The bands played on equal terms both "Dixie" and "The Star-Spangled Banner." The delegations of Massachusetts and South Carolina (the states symbolizing the extremes of abolition and Secession) came into the hall side by side, two by two and arm in arm. Some reporters called it the "arm-in-arm" convention, but angry Republican Radicals, who readily turned to Scripture, dubbed it "Noah's Ark"—"two by two of clean beasts, and of beasts that are not clean, and of fowls, and of everything that creepeth upon the earth." The certainty is that the convention loosed no doves.

From the point of view of men like Littlefield the convention could not have been worse timed for amity and forgiveness. Soon after Milton had told his colored troops good-bye in South Carolina a riot involving similar troops in Memphis, his old station, had resulted in the death of forty-six Negroes, the wounding of many more and the burning of twenty Negro schoolhouses and four Negro churches. And less than a month before the "arm-in-arm" convention a riot around a meeting in New Orleans to elect delegates to that convention had resulted in the death of two hundred Negroes and the injury of many more. As in all such commotions in the South then, responsibility for the riots depended upon who pronounced it, but in the mathematics of murder the Negroes were the ones who died. Undoubtedly, one of Milton's visitors at Mitchelville, Theodore Tilton of *The Independent* spoke as strong partisan but to many angry readers when he said that the convention should be postponed lest the effort to "hold up the President's hands . . . reveal that they are red with blood."

Such attacks were, of course, often unfair to the convention and to President Johnson. The meeting represented the hopes of many that better days had come, that Reconstruction might proceed in peace and concord in the preserved Union. It is not surprising, however, that some like Littlefield who watched in the heat resented the "harmony almost of a saccharine nature" which a historian sympathetic toward Johnson said prevailed. Such harmony was only in the hall. There were many men like Milton in the streets and in the country around Philadelphia, too.

Such men gathered in an answering Loyal Union Convention in the same Wigwam two weeks later. If Milton had prominent antagonists in the first convention, he had powerful and elegant friends in the second. The Union League Club of Philadelphia played lavish host to the delegates and the Union League Club of New York held a mass meeting and banquet in that city to which all delegates were transported free in special cars. Hospitality and hostility combined upon the dictum declared in a statement drawn up by the convention that Johnson in his Reconstruction program had laid his hands heavily upon "every earnest loyalist of the South" and "pardoned some of the worst Rebel criminals. . . ."

Milton was apparently already a member of the Union League, which in the war and after was the secret, political arm in the South of the pluto-patriotic Union League clubs. The clubs had been very active in the recruitment of Negro soldiers. Also, it already had agents in the South, working with Negroes, before Littlefield came home. He became president of the North Carolina Union League in 1868 and in 1870 he presided over the national meeting held at Long Branch, New Jersey, where Grant sometimes maintained his summer White House. Obviously, he had close ties with the Philadelphia Union League Club at the time of the Loyal Union Convention—and probably with the New York Club as well.

Even in that hot and increasingly angry summer, however, Milton's business was lumber, not politics. There must, however, have been many interruptions in his "amiable accessibility" as lumber merchant on Walnut Street. Though he put both together later, it is quite possible that he neglected his profits for his politics. The known fact is that he gave up the lumber business late in 1866 without changing his business address. Evidently he did not run away from buyers to whom he had failed to deliver. The subject was one which disturbed him, however.

Later in North Carolina a newspaper friendly to him stated categorically that: "He is *not* the Littlefield so often spoken of in connection with a lumber transaction in the Philadelphia market." He was the only Littlefield listed in the lumber business in Philadelphia at the time. Obviously, there was some truth in the unspecific charges but the probability is that it was the half-truth from the Sea Islands, where his possessions had been repossessed by others, not from Philadelphia, where apparently no buyers sought to prosecute him. From his point of view, he had been robbed by those who sought to make him out a thief.

In Philadelphia, only greater opportunities seemed to turn him from lumber to oil. Certainly not even "great timbered possessions on the Edisto" offered any such dazzling prospects as the oil lands in northwestern Pennsylvania from which swift fortunes had been made since 1859. Milton may have become interested in oil by the demands for lumber in villages like Pithole, Oil City, Titusville, which became crowded cities almost overnight. Fortunes had been made and lost. Of the 5,560 wells drilled at a cost of between $3,000 and $8,000 each in the first ten years of drilling, 4,374 had been "dry holes." But those who hit, hit fortunes. There was a rush of those who hoped to hit. Speculators far away wanted a chance, too. Others were ready to serve their hopes even at a distance. In 1864 and 1865, in Philadelphia alone, Ida Tarbell wrote, more than a thousand oil companies "mostly bogus" had been formed.

All that is actually known about Littlefield in the oil business is that in 1867 he was so listed in the Philadelphia directory. But to that spare fact other information can be added. Milton was late again. Fluctuations in oil prices were fantastic. In 1859, the year of the first well, oil sold at $20 a barrel. New wells pushed the price down to fifty-two cents in 1861, but in 1863, it had risen to $8.15.

In 1867, Milton's year, it went down to $2.40. The oil bubble burst and, says Miss Tarbell, "it was nothing but the irrepressible energy of the region which kept the business going in the panic which followed." Many crooks took cover but if Milton was involved in the process by which "stocks in companies whose holdings were hardly worth the stamps on the certificates were sold all over the land," no Southerners who searched his record to damn his name ever referred to it. Unpursued and unperturbed, he moved on to a speculation in which not oil for lamps but, as he presented it, freedom in the dark South was at stake.

If oil was going down, political passions were rising higher in a year of startling contrasts. However history is read, some of the best men were engaged in the worst causes then, and vice versa. Light and darkness were often indistinguishable side by side—or arm-in-arm. If many were poor, both pawnbrokers and speculators prospered. Littlefield's companion in the disastrous Florida foray two years before, John Hay, noted the sharp contrasts. Young Hay was to solve all his postwar problems by marrying the daughter of Amasa Stone who made millions, in part, by giving John D. Rockefeller secret rail rebates on oil shipments. But in 1867, Hay was still a bachelor. Washington was "gayer than you ever saw it. Balls nearly every night—receptions without number." But when he went out to the Illinois country, from which both he and Littlefield came, he reported early in 1867 "poverty everywhere. In the East it is still tempered by the fever of speculation. But in the West everything & everybody is flat as a buckwheat cake, *de la veille*. There is no money and no business."

Hay made that report from the country to which Milton had not returned during the same month in which Congress passed the Military Reconstruction Act over Johnson's veto. Congress took over the Reconstruction job, set up military districts, and provided for return of the states to the Union only on a basis of Negro suffrage. Elections were to be called, conventions held. So the South was to be made safe for the Union, and the Union safe in Republican control. The need for that, as the year proceeded, was made even more clear among Republican patriots in Philadelphia. They were determined, with their member Jay Cooke, the staunch Republican and Union financier, to save "the legitimate results & fruits of the war." Such fruits included fiscal policies as well as freedom; and the rights of the freedmen coincided neatly with the needs of the financiers.

"What bad news, sad news tonight," Cooke wrote on the night of the off-year elections in 1867. "Pennsylvania and Ohio gone Democratic and the sad lessons of the war all forgotten. Well, God reigneth. His will and purpose will all be made known and enforced in goodtime."

Neither Mr. Cooke nor men like him in Philadelphia and other Northern cities, however, left such political matters entirely to the will of God. With the Presidential elections and, God willing, Ulysses S. Grant, too, coming up next year there was no lack of political funds in the North. Nor was there any misunderstanding of the political importance of the South in which Negroes, who were or should be grateful to the Republican Party for freedom, would vote. The close shave which McClellan had given Lincoln in 1864 was recalled sharply by the Democratic victories in 1867 in New York and Pennsylvania.

Mr. Cooke's early information about Ohio turned out to be wrong but by a Republican majority of only three thousand votes. Furthermore, Ohio in the same election had defeated a Negro suffrage amendment by fifty thousand, while similar measures were beaten also in Michigan, Minnesota and Kansas. Obviously, with Northern States uncertain, it was time for the dispatch southward of "the emissaries of the Union League Clubs of New York and Philadelphia" which Claude Bowers wrote "have been unfairly denied their historic status in the consolidation of the Negro vote."

After lumber and oil, such consolidation was a business for which Milton, as a militant Republican and a friend and leader of the freedmen, was admirably fitted. In it he had the blessing and the backing of pluto-politicians in New York and Philadelphia. Actually, however, he went south at the end of 1867 not merely as an agent, certainly not simply as an emissary. He set out south upon substantial and by no means entirely unwelcomed errands of his own. He was dispatched as patriot, he went after a profit, but he went not merely as an invader but, in important respects, by Southern invitation.

Opportunity opened when he needed it much. Anna conceived

her second child in March, the same month in which Congressional Reconstruction was born. She was delivered, in the November in which Mr. Cooke was so politically pessimistic, by Dr. Thomas Moore of 108 Tulpehocken Street. The baby was named Calvin Alfred after Anna's father and Milton's cousin, Colonel Calvin Littlefield of Ellisburgh, New York, with whom Milton had worked in filling the draft quota of Jefferson County with Negroes from South Carolina. Obviously, Milton's affection had grown for his first cousin, seven years his senior.

They had, despite the difference in their ages, much in common. Colonel Calvin Littlefield had, like Milton, once been a schoolteacher. He was active in politics and had served three terms as a member of the New York Assembly. Also, Calvin had responded promptly to the defense of the Union as Lieutenant Colonel of the 94th New York Volunteers. After strenuous service in the army in Virginia he resigned as a full colonel in 1862 because of "disability." Apparently after his service he moved with a limp which never delayed him. He was to be active, as Milton was, in railroad matters and later became secretary and treasurer of both the St. Louis and San Francisco and Atlantic and Pacific railroads. In the fall of 1867, however, the joint concern of the two Littlefields was not railroads but prewar Southern bonds. They proposed to buy depreciated North Carolina bonds, get the State Reconstruction Convention to re-assert their validity and sell them on the rise such action would assure.

Calvin brought Milton again into association with the two other upstate New Yorkers who had participated in the draft deal. One was John B. Clarke, selectman of Ellisburgh, who had married into the Littlefield family, and the other, obviously a major, if a silent, partner, was Norris Winslow, of Watertown, New York. The year before, Winslow (whether or not on the profits of the draft deal) had sold out as a storekeeper and established his own Merchants' Bank. He went later into manufacturing, real estate and other enterprises and became, according to John A. Haddock's *History of Jefferson County* (published in 1894), the man who had "done more to improve and build up Watertown" than any other. The Littlefields helped him build it. Also, Banker Winslow was essential in the Littlefields' enterprise.

Calvin and his friends had the money for the business. Milton, however, had the connections necessary for its successful operation. Milton brought his friends from the North and South together shortly after an election on November 19 and 20, supervised by the military commander General Edward R. S. Canby. That election called for a North Carolina Constitutional convention in January and chose the delegates to it. Littlefield's friends from the state were among those named.

Their meeting, like their plans, was private, but it seems highly likely that the new North Carolinians and the upstate New Yorkers met with Milton in the huge and gilded St. Nicholas Hotel in New York where so often afterward Milton's name was scrawled upon the ledger. Generals who could afford it—and some who could not—met merchants and brokers in that hotel which Charles Dickens had called "the lordliest caravanserai in the world." Some fun was made of its golden grandeur. An English comedian refused to put his shoes outside the door to be shined, he said, for fear that they would be gilded. Even those who jeered at its "barbaric splendor" admitted that it went no further in offending good taste than did the rich mansions of the new crop of millionaires. It was a proper place for expansive planning.

The chief of those whom Milton introduced to his upstate New York associates was his old Florida comrade in arms, General Joseph Carter Abbott. A florid, confident man, he was soon to become United States Senator from North Carolina. He had been a successful prewar lawyer and editor in New England before he went off to war at thirty-five, even though Southerners later tried to prove that when he left to fight for the Union he also left unpaid bar bills in Manchester and Boston. Actually he had been Adjutant General of New Hampshire for five years before the war and had served as a member of the commission to adjust the boundary line between New Hampshire and Canada.

Milton had known him at Hilton Head and in Florida where Abbott's regiment had broken at the Battle of Olustee. After that disaster, however, he had been made a brigadier general "for gallant and meritorious services in the capture of Fort Fisher, N.C.," which guarded the port of Wilmington. Abbott had remained in Wilmington as commandant, cleaning up that blockade-running port ("perhaps the dirtiest ever seen"), then settled there as citizen, like Milton, in the lumber business. Wilmington was not unaccustomed to strangers. A student of blockade running, Theodore D. Jervey, of Charleston, has reported that among the stockholders of the companies operating blockade runners were a number of New Yorkers. The tough, long-shot and jack-pot gamble of blockade running under the Confederacy attracted adventurers from far away, some of whom, if not carpetbaggers, were by temperament not greatly different from pirates. The new strangers were not less respectable, even if some local ladies passed swiftly by Chloe Merrick when she came to set up a school.

It was not an irrelevant item at the bond-deal meeting that Abbott's commander in the capture of the North Carolina port was General Joseph R. Hawley, who had served with both Abbott and Littlefield in Florida. Hawley was specially hated in North Carolina because he was a native of the state. He was already politically prominent in the North, however, and in 1868 he served as president of the Republican National Convention which nominated Grant. It was in that position that he produced the epigram much quoted by those who were appalled by the suggestion that United States war bonds be paid in depreciated currency instead of gold. Hawley thundered: "Every bond, in letter and spirit, must be as sacred as a soldier's grave." No such sacrificial security lay behind the bonds in which Littlefield and associates were interested when they met late in 1867 but their determination upon their integrity as a basis for rising prices was the same.

Abbott brought two other gentlemen into the deal with him. Both were men originally from Maine. George Z. French, a heavy man of thirty-five, had set himself up as a Southern planter new-style near Wilmington, as president of what he called the Excelsior Plantation Company. The other much more colorful character was General Llewellyn Garrish Estes, who had ridden into North Carolina with General Kilpatrick's incendiary cavalry and remained to be appointed a collector of internal revenue with the backing of both senators from Maine. Later Estes defaulted on his accounts as collector (to the pain of Abbott who was on his bond) and was awarded a postwar Congressional Medal of Honor for having voluntarily led troops in a charge over a burning bridge at Flint River, Georgia, in August 1864. At the first meeting with Littlefield and afterward, he still looked like a man ready for a desperate charge, but less dependable in the camp. The Raleigh *Sentinel* described him as both "greedy" and "exquisite."

The men from the South were confident of their ability to carry out their part of the bargain. All three had been active the summer before in planning the political convention, with Abbott as chairman, at which the Republican Party was organized with Negroes as an important part of its voting strength. (Negroes by no means constituted all of its strength in North Carolina. The registration under Congress' new stern rules and under supervision of the military showed 106,721 qualified white voters to 72,932 Negroes.) The significance of the new Southern Republican Party and Milton's friends' power in it was not reduced by the sneers of Democrats as voiced by the *Sentinel* that at the first Republican meeting "patriotism and perspiration were profuse." The vote for the constitutional convention to reconstruct the state had carried 93,006 to 32,961. The result was not changed because, as some said, many white people did not vote. Abbott, French and Estes were delegates to a convention to remake the state and, incidentally, to decide what, if any, existing state debt (including the old North Carolina bonds they agreed to buy), the reconstructed state would assume.

To the Yankees, North and South, at that meeting the prospect seemed bright. What they undertook was the highly moral matter of upholding the integrity of bonds which had been issued in good faith before secession. They were in a position to rebuke repudiation and make a neat profit at the same time. Mr. Winslow would be able to buy another carriage, maybe another bank, and go forward in his civic services to Watertown. Others could count their gains. It seems just possible, however, that the Yankees from the South did not emphasize all the possible difficulties to the Yankees from the North. There were some.

Even with Abbott and his associates active in the convention which was to meet in January, the bonds constituted a real gamble. Not all, even among the Radicals, shared the notion that the old bonds should be paid. Some, like Albion Winegar Tourgée, of Ohio, who assisted in writing the State constitution which North Carolina kept long after it rejected him, insisted that old North Carolina, along with its debts, was a dead state, having committed suicide by Secession.

"He would be a fool," said Tourgée, "who would emigrate to North Carolina, if the new State is to be saddled with the debts of the old."

Tourgée became an expert on fools. Later as a successful novelist, drawing his material from his own Reconstruction experiences, he wrote *A Fool's Errand*. His influence was considerable, however, as the time for the convention approached. Milton apparently met the brilliant, erratic, one-eyed Tourgée first at the Loyal Union Convention the summer before where that soldier-lawyer-writer made a venomous and exaggerated speech about conditions in North Carolina which attracted much attention. He could speak effectively, however, and his opposition to the bonds made it clear that Milton and Northern and Southern friends were engaged in no sure-fire speculation.

Tourgée's position showed that even the eighteen carpetbagger delegates were divided on the bond question, as they were on many other things, including offices. If Littlefield and company could control all the Negro delegates, there were still only fifteen of them. In the convention, called and chosen under Negro suffrage, seventy-four of the Republican delegates—a majority of the convention—were white men natives of the old state from which they were to make, in Tourgée's words, a new one. And by no means were all of them the rag, tag and bobtail of the whites. No carpetbagger among them infuriated the Conservatives more than the aristocratic, native William Blount Rodman who was to become a justice of the State Supreme Court. Littlefield could not much hope to influence the lonely thirteen Democrats, or Conservatives as they were called to placate the old line Whigs many of whom still regarded Democrat as a dirty word. That feeling indicated a division which not even the war had eradicated. In some respects it had sharpened it.

So perceptive a reporter as Sidney Andrews was surprised when he came into the state after the war to discover that the old Whig-Democratic division was still very much alive—even "pugilistic," he said.

"To be an 'old line Whig' is to be a perfect gentleman," he wrote, "while to be an 'old line Democrat' is to be a vulgar fellow outside the pale of good society; or, on the other hand, to be an 'old line Democrat' is to be a man of good sense and sound opinions, while to be an 'old line Whig' is to be a conceited fool and bloated aristocrat."

However representative they may have been of others of that political persuasion, Littlefield's friends among the Conservatives when he came to North Carolina were generally old line Whigs. With his carpetbagger associates, he went forward as managing director of the bond project with the purchase of a "large amount" of the old bonds with the agreed purpose to "re-sell them on the rise" which still had to be assured. Littlefield and his partners, of course, had no monopoly of the business. "Wall Street brokers," as he was often reminded later as their reputed agent, were interested in the bonds. Some native North Carolinians, including George W. Swepson, the banker whom Milton was to know much better later, held the bonds in speculation.

Swepson had made a better deal than Littlefield in getting his bonds. He had persuaded the indigenous manager of the North Carolina Railroad to swap him prewar bonds ("old sixies," as they were called) for Secession bonds even after General Johnston had surrendered to Sherman. So he got the old, untainted bonds for practically nothing. That was a kind of bargaining enjoyed, if not always approved, South as North. Other Southerners did not generally hope for quite so much but they were interested in the recuperation of other Southern properties, too, and eager to have Yankee or any other help in the process.

They sought it in Milton. What they wanted, among other things, was that the convention provide state funds to complete and rehabilitate the little Chatham Railroad which ran from Raleigh to some marginal coal fields fifty miles away on the Deep River in Central North Carolina. There is no limit to the extent of dreams among the ruins or promotions in chaos. Thus, they hoped, the battered little Chatham Road, built by the state in wartime but now taken over by private interests, was to become ultimately part of a South-wide railroad system. And the lands along the river, so the scheme ran, were to be made the site of a new humanitarian penitentiary in a state which until then, the new makers of the new state felt, had depended in punishment too much upon the barbarities of the noose, the branding iron and the lash.

The projects did not constitute merely the old ideal of internal improvements nor were they just promoters' dreams. Even irascible but impeccable old Governor Jonathan Worth, soon to be ejected by the Reconstructionists, had been excited by the prospects. He wrote of convicts useful "in excavating the coal and iron ore and in melting and manufacturing the iron ore." (There were some hopes of copper, too.) Thus he thought the enterprise would not only "accomplish the chief object of punishing criminals, but developing the coal and iron of Deep River—supplying to our RRs. the car wheels and rails, etc., and making available to some extent the expenditures of the State in building the dams on Deep River."

The pieces matched together in a Reconstruction dream almost like the later TVA, providing for the prostrate state even more river development advantages—penal reform, railroads, water power, navigation, mining, manufacturing. It was a dream at least as high as the steep banks of the little river. Not all concerned with it were quite as unselfishly motivated as Governor Worth, however. And those who hoped for profit realized most acutely that the project would require money, and money meant continuing investment of state funds in railroad development like that which the state—and other states—had made before the war. That now depended upon the approaching convention. Southerners held on to the railroad. They kept much of the land. But Northern interests, Governor Worth mentioned later, acquired the Egypt Coal Mine. And when Littlefield came south it was generally known that he was, as the Democratic *Sentinel* put it, and the Republican *Standard* for once agreed, "much interested in the Deep River mining region." It was his concern that the convention should be, too.

If Milton had any doubts about his new enterprises, he never showed them. Wherever he went, he carried the atmosphere of the gilded parlors of the St. Nicholas Hotel. He was richly wrapped against the cold when he left Philadelphia in December 1867. In Germantown the wind whistled through the bare trees and on Walnut Street the carts slipped along the icy cobbles. It seemed natural to Milton to be going south again, even in civilian clothes. It is not of record that he carried a carpetbag. One who observed him on the cars which he was to ride so much, north and south, in the years ahead noted that when he settled on a train in those cindery days he always "changed his beaver for a low black cap, which very much changed his appearance." He did not seem much changed as he set out as a veteran of thirty-seven on what Tourgée later called "a fool's errand." His beard was as dark and as neatly trimmed as it had always been since he grew it first in Memphis. But he went to a South which was always more enchanting because of its changes and surprises. Perhaps the greatest surprise always was that it could show itself so little different from other places—even the North.

He left frozen Philadelphia remembering the South, to which he hurried again, in terms of the sun on the Sea Islands. But in the little state capital of Raleigh, no warmth awaited him. On New Year's Eve there was, according to the violently unreconstructed *Sentinel*, "the heaviest fall of snow that we have had in this latitude in years." The *Sentinel* usually devoted more space to politics than to the weather. That paper seemed to grow louder as it got poorer. Even for the *Sentinel*, however, the heavy white fall brought the year to an end in quietness. In the unblemished southern snow, it reported, sleighs were out and their bells jingled joyously in the streets. It would be two whole weeks—until after the convention met—before the *Sentinel* would announce briefly and sourly and normally that "muck and mud are holding high carnival." Then even General Littlefield's immaculate boots might be bedaubed.

CHAPTER IX

Welcome, Stranger

THE IMMEDIATE IMPRESSION General Littlefield made in Raleigh was that of "a man of singular courtesy and intelligence." He could not have received such a testimonial as of that time from a more acceptable source than Kemp Plummer Battle, native aristocrat of about the same age, who had a very high appreciation of Southern traditions, Episcopal theology, classical learning and the dollar. Furthermore, Battle's contemporary judgment of Littlefield as he arrived was endorsed in history by Dr. J. G. de Roulhac Hamilton in his standard work, *Reconstruction in North Carolina.*

"His charm of manner and *bonhommie,*" Dr. Hamilton said of the arriving General, "made his company acceptable to many Conservatives who at first did not question his motives or his character."

Actually, he seemed essential to many Conservatives and to others, too. He was the kind of man who had been sought and awaited. Raleigh was acutely conscious of the need for such development as even Littlefield's manner always promised. Even the Raleigh *Sentinel* was strong for development though its junior editor, Seaton Gales, member of a distinguished American family of journalists, had persisted in calling the United States flag a "rag" and had once retired to his home by a back street to keep from walking under it.

"This is emphatically the age of railroad completion," that paper said not long before Milton arrived. Such expansive possibilities of development did not seem too promising, however. The aristocratic, irascible and rheumatic Dr. William J. Hawkins, president of the Raleigh and Gaston Railroad, had recently made one job for his young nephew, Captain Alexander Boyd Andrews, out of two held before by a colonel and a captain. Twenty other untitled workers had been fired. That was "wise economy," the *Sentinel* agreed, "but it is a hard blow at those thrown out of work."

Other work was not easy to find: "Quite a large number of emigrants passed through the city, on Wednesday, en route to the Northwest." At the time of the new registration of voters (including new black ones) ordered by Congress, the *Sentinel* noted, "General quiet prevails, though many of our colored people have turned politicians, and the white people are mainly looking after bread." Not all was grim. Some lived very well, indeed. Though the leading local hotel was not the St. Nicholas, shortly before Milton scrawled "General M. S. Littlefield—Philadelphia" on the ledger of the Yarborough House, the *Sentinel* referred to that hostelry's proprietor as one "whose reputation as a hotel keeper is almost world wide." That innkeeper's custom of sending choice dishes to Raleigh editors, regardless of their politics, stimulated the local attestation to his world-wide fame.

Milton might have chosen a more famous town. Raleigh had not changed much since one of Sherman's tired aides, Major General Jacob D. Cox of Ohio, had called it the "most attractive town" he had seen in the South: "It is simply a large village with wide streets, each house having a good sized dooryard and fine forest trees embowering the place in the most beautiful foliage." And a few weeks later even the higher authority of General Grant attested that "Raleigh is a very beautiful place. The grounds are large and filled with the most beautiful spreading oaks I ever saw."

Not all the streets were wide and gracious. Though Captain G. W. Pepper, a war correspondent, said that "the spacious Fayetteville Street is lined with stores so solid and elegant that they would not look out of place in New York," a Massachusetts private listed in his diary the principal sections worthy of note as "Frog Level," "Devil's Half Acre" and "Vinegar Hill." The last, he understood he said, derived its name from the people of sour countenance who lived upon it. He must have recorded that for the homefolks. Other men who went there, particularly in the evenings, knew it as a place where the loud laughter of women and piano music came like the chinks of lamp light from the windows of shuttered houses. Raleigh was not Memphis, but there were women in it brazen in gay greed for part of the Union Army's pay. Confederate currency then made neither love nor music on Vinegar Hill.

General Sherman, who still did not regard himself as the nurse of his men, took little note of such matters. With his red beard flecked even more with gray, he was hell bent on his way to receive—with too much generosity, Secretary Stanton thought—the surrender of General Joseph E. Johnston. Sherman had been worried in Raleigh, however, because his "immense host in blue," which had had its taste of fire and pillage in South Carolina, was encamped on the wide hill of the lunatic asylum the night the news came of Lincoln's assassination.

Nothing happened. But the place seemed full of portents. The last time Sherman saw Lincoln, with Grant, on the *River Queen* at City Point thirteen days before Appomattox, the two generals had been unable to assure Lincoln that more blood could be avoided. They feared that Lee might get away from Richmond to join Johnston and that Union victory might require "one more desperate and bloody battle" in the vicinity of Raleigh. No such battle, of course, took place, but within three weeks a bound boy, who had run away from Raleigh, Battle said, to escape prosecution "for stoning the house of an old woman," was President of the United States.

With Raleigh men Andrew Johnson discussed the first Reconstruction proclamation he issued. It provided for provisional government in North Carolina. Some of them knew him. A few already admired him. Most had heard the whispers, originating with those Southerners always surprised at eminence arising from humble birth, that he was not the son of Jacob Johnson, the respected porter of Casso's Inn, but child of his wife, Mary McDonough, by one of the aristocratic Haywoods or perhaps by a former distinguished Chief Justice of the State.

Some of the men from Raleigh thought that even the leniency which Johnson followed was too severe. Since Federal power had proved the Constitutional theory that a state could not secede, he only needed to let its legislature resume its proper and loyal place in the Union.

"There is no one of that body," a consistent North Carolina Unionist told the demurring Johnson, "who might not be led back into the Union by a silken thread."

Two and a half years later when Milton Littlefield arrived, Johnson, perhaps of his own fault, was caught between the advocates of the silken thread and the iron chain. They have remained the standard symbols of the story, but not all of the story itself. There were Southerners restive in the ruins even before Sherman left the South. Indeed, the day before Sherman arrived in Raleigh, young, amiable Kemp Battle, who was to become the long-time president of the University of North Carolina, became a figure for those Southerners who did not forget the cash even when chivalry was cast down.

Battle was one of those excluded from Johnson's amnesty proclamation because he was worth more than $20,000 even at the war's end. But on the day Sherman's army approached Raleigh he busied himself to find "something more valuable than the Confederate currency which I had on hand." For $700 in C.S.A. bills he only got "the poorest cotton umbrella I ever saw and some old railroad pamphlets." It was a good bargain and one which indicated that even in disaster there were those who understood that, come silken thread or iron chain, continuity is a golden cord.

Such an understanding brought Milton and Battle and some friends of his together. Battle had not limited his adjustment to surrender to getting rid of his Confederate currency at whatever bargain he could make. He became quickly the first party in the name of a firm, Battle, Heck & Company, set up to attract Northern men and capital to the bankrupt South. Some in North Carolina were for it and some against it, the *Sentinel* said.

The Heck in the company, Colonel Jonathan M. Heck, was himself a newcomer to North Carolina. He had been, Battle wrote, a land trader in West Virginia and was later employed in the Quartermaster Department of the Confederacy. Oddly after his early capture, however, he was permitted "through the personal kindness" of the Union commander, General George B. McClellan "to bring his family through the enemy's [*sic*] lines" to North Carolina where he was equally ardent as a Baptist, a Confederate and a promoter. Soon after the war's end he was active with his wife in the ceremonial unveiling of a monument over the grave of General Robert E. Lee's daughter Mary, who had died during the war at Warren White Sulphur Springs, a North Carolina health resort which Heck purchased. Also, after the war the *Sentinel,* which was sometimes suspicious of both his Southern patriotism and his Christian piety, regularly referred to him as "Colonel Heck who teaches the Sunday School."

The "& Company," behind their names was significant. Chief figure in it was the rheumatic and relentless Dr. Hawkins, then forty-six, member of one of the richest and most distinguished families of the state. Physician and large landowner, he had turned to railroad operation in 1855 and when Battle, Heck & Company was organized with his backing, he dominated not only the Raleigh and Gaston but the Chatham Railroad as well. Battle, Heck & Company's plans "to break up the business lethargy prevailing after the surrender," as Battle stated them, were to "make known in all feasible ways the lands in North Carolina for sale and to induce Northern people to buy and settle among us." The prospect did not seem unpromising: "There had been expressed by soldiers who had traversed the state much admiration of our climate and other advantages so that it seemed reasonable that an immigration of land buyers could be secured for cultivation of the soil, converting forests into timber, mining, fisheries and the like."

Heck and Battle went north. They secured the endorsement of such a prominent, if sometimes politically sad, gentleman as Jay Cooke of Philadelphia, "who warmly recommended our scheme." They received "favorable notices from some of the great newspapers, equally of course paid for." They opened an office at 62 Broadway. And "we magnified the importance of our enterprise by taking rooms at the St. Nicholas Hotel." In its gilded atmosphere

Milton Littlefield seemed exactly the kind of man they were seeking.

Milton's assistance was more than welcome to such recouping Conservatives. Battle, who retired from Battle, Heck & Company, to become State Treasurer under Governor Worth, thought its operations had been a failure. He wrote that "the cause of our defeat was the rupture between the Republican majority in Congress and the President, ending in 1868 in upsetting the state governments inaugurated by him. The rupture was accompanied by threats of confiscation of vast areas of land and this caused general distrust of Southern titles."

Others did not accept the notion of failure. Littlefield, now interested in Deep River, had had to face such distrust before. Also, now he was on the side which had been turned up by the upsetting of the Johnson program. And that was as important to Dr. Hawkins and his Southern associates in Deep River development and railroad plans as it was to Littlefield. Neither the debonair newcomer nor the arrogant aristocrat was easily discouraged. It turned out at the convention to which Milton came south that neither of them had reason to be.

That was, of course, the "mongrel convention" and "the convention (so called)" to the *Sentinel* which had received the state printing under the state government that was being upset and had little hope that it would receive it much longer. Such monetary considerations, however, did not dictate its policies, though its policies dictated its poverty. Certainly it did not ingratiate itself with the new regime by a reporting of the convention's sessions, marked by the repetition of such phrases as "the nigger delegate from Wake" and carpetbaggers "busier than bees in a tar bucket." It damned most such a new native Republican as Colonel William B. Rodman as an apostate and renegade who with "ability and powers of usefulness, perverts them, for manifestly selfish considerations, to the detriment of his own color, of his former friends and associates, of his State . . . there are no waters of Lethe that shall wash out the damning stain."

The convention barred reporters whose writings, with little wonder, it regarded as insulting. And undoubtedly Littlefield, as the head of what Dr. Hamilton described as "a quiet but influential lobby," shared the indignation of the delegates. He received scant attention at first, however, though the *Sentinel* obviously had him in mind when it reported that "we hear it rumored that the Wall Street New York brokers have presented a number of the Radicals of the Convention with a new hat and a pair of gloves, with other substantial fixings, in consideration of passing the new financial project endorsing the N.C. bonds (many of which are held by the New York brokers) and directing the next Legislature to make provision by taxation, for the payment of the interest on said bonds, commencing January 1st, 1869."

Milton was always one who liked to present little (and some larger) gifts to his friends. He did get the bonds endorsed. While his gain in that enterprise cannot be stated, his associate, General Abbott, later figured that his share alone of the gain amounted to $25,000. Milton was also active in securing the convention's action calling upon the next legislature to create a penitentiary. He and Dr. Hawkins, Heck and others hoped that it would be established on Deep River lands. It was a cause, however, which he could advance in high humanity. Before he arrived, the *Sentinel* had noted without indignation that "hanging by the thumbs is a very common punishment for offenders. We observe that recusant freedmen come in for their full share on our streets. We understand some of them say it is 'worser dan de cowhide old Massa used.' "

Milton was for development as well as humanity. Perhaps most important, as leading to later things, the convention passed an ordinance directing an exchange of state bonds of $1,200,000 for an equal number of bonds of Dr. Hawkins' Chatham Railroad. Furthermore, the convention gave to the Chatham Railroad all the state's interest in the Cape Fear and Deep River Navigation Company in the area served by the railroad on the rivers.

Milton's activities dealt with details of the convention. Its primary business which roused the most fury was the drafting of a Constitution which enfranchised the Negroes as it had to do under the Reconstruction Acts. That Constitution extended the democracy of white men, too. It provided for popular elections, removed religious tests for officeholding, and provided for the first time in the state's history for "a general and uniform system of public schools" (a proviso kept intact until 1956 when new fear of racial integration in the schools caused its removal). Provisions in the new Constitution, wrote Dr. Hugh Lefler of the University of North Carolina in 1956, "were in line with progressive legislation in Northern states." Perhaps the greatest tribute to the document is that, though often amended, it remained in 1958 the basic law of the state.

The Raleigh *Standard,* which was as violently Radical as the *Sentinel* was Conservative in its policies if not in its reporting, certainly did not speak a universal opinion when it characterized the convention as "one of the ablest, most dignified and most patriotic bodies that ever assembled in the State." Indeed, *The Charlotte Democrat,* which shared less violently the *Sentinel's* views, declared that the convention accomplished its work amid "disgraceful scenes, disgusting even had they been enacted in a brothel." It was at its adjournment, in dignity or disgrace, that Milton first emerged in the aspect of diabolism always afterward attributed to him by the Democrats.

With the Constitution passed and signed, *The Charlotte Democrat* said in a classic account of the occasion, a leading delegate moved for a recess, "flourishing at the same time in his hand, a Freedmen's Bureau song book." Then began what the *Sentinel* called, "Disgraceful Closing Scenes . . . Cornfield Dance and Ethiopian Minstrelsy!! Ham Radicalism in its Glory!!" The delegate with the songbook struck up, "We'll Rally Around the Flag, Boys."

"Immediately the desk was surrounded," said *The Charlotte Democrat* in its account, "by a crowd of inside and outside Negroes, of both white and black complexion, who lent all the power of their lungs to the chorus.

"As the song continued the excitement increased—hands were joined all around and a regular African cornfield dance ensued. Each man commenced singing his own song. Among the ditties that could be distinguished in the terrific din were such as 'Sal's in the garden sifting sand,' 'Come out of the wilderness,' 'Yallow gal, can't you come out tonight,' 'Hang Jeff Davis on a sour apple tree,' 'Old John Brown,' 'Yankee Doodle,' 'Hail Columbia,' 'Star-Spangled Banner,' 'Sound the timbrel,' etc., etc."

This was not the first or last official session in North Carolina which ended in song. It was at that point, however, that Milton made his publicized entrance upon the state scene: "General Littlefield being called on arose and expatiated 'a la spread eagle' and concluded his harangue by singing something to the tune of 'Old John Brown's Soul is Marching On,' the house at his request joining in the chorus." Perhaps that occasion terminated the complete quietness of Littlefield's lobbying, and certainly from that point on in order to be effective something more than quietness was indicated. For Littlefield and his friends, Hawkins and others, to profit, the new Constitution which had been shaped in the resounding Capitol had to be ratified by the people, as enfranchised, in the state.

There was a violent thunderstorm in Raleigh on the very hot March day after the convention adjourned. It seemed like accompanying music to the *Sentinel*'s fury in an article headed "Black Mail" which was a thinly veiled charge that Milton had corrupted delegates at the convention. "People of North Carolina!" demanded that journal, "Are you ready to be thus bought and sold by New York Brokers?" While Milton would not have approved the question he was ready as activator and orator ("among the most active of the Republican orators," says Dr. Hamilton) to seek the answer in that campaign in which he began to receive the undiluted venom of the Democrats. If that was the beginning of his undoing, it was, then, contribution to his power. For it was in that campaign that he became the close friend of William Woods Holden, Republican candidate for Governor.

The physically frail, neat, nervous Holden was hated then. He was impeached later. But if Holden was a "political chameleon," as thought Jonathan Worth, who had defeated him for Governor, Holden was in 1868 still the most brilliant, if erratic and vindictive, politician in the state. Not quite fifty then, he had been born in obscurity (as it is politely said) in Orange County, home of many of the state's richest and most prominent men. As a boy of nineteen he had become a printer, then an editor whose writings attracted much attention, on the Raleigh *Star*, the leading Whig paper. In 1843, damned by the Whigs as a turncoat, he became at twenty-five editor of *The North Carolina Standard*, the leading Democratic paper.

It does not seem basically strange that a man of Holden's origins should realize among Whigs that he was a Democrat at heart. And as democrat among Democrats, he led that party, until then a minority, to strength in a compaign for universal suffrage for white men. Though he more than anyone else built the Democratic Party in those years, he was denied its nomination for Governor. Even many Democrats were profoundly shocked by his proposal that slaves be taxed at the same rate as plows and pots and pans. Holden did shift undoubtedly, however, from extreme views on Secession to the leadership of the Peace Party in North Carolina. As its candidate he attracted much attention in the North when, running on a peace platform in 1864, he secured 29,000 votes in the seceded state against 43,000 for the popular soldier, Zebulon B. Vance, whom Holden himself had supported in 1862.

Edward Everett, who spoke with Lincoln at Gettysburg, mentioned the North Carolina situation in his longer, less remembered speech. He was certainly speaking of Holden when he said: "The heart of the people North and South is for the Union. Indications, too plain to be mistaken, announce the fact. . . . In North Carolina the fatal chain at length is broken. At Raleigh the lips of honest and brave men are unsealed, and an independent press is unlimbering its artillery. The weary masses are yearning to see the dear old flag floating again upon the Capitol, and they sigh for the return of peace, prosperity, and happiness which they enjoyed under a government whose power they felt only by its blessings."

It was not strange that he was Johnson's choice as provisional Governor, and those who distrusted Holden did not find it strange that Holden then turned to Johnson's enemies in Congressional Reconstruction. He did shift. He had come from a stern position with regard to the freedmen in 1865 to an advocacy of unrestricted Negro suffrage in 1867. There were strange aspects of the chameleon about him; there was a strange anti-aristocratic consistency about his life, too—perhaps not strange in a man often rejected. He was vitriolic and sensitive, combative and lonely. "No one," says Dr. Hamilton of him in the Reconstruction period, "charged him with personal financial profit, but he screened and protected the guilty." Perhaps he was susceptible to flattery from men like Littlefield. But in Littlefield he found a man ready to fight by his side. The attacks on both came quickly.

"Radical Club House," headlined the *Sentinel*, in the week in which the convention ended, of the Republican headquarters Milton helped set up. And in one of its first mentions of Milton since his arrival in the city that paper went on to describe the club as "a drinking saloon, where we presume votes are to be bought from blacks and mean whites, in the heart of the city, on Hillsboro Street, in the midst of the private residences of many of our best people."

In the little capital, Hillsboro Street then was a wide, genteel thoroughfare running to the Capitol and as such would have seemed an odd place for trafficking in the votes of blacks and mean whites. As the club opened, however, the *Sentinel* unhesitatingly predicted its character: "Here, the orgies of Bacchus are to be held, night and day, we suppose, during the campaign. On Thursday afternoon there was a large gathering of Negroes and scalawags, to raise a Holden-radical pole. Exciting speeches were made, we learn, by Gen. Littlefield and others, whose names we have not heard, amid uproarious noise and huzzas, much to the discomfort of the quiet people of that neighborhood. Subsequently, after night, a procession was formed, led by a Negro band . . . which proceeded through the streets huzzaing and screeching, making night hideous."

Night was not entirely appropriated by the Republicans. Three days later with a good deal less indignation the *Sentinel* reported another event in the same general neighborhood:

"Hanging in Effigy—On Sunday morning, March 22, an effigy was found by early risers we learn, hanging from one of the trees in Capitol Square, which, judging from a placard posted on the figure was designed to represent Mr. W. W. Holden. The silly thing was soon cut down, and need have aroused none of the excitement which, it seems, it subsequently gave rise to."

The *Sentinel* minimized the incident. It scoffed at complaints made to the Mayor "against a number of worthy young gentlemen in this city of only *suspected* complicity in the affair." The two affairs, however, indicated the beginning of the subterranean warfare which attended the politics then and thereafter. It is quite possible that Milton's open Republican Club was related to the secret Union Leagues being formed throughout the South, particularly among the Negroes, by the Republicans. Milton was definitely involved in such activity as well as in political meetings throughout the state. And the hanging of Holden's effigy seems quite as undoubtedly related to other undercover activities of his enemies. Soon Raleigh also awoke to see night-placed signs:

K.K.K.

Attention! First Hour! In the Mist!
At the Flash! Come. Come. Come!!!
Retribution is impatient! The grave yawns!
The sceptre bones rattle!
Let the doomed quake!

It is commanded.
2nd G. C. OF BL. HOST

The doomed then did not quake. Indeed, every evidence is that in that campaign in North Carolina Milton moved as confidently as he had walked on Walnut Street in Philadelphia. He spoke to large gatherings of Negroes and white men, too. Sometimes he seemed to catch the admiration even of the angry *Sentinel.* It was then that the question began to grow, "Who is General Littlefield?" And the *Sentinel,* recounting all the rumors about Littlefield as lobbyist, Wall Street agent, bond buyer, Northern Republican fund dispenser, Deep River speculator and manipulator for the Chatham Railroad, gave its almost amiable answer: "We judge he is a shrewd Yankee, good at demagoguery and management, and equally expert at making a speech, getting up a club house, maneuvering as a lobby member, or singing 'Old John Brown.'" It was Holden's *Standard* which answered the question in that campaign much more seriously.

"General Littlefield," Holden's paper declared, "is a *Great*-field, physically and mentally, a man who has earned his title of General by his sword. A Yankee? Yes, if you call New York State people Yankees, but a Yankee who brings capital to North Carolina, and brains to work that capital. . . .

"The charge brought against the General seems to be that he owns land in the Deep River Valley, and was interested in getting an appropriation for the Chatham Railroad. Does no one else own land on either side of that 45 miles of railway? Is no one else interested in getting coal here, at one-half what you are now paying for it, or do you prefer to import your coal from Pennsylvania to employing hundreds of your idle men to work a mine in your state, because Northern men are interested in it; and if the General has large interests at stake, does he not bear his proportion of the taxes?

"Again this cry against paying the interest due on the State Bonds. Is repudiation ever honorable? If it is, why not repudiate the whole. You had the money on your faith, used it, reaped the benefit from it, and now abuse Wall Street because they want their own. . . . Immigration is what you must have, but how can emigrants [*sic*] feel any confidence in a state which repudiates its debts? Prove to them that you mean to deal fairly and honorably by them, and you will soon have enough pouring in to work your now neglected plantations.

"What a short-sighted, suicidal policy you are pursuing when you vote against the Constitution, send away Northern men, and Northern capital for fear, they may get a foot-hold in the State. Where a man invests his property, there his interests lie, and, of course, it can be but a little while, before his interest, and the interest of the State is one, and he will work for North Carolina quite as energetically, as many of these native North Carolinians are now doing who, because by their own acts they are disfranchised, and cannot vote, sit by and growl at all who can."

Such a statement might almost have been written as an early advertisement for Battle, Heck & Company. It was much more important, however, as the declaration of the opinion of the paper of Governor Holden who was elected 92,235 to 73,594 when the Constitution was ratified by approximately the same vote late in April. Despite the rising rancors, it was a quiet election. The "best order prevailed" admitted the *Sentinel* in praising a Federal Army officer for his action in one minor difficulty. But Federal troops did not control the election. At the beginning of 1868 the total number of Federal troops in the whole state had come down to 1,078 officers and men. Indeed, at the time of the election many Union officers were more popular with the Conservatives than they were with the Radicals.

After the election Jonathan Worth, who was soon to be removed from office by the military, wrote Colonel J. V. Bomford, commander of the post in Raleigh, that he felt it his duty to say: "I heartily concur in the judgment of every virtuous and intelligent man in this community, that your whole conduct, official and social, has been such as becomes a veteran officer of the United States Army—always strictly performing your duty—always urbane—and eschewing partisan politics so thoroughly that I do not know what are your party predilections, if you have any."

The outcome of the election was difficult for the Conservatives to explain. The *Sentinel* tried: "Money, which, in times like these, when the great body of the people are in a condition so needy, was a most potent weapon employed by the Radicals. The Northern bondholders were ready to pour out money without stint, and every means was employed to spend it freely, where it could effect the object. . . ." But it added underlining the point: "*The defeat of the Conservatives in the late election is not chargeable to the blacks* . . . with a registered white majority of nearly 40,000, the defeat of the Conservatives is chargeable, of course, to *the white men of the state.*"

The election ratified Milton's speculations but an even more important result of it was the sale to him of the *Standard* by Holden. That, of course, was no mere financial transaction. Feeling that he could not continue both as editor and Governor, Holden required a successor who shared his views. His own son, Joseph W. Holden, a hard-drinking, belligerent poet miscast in politics, already was assured of the speakership of the House of Representatives in the approaching legislature by a deal by which Milton's old friend, General Abbott, was to go to the United States Senate. Littlefield was a fighting Radical upon whom the older Holden knew he could depend. Not long after Holden sold Littlefield the *Standard,* the General succeeded him also as president of the state council of the Union League.

The purchase of the paper required money, nevertheless. The *Standard* had been profitably petted by Union commanders who regularly published their orders in it. Its prospects for the state printing under the Republicans could be set down as a certain asset. Before and after Reconstruction this profitable business automatically went to a chosen party organ. It could mean the difference between journalistic life or death. One Conservative paper had recently expired in Raleigh. The *Sentinel* was not having an easy time when it reported rumors that Holden had sold the *Standard* to Milton "for the large sum of $20,000."

"The price was certainly a *good* one," the *Sentinel* added almost in awe.

The *Sentinel* was only guessing and reporting rumor. The actual price, says Dr. Hamilton, was $40,000. Furthermore, ostensibly the paper was sold to an "N. Paige & Co.," when it became the property of Littlefield. Obviously, its actual, if unnannounced purchaser, Milton needed more money than he had in hand—or wanted to tie up in it. The nagging *Sentinel* insisted that, behind Littlefield "the *Standard* is now owned and controlled by the owners of *The New York Tribune,* i.e., the bondholders and leading radicals of the North." *The New York Tribune* that spring was, indeed, supporting with intemperate zeal Congressional Reconstruction and the impeachment of President Johnson, though Horace Greeley had not long before roused Radical ire by signing Jefferson Davis' bond. The Union League of New York then considered a proposal to censure him as a member. The *Tribune* lost subscribers. But if any such New York money was available to Milton, he still needed more. And he went to the Raleigh National Bank, controlled by George W. Swepson, in quest of it.

In view of his later familiarity about the bank and the easy way in which he then drew its funds, the occasion as described afterward by the bank's punctilious puppet president is significant. He gave the handsome Milton a banker's glassy eye.

"Being president of the bank," that gentleman, R. W. Pulliam, told an investigating committee in 1871, "it became my duty to enquire into the pecuniary condition of every man who proposed to do business at the bank. Gen. Littlefield became a dealer by making deposits from time to time, which he drew out as other dealers were in the habit of doing, but when he proposed to make a formal loan of the bank, which he did at the time he purchased the *Standard* office of W. W. Holden . . . his application was rejected upon the ground that he owned no property and controlled no money belonging to himself or others, that would justify the bank in making a loan to him."

And he added: "The rejection of the application was approved by the Board of Directors of the Bank, including G. W. Swepson who was absent at the time the application was made, but on his return expressed his decided approbation of the course of the officers of the bank. The rejection was also known to Governor Holden. At the time, Littlefield was generally regarded as an adventurer and without any means whatever."

Pulliam's memory may have been colored by later events. There is some other evidence, however, of Swepson's "decided approbation" of his subordinate's decision that Milton was then only an adventurer without means. That was provided by a lady whose acquaintance with Milton extended from before that time across the years of his accusation in the South at least until 1871. It would be ungallant even now to describe Ann Cavarly as an adventuress. She was young, pretty and it is in the record that she came to North Carolina not with a carpetbag but with a bonnet box and a Saratoga trunk. She knew everybody in the state bond deals, apparently Milton best of all. She had come to Raleigh about the time Milton had with her husband, J. D. Cavarly, who seemed a mousy young man beside Ann, but who had enough money to speculate on occasions in $60,000 and $100,000 worth of bonds. Ann had a niece at St. Mary's, Raleigh's fashionable school for well-bred young Southern ladies. The Cavarlys lived at the Exchange Hotel near Milton's Republican Club, but were often seen in the parlors of the Yarborough House, too.

Ann Cavarly (sometimes her name was also given as Anna) told later of a talk she had with Milton, a month after the election, in late May 1868. He had been north, perhaps to receive plaudits for his part in the North Carolina Republican victory from deeply interested political associates there. Certainly in Philadelphia he saw his own Anna and the boys. There are no records, but the timing suggests that he may also have gone back to Illinois for the Republican National Convention in Crosby's Opera House in Chicago which nominated Grant.

That was the occasion on which Milton's one-time superior, General Hawley, made his famous epigram about the crime of repudiating bonds. Also, of course, the convention "congratulated the country on the assured success of the Reconstruction policy of Congress." Certainly Milton approved—as his own actions were approved by—the convention's declaration that "the guarantee by Congress of equal suffrage to all loyal men at the South was demanded by every consideration of public safety, of gratitude and justice, and must be maintained." Milton would have been the first to agree also to the convention's additional statement which was less a gesture of conciliation than a statement of requirements: "We favor the removal of the disqualifications and restrictions imposed upon the late rebels in the same measure as the spirit of disloyalty will die out, and as may be consistent with the safety of the loyal people."

His business operations seemed normal, though comparatively trivial, in the North. That was the year in which the Erie War, attended by every type of corruption in the New York courts and assembly, began between old Cornelius Vanderbilt and the tough triumvirate of Daniel Drew, Jay Gould and Jim Fisk. Boss Tweed that year put his Governor in the New York State House. Oakes Ames had started, as 1868 began, putting shares of the Crédit Mobilier where, as he said, "they will do the most good to us"—in the hands of members of Congress and other prominent Republicans.

Milton probably would have shared then the views expressed later about Ames—applicable to Milton also—by the historian Allan Nevins that the bigger operator was "a product of his time, and his ethical perceptions, like those of other business men of the day, were blunt. He declared that he believed his sales of stock to Congressmen were the 'same thing as going into a business community and interesting the leading business men by giving them shares.'" No North or South geographical location altered such practical views.

In confident and increasingly expansive mood the General came back to the Yarborough House in Raleigh where Mrs. Cavarly saw him soon after he arrived. She was anxious to tell him of a proposition Swepson had made to her husband. The banker, she told Milton, had proposed that young Cavarly become president of the North Carolina Railroad, which the state had built westward from Raleigh before the war. An able old-time Whig, Giles Mebane, who had married the older sister of Swepson's wife, had secured the legislation which inaugurated the railroad. Now Swepson proposed that Cavarly, as its president, should run the railroad for about six months, then go into bankruptcy himself and put the road into bankruptcy. At that time he was to let Swepson and associates buy it.

"This was at the Yarborough House," Mrs. Cavarly told Littlefield. She had waited there while Swepson and her husband talked, then listened dubiously when Cavarly reported the proposal to her.

"Immediately I went into the parlor, where I had a conversation with Mr. Swepson on the subject. He told me that he supposed I had heard the proposition he had made to Mr. Cavarly, and said that he thought Mr. Cavarly would make a good president of the road."

As she told Littlefield about it later, she was protective, dubious, suspicious.

"Yes, I heard," she told Swepson. Then, knowing he was one of the private stockholders in the road, she added, "You seem determined to own the whole road."

Swepson was in his middle-forties then. He was "considered wealthy" according to Governor Worth, who used his words prudently and thought of money carefully. The banker smiled at the young woman.

"Yes, and all the other roads in the State."

Ann remembered her reaction to his soft-spoken confidence.

"You can't own the Raleigh and Gaston Road," she said, of the north-south line controlled by Dr. Hawkins.

Even Swepson hesitated, "No, all but that."

Then he seemed both excited and persuasive.

"There is more money to be made by the sale of the North Carolina Road than from all the other schemes put together."

When she told Milton as soon as he returned it was obvious that the conversation had confused her and frightened her a little. He laughed and put his hand reassuringly on her slim shoulder.

"Swepson," he told her, smiling above his beard, "made the same proposition to me."

Milton did not accept it. If he seemed an adventurer at Swepson's bank, his plans did not include making himself expendable in six months for Swepson's purposes. He got the money for the *Standard.* Indeed, by midsummer he had money enough to change it from a semi-weekly to a daily. Swepson, testifying in a lawsuit, later verified Pulliam's story of the refusal of a loan to him. He added, with apparent irrelevancy, that he "never understood that Dr. Hawkins had anything to do" with the purchase of the *Standard.* Dr. Hawkins, however, seems to have been under fewer illusions than Swepson about Milton's dimensions as adventurer and as to the property at his disposal. Within the year when questioning about Littlefield grew sharper, Dr. Hawkins publicly declared his faith in Littlefield's responsibility.

"I know he has considerable property," he said. Some was on Deep River where the doctor-magnate had investments, too.

Dr. Hawkins made even more convincing statements about Littlefield's responsibility privately. An old friend, General W. G. Lewis, who had become president of the little Williamston and Tarboro Railroad after leaving the Confederate Army, discussed his hopes of getting state aid from the approaching legislature with Dr. Hawkins.

"I was told by Dr. Hawkins," General Lewis reported, "that General Littlefield, he thought, had great influence with the Legislature, and was advised by him to see Littlefield and procure his aid in getting the bill through that body."

"This," the Brigadier-railroader hastened to explain later, "was before Littlefield had become in bad odor in the State. I saw Gen. Littlefield and retained him as the attorney for my company to get the bill through the Legislature. I was to give him a contingent fee, no definite sum being fixed, but I promised to pay him the same in proportion as was being paid by other companies for like services."

Others were impressed with Milton's courtesy, intelligence and effectiveness. With him at its head, there was demand for the "well-organized lobby" which, Dr. Hamilton says, was then "crying aloud for the prosperity which could only come through the building of railroads and the issue of State bonds for the purpose." It did not cry alone. Even the *Sentinel* reported that times were dull in Raleigh and North Carolina: "Many of our mechanics are idle and the prospect of improvement is exceedingly discouraging. In the meantime provisions are scarce and high and money exceedingly scarce." Its editor regretted "to witness such evidences of want and poverty, as we see every day in the throng of black, and occasionally white, men, women and children as collect around the office of the Freedmen's Bureau." But Dr. Hawkins' Raleigh and Gaston Railroad paid a three per cent dividend the week before the legislature met.

Governor Worth gave up his office to Holden under "military duress" on July 1. The next day the legislature, already called by Holden under Congressional authorization as Governor-elect, ratified the Fourteenth Amendment, necessary to the state's restoration to her place in the Union. And on the Fourth of July, Governor Holden delivered his inaugural address, Hamilton said, to "an enormous audience, composed, for the most part, of negroes." No black government convened, however. Only 19 of the 170 members of the new legislature were colored. Hamilton estimated that the number of carpetbaggers in both houses amounted to twenty-seven. Thus, the native whites accounted for well over two-thirds of the membership and a substantial majority even of the Republicans, according to his figures, were native Southern white men.

Holden's audience was no solid black mass, though it was the Democratic custom to report all Republican crowds as such. (Governor Vance, whose popularity even with the well-born was not always based on elegance, once said that when he debated with a Republican at a rally largely attended by his opponent's supporters, he felt "like a grain of rice in a bushel of rat turds.") Undoubtedly there were many and varied Negroes present. There were whites, too, some sneering but many arrayed for a triumph. Holden himself, the *Sentinel* reported, wore "white breeches and a palmetto hat." Some ladies delicately fanned themselves on the July day and many parasols made bright spots in the crowd. There were bonnets as becoming as any of Mrs. Cavarly's. General Littlefield, of course, saluting friends and jesting even with political enemies, was dressed impeccably for the occasion. He was handsomely solemn when Holden spoke, and he listened without change of expression when the new Governor took occasion to defend carpetbaggers, stating, as Dr. Hamilton reported, "what was a fact, that most of the leaders in the history of the State had been born elsewhere."

Reconstruction was legally over—and just begun. Littlefield was already planning a new building for the *Standard*. And Swepson, though he kept his residence at the village of Haw River near the center and the shops of the North Carolina Railroad, was spending more of his time in Raleigh. At the bank where Milton had been turned down, the quiet capitalist was accessible to a diverse company of politicians in his office on the second floor behind the door at which sat his clerk and record keeper, a silent rabbinical-looking Jew named G. Rosenthal.

CHAPTER X

Bonnet Box and Saratoga Trunk

IN SEPTEMBER, 1868, in the cars going north," Ann Cavarly reported demurely later, "General Littlefield told me that Dr. Hawkins had given him a hundred bonds for getting the Chatham Railroad bill through the Legislature; that he was to have paid him 5 per cent., but that he had only sent him one hundred bonds when he ought to have sent him two hundred. I know that he sold the bonds two days after for 67 cents in the dollar."

Riding with a lady on the bumpy Raleigh and Gaston Railroad, it is not known whether Milton sat bareheaded, in his beaver, or wore the black cap he customarily put on in the cars. It is certain that he was in expansive mood that September day. The passing North Carolina scene outside the train windows was pleasing to him. Though he always looked at the land with an appraising eye, he had, as his scrapbook indicates, a poetic appreciation of landscapes, too. The fields were still green. The crops were coming in. Also, he looked at the land as one who had recently bought a farm in that area. He had purchased it, he said, for his New York relative, John B. Clarke, who wanted to live in the South. Clarke never saw the place, and the *Sentinel* insisted that Milton bought the land on which it said that kildees starved and "the very squirrels go about crying all the fall for the scarcity of food," only because its owner was a member of the committee to pick the site for the penitentiary.

Underfed kildees and starving squirrels were political figures in the *Sentinel's* columns, but that paper gave one of its occasional unpartisan nods at nature in a brief item headed "Wild Pigeons." Lowering its lash against the Republicans momentarily, it reported: "Numerous flocks of these migratory birds have been passing Southward over this section within a few days past—a sign, the old folks say, of a hard winter."

Littlefield and Mrs. Cavarly, however, were headed north. There were no signs of hard times on Milton's calendar. The $67,000 which he had received from Dr. Hawkins for securing the passage of a bill giving the Chatham Railroad two more million dollars in state bonds, was only one item in the accounting of the summer behind him. And though it turned out that September was a good month for him to be absent from North Carolina, the months ahead seemed even more promising. He talked expansively to Ann, as she later reported. He never testified as to what she said to him. It is clear, however, that prospects then were not quite as pleasing to that young woman. She was less like the pigeons than the Carolina mockingbird which made its nest in any convenient bush or tree, but seemed to sing best imitating the notes of every other bird, from a plum tree covered with honeysuckle.

Her summer had been a good deal less profitable than Milton's. She had been engaged in a promising enterprise with a Captain J. B. Plummer, of Portsmouth, Virginia, who had introduced her to John Gatlin, member of the legislature from the plantation county of Gates. Gatlin thought they could buy and sell at a profit some of the same old state bonds in which Milton and his friends had speculated. They were expected to go up again when the legislature ratified, by appropriations to pay the interest, the endorsement given them by the convention. But after Ann's husband went off to attend to the matter, Gatlin briefly reported, "Mr. Cavarly's trip proved a failure." It was a fiasco more disappointing to Ann beside the evident successes of others.

Unless Milton told her everything, as her testimony sometimes suggested, Ann had no way of knowing what Milton had done about the same offer made to him as Swepson had made to her husband with regard to the North Carolina Railroad, the chief east-west line. Though the fact was only whispered then, she did know, as others did, that Littlefield seemed much at home in Swepson's bank. He no longer went into the Raleigh National Bank, with his beaver in his hand, to ask a loan from Swepson's subordinate. Already he was one of the most familiar of those who frequented "a room upstairs . . . which was a private room set aside for the use of Swepson and his friends."

The room could be entered by "a back or private way." Often coming that way Milton only needed to nod at the inscrutable Rosenthal, keeping a special ledger in which he entered sums, regularly and almost casually, drawn by Littlefield for himself and his political friends. In a matter of months Rosenthal's ledger showed $240,000. It was not strange that Swepson came to be known as the "paymaster" of The Ring, as the combination of Swepson, Littlefield and their associates was called by their enemies. The odd thing was that in the summertime in Raleigh when even the most private doors stayed open to catch the least breeze, when no dog barked unnoticed, when guarded business was a source of perpetual rumor, Swepson's rôle remained secret so long.

Swepson had a reputation for reserve which was fortified even by his occasional outbursts of apparent frankness and generosity, as when he proposed the job for Cavarly. Once in a while he boasted of power, on one occasion even tapping his pocket to emphasize a claim that he kept needed decisions of the State Supreme Court there. Often his apparent candor served his reticence. Late in 1868, when Swepson was hand in glove with Littlefield, former Senator Thomas L. Clingman, whose services Swepson was also finding useful, said that the banker told him that he did not trust Littlefield "at all and meant to have nothing further to do with him as soon as he got clear of some matters in which he had been previously engaged." It seems certain, however, that even when he agreed that Littlefield should get no loan from the bank because he was an adventurer without funds, Swepson was already engaged in operations which depended much on Littlefield.

A certain awe surrounded Mr. Swepson who was, as Governor Worth put it, soon after the war, in a letter to an inquiring nurseryman of Bridgeport, Connecticut, "in our impoverished state" regarded as wealthy. Swepson bought many more things than shrubbery. He bought up almost as a favor properties which some less fortunate citizens sold in desperate auction sales, a "melancholy feature" which the *Sentinel* said became "perfectly epidemic." Much could be bought by a man with money at such sales. Swepson had agents telling him about particularly good opportunities as far off as Columbia, South Carolina. And as early as the summer after surrender the *Sentinel* was "highly gratified to learn that through the energy of G. W. Swepson, Esquire, of Alamance" the First National Bank of North Carolina was organized. Soon afterward with Pulliam, who turned down Littlefield's loan, he also opened a wholesale merchandise business. Citizens who weighed their words less carefully than Governor Worth knew that Swepson was rich in the ruined South.

His social position equaled his wealth. He had been born a Virginian, which sometimes seemed to provide a status and not merely an address. Then as a young man he had moved just across the line to Caswell County, North Carolina, a center of large plantations and many slaves. There, when he was twenty-three, he married at Oakland Plantation, Virginia, the sixteen-year-old daughter of Bartlett Yancey, who in his day was one of the state's chief citizens. The marriage gave Swepson important connections.

Virginia's cousin, raised as her brother, was Rufus Yancey McAden, who was to become a prominent Charlotte banker who worked with Swepson when his prospects seemed best and was able to help Swepson when his troubles seemed worst. Virginia's older sister had married the already mentioned Giles Mebane, prewar power in finance and Whig politics, who in 1849 had been instrumental in launching the state upon the building of the North Carolina Railroad.

The first train on that road, said a history of Alamance County, where it maintained its shops, "bore the name of that grand old man and noble statesman, Giles Mebane." He met the pattern if not the conventional picture of the Southern aristocrat. When Sidney Andrews observed him at the state convention in October 1865, Mebane was talking sense but gesticulating much "with his right hand, between the thumb and first finger of which he held an immense quid of tobacco taken from his mouth when he rose to speak."

George Swepson never gesticulated with a quid. He was as neat in his habits as in his dress. He spoke softly through thin lips except upon occasional outbursts of profanity in excitement or panic. Before the war he had quietly amassed a fortune in the new industry of the already changing South. He owned cotton mills. A town in Alamance County was named Swepsonville. Also, he was partner in a brokerage firm, Swepson, Mendenhall & Company, in New York.

Too old, if not too physically timid, for soldiering, Swepson did not become an outspoken peace man like Holden, but with the aid of McAden, then his lawyer and mill partner, and advertisements in Holden's *Standard*, he began to liquidate his properties long before the collapse of the Confederacy. It seems certain that he did not keep the proceeds in Confederate currency or invest them in ephemeral patriotic securities or at the last, after Battle's fashion, in cotton parasols. Indeed, Dr. Hamilton in his *Reconstruction in North Carolina* says that as early as the end of 1864 Swepson was "entering upon the financial operations which during the next few years were to do much toward the financial ruin of the State."

It was then that Swepson made a contract with officers of the North Carolina Railroad, which owned $58,000 in North Carolina antewar bonds. It provided for the exchange of Secession bonds for prewar ones, at the rate of two for one, to the amount of $25,000. Later, he contracted for the remainder at the same rate. The complaisant managers of the railroad's sinking fund let him make the swap even "after General Johnston's surrender had made them [Swepson's new bonds] practically worthless. He bought them by this exchange at three per cent of their face value."

Swepson (nobody ever called him George) had in addition to his other activities resumed his operations in New York early in 1866 when his trusting friend Governor Worth discovered, as he wrote him, a "villainous transaction." It involved two of Swepson's later North Carolina associates in railroad manipulations, who bought a large amount of state-owned cotton for 33 cents and resold it quickly at the market price of 47½ cents. The deal was handled through Swepson, Mendenhall & Company, 79 Pearl Street, New York, but Worth (though he forced the profiteers to disgorge) never suspected Swepson.

Later Worth expressed the view that the "amiability" of Kemp Battle, then State Treasurer, led him to exhibit too much leniency toward the villains. Apparently amiable or gullible himself, Worth, until he died, had no doubts about Swepson. In the midst of the summer session of the legislature in 1868, as a sick and financially insecure old man, he wrote that "Mr. Swepson, when I last saw him, was meditating the plan of getting up here a Savings Bank, on a large scale and offering me the Presidency." Mr. Swepson seemed always to give the impression that his plans included the hopes of others.

Ex-Governor Worth wrote that letter to A. S. Merrimon, then and later Swepson's lawyer, on August 21, 1868. It was the same day on which a committee was named by the legislature to select a site for the penitentiary. That was significant as it pointed a first matter in which Swepson and Littlefield were associated. Littlefield had been interested in the Deep River lands when he arrived in Raleigh. Swepson had bought an interest in the Deep River Manufacturing Company, set up to develop the lands along the Chatham Railroad, in which the other stockholders were Littlefield, Colonel Heck, and Captain A. B. Andrews, nephew of Dr. Hawkins. Heck thought then that Littlefield was "a special friend" of the Chatham Road. On one occasion Littlefield thought that Heck, as Hawkins' messenger, pocketed half the bonds Hawkins owed and sent him. But Dr. Hawkins was also Swepson's friend and a director of his bank. Perhaps he persuaded the banker of Littlefield's value. Certainly about the time of Milton's talk with Mrs. Cavarly about the North Carolina Railroad, he became in larger matters the "special friend" of Mr. Swepson.

At the beginning of the summer session after Holden's inauguration The Ring was already in operation. Littlefield was everywhere evident as its personable "lobby lawyer." Many knew that Swepson was its paymaster. That businessman said later, however, that he only entered into this arrangement when he was informed by Littlefield that he could get no legislation "unless I entered the same arrangement . . . the other railroad presidents had made, to pay a certain per cent (ten per cent in kind,) of the amount of the appropriations." When he entered the deal Swepson was not a railroad president. And clearly he joined with enthusiasm.

He allowed legislators to cash their *per diem* at his bank without any discount. With his aid Littlefield was ready to make loans to needy legislators with little expectation of repayment. This, says Hamilton, made Littlefield "the idol of the carpetbaggers and corrupt scalawags, while his Radicalism commended him to Republicans who were not tainted with dishonesty." The most respectable Conservative lawyers, including Merrimon and Battle, drew the legislation which The Ring presented (always only in the capacity of attorneys, both strenuously insisted later).

Much indignation was expressed about Littlefield's hospitality to all comers in "the third house," a bar which he maintained in the west portico of the Capitol itself. Cavarly testified that liquor and cigars were kept there . . . "as I think, from the number of bottles in the room." More robust citizens knew so by the drink. Professor Hamilton wrote of the convenient bar that "mere words cannot adequately express the disgust and hatred felt by the respectable people of the State, outside the legislature, for this open shame in the Capitol. There is, however, no doubt that many Conservative members daily enjoyed the hospitality of the 'third house,' though without surrendering any right to condemn it in public."

Dr. Battle in his memoirs indicated that it was not the first time liquor had been served for purposes of persuasion in the building. It was probably not the last. And even the outraged *Sentinel,* whose reporters were sometimes thirsty, too, did not mention the matter until the session was nearly over. Then it noted that the bar had been "accessible to anybody who desired to drink something stronger than water, and a large majority of this moral legislature stepped in often and took 'sugar in their'n.'"

Such hospitality alone did not account for The Ring's effectiveness. Hamilton named seven legislators, including a preacher, who he said Swepson and Littlefield "had bought for their joint use." By no means all who favored the railroad legislation were crooks, however. There was an honest, even traditional faith in railroad development by the state and even the *Sentinel,* while shouting its suspicions of the carpetbaggers, expressed the belief that "the railroad schemes of the State, if prosecuted and managed with ability, will be safe investments, and ultimately will vastly improve the ability of the State to meet its obligations."

Littlefield had varied lieutenants. Senator Abbott and General Estes, partners in his original bond speculation, aided him. Estes read the legislature letters from Battle and Banker Pulliam approving appropriations to pay the interest on the old North Carolina bonds. Milton had other less reputable allies. There was John T. Deweese, considered by Conservatives the "most obnoxious white man" on the North Carolina scene, or as the *Sentinel* described him, "the Leviathan of fools." Deweese, who had arrived as an undistinguished soldier, bought off a more popular Negro candidate in order to go to Congress and there later was caught selling cadetships to West Point. *The National Intelligencer* described him as small in stature, bobbing his head vigorously, like a pendulum backward and forward, and demanding troops to protect new loyal Southern governments. The rebels still had "them guns," he said. Holden once warned Swepson not to pay a sum Deweese claimed was due him. Afterward in Indiana, having turned Democrat, Deweese made an elaborate, almost boastful confession of his sins in Raleigh excusing himself on the ground that he was then "a green country boy," though he was thirty-three in 1868. In Raleigh, and as Congressman in Washington he was ridiculous, offensive and demanding even in the eyes of his carpetbag associates—yet his picture somehow survives as the portrait of them all.

A scornfully different man was Major General Byron Laflin who, as chairman of the Committee on Internal Improvements, was the floor leader of The Ring. Governor Worth called him a "miserable fop," but the *Sentinel*, which did not love him, quoted another description: "Laflin, with a face all purpled over with claret, a splendid mind, a stooping form dressed à la Byron, and an eye among the best and most beaming that ever was set in the head of man." He declined to flatter fools. In the legislature, he lashed out at members of his own party whose requests for leaves of absence, he said, reminded him of the three months' men in the Federal Army after the first Battle of Bull Run, "They all wanted to go home."

Laflin apparently had no such desire. His wife had died in Pittsfield, Massachusetts, the fall before. He was a man at loose ends, careless, contemptuous and dissolute. The *Sentinel* was perhaps justified later in describing him as "the big dog of the concern who lays about loose in the city of Raleigh, laughs, loves and drinks whiskey." He kept, that paper said, "bottles, baskets, demijohns and rundlets of whiskey." His "fallen fair associates," it added, called him Prince Laflin.

Littlefield found him effective. Despite the *Sentinel's* slurs about Laflin's title he had been brevetted Major General after splendid war service. And perhaps more significant from Milton's standpoint, he was the younger brother of Congressman Addison Henry Laflin, graduate of Williams College, who was described in the political broadside damning the Jefferson County draft deal in 1864 as head of the political organization to which Milton's friends there belonged. The Laflins were not the offscourings of Northern society from which, in Southern presumption, all carpetbaggers came. They were an old papermaking family in the Berkshires of Massachusetts, and the year before the war ended the Laflin brothers had sold a paper mill they owned in Herkimer, New York, to Warner Miller who developed there many processes which made newsprint plentiful and cheap. The Laflins had helped Horace Greeley found *The New York Tribune* by granting him at the outset three months' credit on the paper he needed.

The Ring delivered that summer. Laflin swept past objections that new bond authorizations for Dr. Hawkins' Chatham Railroad would make the state responsible for $3,200,000 on a short, bob-tailed line. Other railroads which had engaged The Ring's help got what they wanted. Finally, and most important to Swepson and Littlefield, the Western North Carolina Railroad running unfinished into the mountain wilderness was divided into two parts and its capital stock, of which the state was pledged to take two-thirds, was increased to $12,000,000—$6,000,000 for each division. Littlefield was named one of the commissioners to set up the Western Division of the Western North Carolina Railroad which was then only a paper project in difficult mountains. It provided the fulcrum for greater plans.

Littlefield had a right to be contented when he rode north in the cars with Mrs. Cavarly. Apparently he did not tell her everything. It was, indeed, a long time before he told anyone of his schemes with Swepson after the banker had made his approaches to both him and Cavarly about the North Carolina Railroad. The Cavarlys had shied away from a dangerous project. Littlefield and Swepson modified it. In the Western Division of the North Carolina Railroad, they moved on a project of manageable proportions, less under the immediate eye of the state. Their purpose was not, Littlefield told an agent of the state who later followed him to London, as some supposed just to grab the bonds "without any intention of building a road."

"He told me I was mistaken," the representative of the state said; "that I did not understand the plan fully; that it was the purpose ultimately to build the road, but to do it upon mortgage bonds and otherwise so leave it in debt as to enable themselves to buy it when sold for debt, and in the meantime that the money was to be used in speculation and otherwise in order to strengthen themselves to buy it."

Even then Littlefield was not quite candid. Funds from the bonds of that road were to be parlayed in the purchase of other railroads. What they planned was not a quick fraud but an imperial design, not unworthy of more famous gamblers in American railroads at the time. September 1868, when Littlefield went north, was a time for quietness, however. There was "a disposition on the part of the plunderers," Hamilton said, "to avoid offending public sentiment as much as possible and to wait until the regular session, which would begin after the election was past" and in which they confidently expected Republican victory. Though the people were quiet, feeling among politicians was high. Democrats for some strange reason seemed to have high hope that they would elect, over Ulysses S. Grant, Horatio Seymour, who had been nominated by the Democratic National Convention which met in a conglomeration of symbols on the Fourth of July in Tammany Hall! Campaigning began early.

General Littlefield was busy with the legislature in August when, according to the Democratic paper in Raleigh, "the whole city was one blaze of light and enthusiasm" in a state rally for Seymour. "Bevies of fair young ladies" had given the finishing touches to "the garniture of flowers and foliage and flags" in the convention hall. Horsemen wearing sashes met the arriving delegates. There were transparencies, a "great torchlight procession," a balloon ascension. The Conservative South arrayed its beauty and chivalry, oratory and white supremacy.

The *Sentinel* noted, however, that "the New Hanover delegation was accompanied by a detachment of the colored Seymour and Blair Club of Wilmington." That represented a wan hope of dividing the colored vote. At that time a demonstration was made by some Negroes against the parade and "only the forebearance of the crowd and the efforts of A. H. Galloway prevented a riot." That Negro Republican legislator, even the *Sentinel* said, "deserves great credit for his prompt rebuke to the disorderly men of his color, and his efforts to restrain their violent and insulting exhibitions." The *Sentinel* did not restrain itself the next month in reporting the Republican rally for Grant which it described as "The Congo Mass Meeting."

Littlefield was not present. That seems strange. He had been elected president of the Union League the month before which made him in effect the chief of Black Republicanism under the Governor whom he succeeded. Mrs. Cavarly dated his September departure, however. His absence was corroborated by the fact that at the time of the meeting that highly literate carpetbagger, Albion Tourgée, had to turn to Swepson for help because Milton was not there to advance him a loan. Though Milton had the Hawkins bonds to dispose of at the time, it seems just possible that a better reason for his absence was that he anticipated unpleasing possibilities and was content to be away. The *Sentinel* which would not have missed him did not mention his presence at the mass meeting.

"Nigger As Good As A Horse" was one of its first headlines over its news report of the meeting based on an allegation that Governor Holden, the colored man's friend, had made his stable available as sleeping quarters for some of the thousands who attended. (Five thousand the *Sentinel* said; fifty thousand, the *Standard*—which was about as close as the two papers ever got together on the truth.)

The *Sentinel* stopped just short of charging cannibalism but it let itself go in describing the night of the "fetich convention" around the Capitol Square: "A mass of yelling, cursing Negroes filled the beautiful grounds, and swarmed in the various rooms and offices of the building, while dancing, speaking, shouting and grotesque and Ashantee performances ran riot . . . The Senate chamber was filled with Negro women lying on the floor or reclining in the chairs—a Negro with a bludgeon, acting as sentinel at the door, to keep off amorous colored swains . . . almost every porch and sheltered corner in the city might have been seen filled with Negro men and women, huddled together to sleep in heaps."

It recorded no disorders. The Governor's son was reported—absolutely falsely, that often-harassed young man said—as saying, "Go to the polls, armed with guns, pistols, and bludgeons and vote. Implore the God of Turpentine to shower down torches or flames upon the dwellings of the rebels." However, one complaint of the Conservatives was that the proceedings were improperly too judicial with Supreme Court Judges Reade, Dick, Rodman, and Settle (all native, white Republicans) taking part. The speaker of the occasion was that distinguished native of North Carolina, then Governor of Connecticut, General Hawley, with whom Littlefield and Abbott had served in the war.

Outside the cities Republicans reported that the Ku-Klux rode and Conservatives spoke much of the outrages of the Union Leagues, but in September Littlefield's *Standard* really aroused the furies by touching the sensitive nerves around Property and Southern Womanhood. In view of his Sea Island experience in the settlement of freedmen, it is likely that Milton himself wrote an editorial called, "Retaliation" which appeared on September 2. Directed at what the writer called "this wholesale crusade of oppression carried on against the colored race to starve him into voting against his choice," the editorial presented "one efficient remedy." It proposed that in counties controlled by the Republicans, Negro craftsmen build at public expense villages for from five hundred to fifteen hundred colored paupers. Then "let the county paupers be moved in and be provided with houses and food at the expense of those who have made them paupers. Let the tax be so laid as to affect only the large landowners" to the end that "the oppressive landholder will be compelled to throw his broad acres upon the market to raise money to pay the taxes . . . and give the poor a chance to buy land."

The other editorial appeared while Littlefield was out of the state but its attitude of levity toward chivalric pretensions suggests his hand. It appeared on September 19, the day after the *Sentinel* had made the "Congo Mass Meeting" sound like an orgiastic festival. An off-beat injunction to Republican campaign workers, it ran:

> Work
>
> But whatever else you work, don't forget to work among the women. The Confederacy wouldn't have lasted a year if it hadn't been for them. One good rebel woman is worth a dozen rebel men. Go after the women, then. They will make their husbands and their lovers shout for Grant and Colfax until they are hoarse, if you will manage to replace some of the diamond rings and laces Frank Blair stole from them when he was here. And don't hesitate to throw your arms around their necks now and then, when their husbands are not around, and give them a good ——. They all like it, and the Yankeer you are the better it takes. Our experience with female rebs is, that with all their sins they have a vast amount of human nature, and only want to have it appreciated to be the most loving creatures imaginable. Scalawags and carpet-baggers! Don't fail, therefore, as you canvass the State, to look after the women. You are all good-looking and they know it, but with native modesty, like sweet New England girls, they like to be approached first. Don't be afraid of their eyes—they glare like young leopards by daylight, but under the moon no blue, death-stricken fawn is half so tender or half so deep. Don't read Judge Pearson's letter to them, but give them Byron and Shelley in volumes, and you will have them in your arms, if not in your party, in less than a week.

The paper had hardly reached the streets, a historian reports, before indignation rose to the dimensions of a lynching bee. The *Sentinel* automatically sounded its outrage. It resounded in Washington where *The National Intelligencer* declared that the wives, daughters and sisters of brave, honorable Southerners were "thus marked out as the prey of the spoiler and the libertine" by Wall

Street and its speculators. N. Paige, the ostensible proprietor of the *Standard,* felt it wise to leave town. He was succeeded by one John B. Neathery, who carried a derringer. The absent Littlefield was not bothered when he returned, but the *Sentinel* in his absence said that when an unnamed gentleman had questioned Milton about the truth of another piece, he had replied that "he did not write the article, but, if he had, and had told a lie, he would stick to it."

Despite the thunder in the documents, the campaign was a quiet one. Holden asked for troops to "inspire a salutary terror" in Rebel Ku-Kluxers. Littlefield, a press dispatch from Washington said, had been to Grant's headquarters to urge military forces to preserve the peace. Actually, Hamilton wrote, "the apathy of the voters was unusual." And if Littlefield was worried, he did not let his political fears interfere with business in hand. With Swepson in mid-October he went to Morganton in the foothills of the red and golden mountains for the organization meeting of the new Western Division of the Western North Carolina Railroad.

Other amenable or innocent friends of Swepson met them there in a pleasant, verandahed hotel, the Mountain House, on the night before the meeting, and then arranged all the details including Swepson's election as president on the following day. They were careful about stockholders; they hand-picked the directors. Littlefield took $200,000 worth of stock, later raised it to a million, without ever putting any hard cash into the coffers of the road. Bona fide stock subscriptions, Dr. Cecil Kenneth Brown found in a study of the road's history, amounted to only $8,000.

There was not even a whisper of scandal. Indeed, the always suspicious *Sentinel* said of the road's new officers, "These appointments give undoubted assurance of energy and skill, and the public may expect the completion of the road in the shortest possible time, if no unforeseen impediment presents itself." No impediment was visible. Indeed, Littlefield was greatly strengthened as railroad speculator and politician shortly thereafter by an electoral landslide for Grant. North Carolina went Republican by 96,222 to 83,746. The capital county of Wake went for Grant 3,433 to 2,953. Yet the Democratic organ there reported that "from every section of the State the news is that the late election was one of the most quiet we have had. In this city it was remarkably so,—no one either white or black, manifesting any disposition to violate order. . . ."

Quiet was what Swepson and Littlefield required. They had their railroad but some doubts had been cast upon the validity of the state bonds they were to secure, on the ground that the Act passed by the special session in August had levied no tax to pay the interest. Rumors had spread that the interest would not be paid on the state bonds due in January. In those days Swepson, however, seemed a man who could make a profit even on his troubles. Governor Holden sent out a letter stating that all interest would be paid on time. Holden did that by selling $180,000 in North Carolina Railroad bonds which the state had received as its dividend from the road Swepson had first planned to buy. Knowing of Holden's letter in advance, Swepson, along with one of the same men Governor Worth had caught in the "villainous" cotton transaction in 1866, bought those bonds at a price far below par, soon sold them at a large advance.

Such measures, even at a profit, could not be counted on to maintain public confidence in the bonds Swepson and company expected to receive. Therefore, at the session of the legislature, convening on November 16, Swepson, depending on Littlefield, planned legislation to confirm the railroad bond Acts of the special session and levy a tax to pay the interest. Also, in their more confident mood, they proposed to boost the capitalization of their Western Division of the Western North Carolina Railroad from six to ten million—with the state still pledged to take two-thirds, payable in state bonds. The validity of other bonds, including those of the Chatham Railroad, was to be insured also.

For this legislation Swepson was to pay, as Dr. Brown put it, "to Littlefield, or through Littlefield to the legislature . . . the sum of $241,713.31." The plans were endangered, however, by the small sum of $12,037.53 which Swepson invested in another enterprise. That sum later showed up in the complex accounting of the Western Division, for Swepson's stock in the Deep River Manufacturing Company which wanted the state to take lands along the Chatham Railroad as the site for its new humanitarian enterprise, the state penitentiary.

All seemed calm among carpetbaggers and scalawags as the legislature reassembled. Indeed, any action by interlopers in the traditional life of the state was overshadowed by a roaring row between such old-time North Carolina businessmen as George W. Mordecai, president of the long-established Bank of North Carolina, and Swepson's relative, R. Y. McAden, over the affairs of that tottering institution. But a week after the session began the *Sentinel* reprinted an item from *The Roanoke News* about the purchase by a legislative committee of the Deep River site for the penitentiary. The state was paying $12.50 an acre in state bonds, the item said, for cut-over land "that would not bring at auction today one dollar an acre." The *Sentinel* seemed cautious in its comment: "Not having examined the premises and being ignorant of the value of the property, we express no opinion, but we find that the purchase of the 8,000 acres of land creates universal surprise and general indignation."

Surprise and indignation were both compounded before the month was out by the introduction in the legislature of a resolution for an investigation of charges of bribery and corruption, particularly in relation to acts concerning the Chatham Railroad. Surprise in the state and indignation among Republicans in the legislature were increased because the resolution was introduced by a carpetbagger, Senator W. H. S. Sweet, of Craven.

"I am able to prove conclusively," Sweet said, "that votes of members were bought during the last session of our General Assembly for dollars and cents."

Swiftly, a Republican moved to expel Sweet from the Senate. An effort to remove him from his own investigating committee failed only by the vote of the Lieutenant Governor which broke a tie. But Sweet had friends in Raleigh. In the summer he had voted to reimburse officials at the state lunatic asylum for money they had spent for the care of patients during the war, recalling that as a Union prisoner in Raleigh he had been given comfortable quarters in the institution for the insane. Democrats praised his position. So did every Republican paper in the state except the *Standard* which attacked him brusquely and bitterly. But Milton's paper did not require his greatest efforts in the matter. He learned long before the public did that Sweet's information came from Ann Cavarly.

Littlefield did not mention this in the *Standard*. Neither Ann nor her husband spoke of it when they testified later before the State

Fraud Commission. The facts did not come out until nearly a month after they occurred and then only by gossip and report recounted jubilantly in the *Sentinel.* That journal, then just embarking with new, tougher editorship upon an even sharper campaign against the carpetbaggers, learned that in the week after Senator Sweet made his charges, Milton was not merely an indignant politician. He was also an active and persuasive gentleman dealing with a lady who at that point seemed less susceptible than bankers, railroad presidents or legislators.

"Mrs. Cavarly knew of bribery and corruption," the *Sentinel* reported. "She so spoke to carpetbag members. She suggested a committee of investigation; carpetbag members declined to move for the committee. She talked to Senator Sweet. He moved for the committee. When the committee is raised General Littlefield is a frequent visitor at the Hotel where boards Mrs. Ann Cavarly. He is known to have been closeted, yes, shut up with her in the Exchange Hotel—holding more than one interview with this lady, her husband being cognizant of the fact."

Suddenly, it was the turn of the Republicans in North Carolina to be shocked at the bringing of a lady's name into such a story . . . "closeted" in her room with the handsome General! Governor Holden was indignant. The *Standard* thought such journalism, involving a lady, deserved the rebuke of all honorable men. The *Sentinel* was not disturbed.

"We don't know the lady—" said that unrepentant paper—"we never saw her—we should have a mean opinion of ourself, if we should write that which gubernatorial or carpetbag malevolence could torture into an attack upon her deportment as a proper wife. . . ."

However: "This lady spoke to more than one carpetbagger of bribery and corruption. She was warm and indignant about it. She was for investigating it. One carpetbagger required her to make an affidavit of bribery and corruption before he would move for a committee of investigation. Her conversations with the *Standard* man, Gen. Littlefield, and her sudden exit from the city is all we intended to speak of and nothing more; that is all we know and all we intended. . . ."

It recited with evident gusto what it knew:

"On Monday the 7th day of December, cold, dark and rainy, Mrs. Ann Cavarly at 20 minutes before 8 o'clock, leaves the Exchange Hotel, takes the Omnibus for St. Mary's school to visit her niece; instead of returning to the Hotel, she went to the depot,—at 20 minutes past 9 o'clock she took the train for Richmond, without husband or attendant, carpet-bag, night cap or night gown, without the knowledge of the landlord or of a single boarder at the house. On the next train followed her bonnet box and Saratoga trunk."

That passage reveals much. St. Mary's was not merely Raleigh's fashionable school where young Episcopal virgins were tenderly educated. Also it was the school in the South which, during the war, Robert E. Lee chose for his daughter Mildred, whom he called, "my light-bearer." It was perhaps there that she learned, in addition to English, some Latin, music and Ornamental Needlework, the ability under any circumstances to appear "glorified in crinoline."

Mrs. Cavarly's visit to her niece at the school suggests much as to her own quality. But her secret departure from it indicates other qualities as well. According to the history of their school, St. Mary's girls learned that the depot to which Ann went was remote, "surrounded by warehouses, and afforded no waiting room." But as the girls discovered as they came to school, "there were plenty of horse-drawn hacks and an omnibus awaiting them . . . and amid the distracted calling of drivers and waving of whips the travelers took possession of the omnibus and were driven to St. Mary's." Ann Cavarly took the reverse trip in the dark. No evidence remains as to whether anyone met her, though few ladies would have wished to be there in the night alone.

"When Senator Sweet asked her husband," the *Sentinel* said, "when she would return and if she had relations in Richmond, Mr. Cavarly said she had none and would return in a day or two. Yet the fact is, and we know it to be so, she has engaged board at the Spotswood Hotel in Richmond for a month. And thus did Littlefield triumph over Sweet. Thus did wickedness triumph over virtue; and falsehood over truth. . . ."

Ann was gone. The Spotswood Hotel in Richmond to which she had retreated was something special after the Exchange Hotel which, even in Raleigh, was only a superior boardinghouse. The Spotswood was the hotel to which Mr. and Mrs. Jefferson Davis went on the day of their arrival as first lady and gentleman of the Confederacy. It was a hotel in which General Lee had had quarters. After the war when Mrs. Cavarly arrived it still was Richmond's finest hotel.

In Raleigh the Deep River penitentiary site was a casualty of her departure. It was abandoned though much of the $100,000 in bonds paid for it had gone north, too, in the possession of an obscure character, a wood dealer and wagoneer, named D. J. Pruyn (member of a well-known Hudson River family), who also lived at the Exchange Hotel and handled the sale of the land, as his own, for Colonel Heck and friends. The penitentiary was a detail which could be, so far as Littlefield and Swepson's greater plans were concerned, charged off to profit and loss. More important to them, Byron Laflin easily pressed through the legislature the railroad bond legislation they required. Early in the next year Swepson asked and secured a first batch of $4,000,000 worth of state bonds from the State Treasurer.

There was no big snow as that year ended. But for many there was verification of the sign of a hard winter which the old folks had seen in the flight southward in September of the masses of migratory wild pigeons. One detail in the record, however, brightened the time. Three years after Ann left Raleigh on that cold, dark night of December 7, 1868, Swepson was asked by interrogators to explain an entry in the Littlefield ledger which Rosenthal kept for him. He put a thin finger on the item in the book.

"As to the charge for diamonds, December 11, 1868," he said, "I bought some diamonds in this city from some persons whose names are not remembered by me, at the request or by the direction of Gen. Littlefield, for him, and I paid for them."

That was only one item in a very large book. His explanation remains cryptic.

CHAPTER XI

Darkness at Midday

GENERAL LITTLEFIELD had departed, heading northward and stopping in Richmond, presumably at the Spotswood Hotel, when Senator Sweet rose at a session of his investigating committee. The Senator seemed baffled. Mrs. Cavarly was gone. Now he reported that "a person of prominence, connected with the *Standard* office, had absented himself from the city, and could not be found; that this person, connected with the *Standard,* it was thought would throw light upon the bribery and corruption business—the buying and selling of votes of members of the General Assembly."

Then a new, more strident voice sounded from the *Sentinel*: "No senator was at a loss to designate the absent man. It is Gen. Littlefield, who, it is said, with Wall Street brokers and bondholders of the State, owns the *Standard* as an organ to advocate and defend all the reckless plans and projects in the State, ostensibly for its improvement, but in truth for the plunder of its treasury."

The thunder at plunder from the dingy offices of the *Sentinel* came from the pen of its new editor, former Confederate Congressman and cavalryman Josiah Turner, Jr., who at forty-eight had turned in a combative career to journalism. That shift from saber and legislative seat to pen was less strange, however, than the fact, then secret, that Turner began his editorial baying at what he insisted were Littlefield's flying heels, with money which he had borrowed from Swepson for the purchase of the paper. Turner blandly and bluntly denied as long as he could that his money came from Swepson. Even Swepson realized, when that fact at last came out in a belated effort to collect his debt, that some explanation was due public curiosity or general astonishment. His explanation left a mystery still. Undoubtedly, with the childless banker blood was thicker than water. And beyond consanguinity, he valued the importance of family relationships in the South.

"Giles Mebane's brother married Mr. Turner's sister and Giles Mebane and I married sisters," he said.

That apparently seemed to him, as he presumed it would to his hearers, an adequate explanation. Also the loan seemed good. Though Joe Turner got the money, the banker required that the note be signed as principal by the new editor's father. Before the war that old gentleman had been the second largest landowner in aristocratic Orange County in which Governor Holden, whom Turner hated most, had been a man without family who became a prewar Democrat. Other items undoubtedly also went into the transaction. Swepson like some other men feared the violent, vituperative Turner. Also, as a banker, Swepson regarded loans as favors and generally expected favor as well as interest in return. Almost casually when he made the loan, he made a condition which, as he repeated it later, sounded only patriotic.

"I requested him that nothing should go in the *Sentinel* to damage the credit of North Carolina bonds. And he agreed to it."

With the money in hand, Turner clamped on his hat and hurried down the back stair from Swepson's private office. He was an impressive figure. Judge Robert W. Winston, of Raleigh, a boy at the time, put in his memoirs, *It's a Far Cry,* the impression made upon him by Turner as being in those revolutionary times as spectacular and fearless as Danton.

"Of revolutionary proportions," Judge Winston wrote, "with a forehead not unlike some cathedral dome, eyes deep set, a cavernous mouth and a voice that carried conviction, Turner's presence was masterful."

And he was believed to be secretly more than he openly appeared. Young Winston remembered a morning in the late 'sixties, when Turner spent a night at his father's house. Coming into the dining room for breakfast, he greeted Winston's mother.

"Good morning to the queen of the household," he said, with a bow.

And she replied quickly, "Good morning to the King of the Ku-Klux."

Turner under oath denied his right to the title. It was conferred or at least publicly attached to him by the *Standard*. Many, including Governor Holden, believed that he held some such position. No dissemblance marked his editing. He hit hard and wide, unmasked and by day. It was a month after he took Swepson's money, however, before he coupled Wall Street brokers and North Carolina bondholders together in evil machinations. Swepson gave no evidence that he noted it, but within half a year Governor Holden, who obviously knew something about the loan and who hated Turner quite as much as Turner hated him, wrote Swepson.

"I see," Holden wrote, "Turner copies article charging that Littlefield and Swepson have swindled the people of Florida. My advice is to crush him. He will sting you as long as you nurse him."

As a man whose deviousness amounted to genius, Swepson had profited more by nursing than crushing. He stayed out of the path of verbal fisticuffs in which Holden was often involved. And the financier gave no evidence that he was disturbed when Turner soon after he got his loan stepped up the already habitual attack of the *Sentinel* upon his partner Littlefield. Whether or not Turner was the King of the Ku-Klux Klan, Littlefield was the president of the North Carolina Union League. Turner's attack on him came with a blast:

Notice Extraordinary
$50,000 Reward!!!

> The Editor of the *Sentinel* will pay FIFTY THOUSAND DOLLARS for the personal appearance of Gen. Littlefield, Editor of the *Standard*—said Editor to be delivered to Senator Sweet, as a witness to go before the Legislative Committee, to testify as to the alleged bribery of certain members of the General Assembly who Senator Sweet, on the floor of the Senate has already declared, received dollars and cents for their votes.

The notice added by way of description of a wanted man: "When the editor left, he had in his left hand a small carpet bag." It stated further almost as a smirk at its own bombast: The reward "to be paid in Confederate money, new issue!"

In retrospect, as it must have been then, Turner's humor provides a saving grace for his savagery. Often he himself would have seemed ridiculous save that he worked much in ridicule. But he was deadly serious in his efforts early in 1869 to prove that rats were leaving the ship. He was energetic, too. He gathered the gossip on which he based his story of the nighttime departure of young Mrs. Cavarly though he piously said that "we hope it was only a modest woman's aversion to appear as a witness that caused her sudden departure from the city." He pointed out gleefully, however, that Littlefield followed her to Richmond while "his dirty paper declared the 'character of the General Assembly as a body is vindicated.'" Also, the *Sentinel* heavily underscored the coincidence that some of Littlefield's minor associates, Pruyn who had sold land for the penitentiary and a "Judge Alden, of the Governor's Reconstruction staff," fled from the city at about the same time.

They went, the *Sentinel* reported, "in a fine carriage, drawn by a span of fine bay horses" to a station on the railroad near Raleigh where "the carriage stood in the woods until the train came." Then: "Pruyn went in at one end of the car, and the flying Judge at the other." Pruyn went to Washington where Mrs. Cavarly saw him later. Alden was obscure in Raleigh; he seems to have disappeared permanently, but the *Sentinel* itself later gave a second explanation of Alden's flight very different in its relation to Littlefield. Then, it said, he was not following but running from Littlefield because he had defrauded the General in a matter involving a note and a $2,000 diamond breast pin. Dollars and diamonds and departure seemed much mixed up in Raleigh at the time, even without the help of Turner's running—or galloping—commentary.

The truth then, so far as the ordinary citizen and newspaper reader was concerned, was not made more certain by the counterattacks of Littlefield's loyal *Standard* staff in his absence. As that journal saw it "the annals of delusion, misrepresentation and falsehood" would have to be ransacked to find Turner's equal. He was an "arch defamer" and "a notorious libeller of patriotic Northern men." Only "vulgar manners and vicious habits" had to be added to the conventional portrait of a scoundrel to provide a description exactly corresponding to "the reckless and worthless creature, whose high sense of honor and chivalric spirit move him to grossly misrepresent a gentleman who is unavoidably absent from the city on pressing business." As a final fling, the *Standard*'s writer suggested that no one should talk of another's departure who had "retreated precipitately from the presence of a corporal of the Federal army during the war." In the midst of its own bombast, however, the *Standard* put the essence of its position and Littlefield's often proclaimed purposes.

"General Littlefield and his friends," it said, "do not need, neither do they desire, a defense in these columns. Since their arrival in North Carolina the most beneficent results have followed. Manufactories and internal improvements have been fostered and augmented, commerce has been increased and extended; native industry has been cherished and rewarded; the value of lands greatly increased, and all classes of our people are looking forward to the future with a pleasing hope of bringing up their families for still better times and a greater prosperity. Such are a few of the effects produced by the activity of a few Northern gentlemen who either came into the State with brigades of soldiers or with their pockets full of money."

Undoubtedly the hope of jobs had a greater appeal than jeremiads for many Southerners in those days. The indignation of his own paper probably protected Milton less than the fact known even among Turner's supporters that he had talked almost as roughly about Jefferson Davis. The General was aided also by a widespread impression that some personal resentment against Governor Holden as an upstart and Whig turncoat entered into Turner's scornful opposition to him and so also to his friends, including Littlefield. Milton was aided even more when Turner's charges ran against the testimony of such a substantial citizen as Dr. Hawkins. If Littlefield was gone, Hawkins was present. He testified he had not given Littlefield Chatham Railroad bonds but had sold him $60,000 worth and received his draft for it.

"Is there anyone so credulous," Joe Turner demanded, "as to believe that this $60,000 draft is ever to be paid, or was ever intended to be paid?"

But the full-bearded Hawkins was unshaken on the stand.

"I believe he is responsible," he said of the General. "I know he has considerable property."

The General even then was preparing, to Turner's editorial and business chagrin, to give evidence of it. When Turner traced him romantically and politically to Richmond and Mrs. Cavarly, Littlefield was traveling much on political and financial business, too. Turner would have given his pistol hand if he could have known then of operations which carried Littlefield to Florida where he had knowledge and acquaintances from his wartime service in the South.

In November 1868, not long before Swepson made his loan to Turner and was expressing distrust of Littlefield to former Senator Clingman, he said, so Clingman related later, that he had sent Littlefield to Florida "last winter—but he accomplished nothing" in connection with "a chance for a great speculation there in three railroads." That would have dated the Littlefield-Swepson association from the time of Littlefield's supposed first arrival in Raleigh—before, Swepson later said, he turned down Littlefield's loan in connection with the purchase of the *Standard*. Perhaps Swepson's or Clingman's memory faltered. The Republicans did not come into power in Florida until June 1868. The railroad manipulations only began then. The certain fact is that while Turner was fulminating early in 1869 about Littlefield's absence—though not yet mentioning Swepson—the three Florida railroads were purchased with funds, derived from the bonds of the Western Division of the North Carolina Railroad, which Swepson was then receiving. He had achieved control of those roads, Paul E. Fenlon wrote in the *Florida Historical Quarterly*, "without the expenditure of a dollar of his own funds."

The deal then was Swepson's only, not Littlefield's. It was a part of the banker's wide Southern operations like those in which he bought stock and sought control of the Carolina National Bank of Columbia, South Carolina, and considered investments in national banks at Tallahassee and Jacksonville in Florida. A South Carolinian hoped he was going to start a fire and life insurance company. He was preparing, with Littlefield this time, to establish a new State Loan and Trust Company of North Carolina. Swepson sought and received little publicity in these matters. Evidence of some of them remains only in his correspondence. "I generally keep my letters," he said later. However, then he welcomed—even sought—the publicity he received in Florida where he so wanted to be welcomed that he was ready to extend railroads to the horizon of Florida's hopes, "contribute fifty thousand dollars" for the construction of a "first class hotel" in Tallahassee and was considering establishment of a line of steamships to ply between New York and Jacksonville in connection with extension of the railroad to the west "at his own expense."

In Raleigh Turner kept the light of publicity on Littlefield and sometimes seemed to make light where he had none. There was an illumination, however, which Littlefield did not mind about reports of his presence at the inauguration of Grant. Milton had no desire to conceal the fact that he was one of the packed crowd which sped Grant "down Pennsylvania Avenue in one long shout." He happily subscribed to the view, which angry and dying old Governor Worth wrote "in despair," that the election of Grant was "a national endorsement of the Congressional plan of Reconstruction." At Willard's, in the Ebbitt, on the crowded streets, Milton himself was a gleaming symbol of that endorsement.

Mrs. Cavarly, she said later, was at the inauguration receiving as usual the confidence of carpetbaggers, this time from Pruyn who told her he was "satisfied with his operations in North Carolina." He had "sold the bonds he got in the Penitentiary business, I think he said, for 60 cents on the dollar." The pendulum-headed Congressman Deweese, however, told her and Taylor Soute, a Maryland banker, that Pruyn could not be held responsible because he "has nothing."

The *Sentinel* reported that General Byron Laflin was also in Washington for the occasion—"such visits give this illustrious General so much red in the face that blushing can't change his color." However florid Laflin was, he shared Milton's presence and prominence, the paper said. And undoubtedly while Milton was there, he saw his brother John who that year secured a copyright on a steel engraving made by Gudger of his much-praised portrait of Lincoln. John had left the government service and maintained both a studio as "artist and publisher" on Twelfth Street and a residence on New York Avenue. Prominent people came to see his pictures.

Pleasant as was Milton's participation in the celebration as Grant arrived and Andrew Johnson (with whom Grant would not ride) departed, Milton showed no reluctance about returning to Raleigh. Nobody sought to collect the price in Confederate money which Turner had put upon his head. And Turner mentioned the reward no more. Despite his clamor, that angry gentleman was having his troubles. Obviously, then, the people he was laboring to save were giving him no overwhelming financial support. His fever did not seem generally contagious. Two days before Milton returned, its proprietor took the *Sentinel* out of direct competition with the *Standard* and made it an afternoon paper. On Milton's return there was almost a sound of respect in Turner's sneers.

"Home Again—General Littlefield has returned," he said.

"We saw him with Abbott, of New Hampshire, get out of the 'Buss' as the Yankees call it." Apparently good Southerners still said "omnibus" which was perhaps justified by such a "six-horse omnibus" as the Yarborough House sent to meet all trains. On this bus ride Littlefield was accompanied not only by Abbott but also the other gentlemen in whose partnership he had first come to the state: "Carpetbagger French (big Ingin) and Gen. Estes, of New York, via New Hanover, went to meet them at the depot."

Turner had his nicknames for almost everybody he hated which required a good many nicknames. He hung a variety on Laflin as a lady-killer and wine-bibber. Even minor characters in Turner's demonology received them. Turner was as suspicious about state purchases for costly furniture as he was about railroads and bonds. So he called General Estes' brother-in-law who became Holden's Secretary of State, "Ipecac" Menninger based on a joke he made about him: "Now we ask Dr. Grissom, of the Lunatic Asylum, if it takes fifteen grains of ipecac to make the child throw up the cake, how many grains will it take to make Menninger throw up the cushions and the carpet?"

For Littlefield, however, he had then no nicknames. He was "the distinguished lobbyist who was presented by the Grand Jury of

Wake County for attempts to influence the Legislature with whiskey and money." Turner knew that a Conservative attempt to indict Littlefield had failed but he never forgot it, blaming failure not on a lack of facts but the presence on the bench of a Republican judge whom he customarily called "Greasy Sam" Watts. Still in his charges against Littlefield, Turner wrote like a man who respected his adversary even in his wickedness. He wrote: "Littlefield does not concern himself with small grabs, with him it is 'neck or nothing.'"

Though Milton's paper lambasted Turner in return, Littlefield personally seemed magnificently oblivious of the Democratic editor. He took no part in a street encounter between Turner and a group of infuriated Republicans, including the Governor's son, "Ipecac" Menninger, Pruyn, Laflin and one of Swepson's native business associates. After Turner drew a six-shooter on his antagonists, the incident ended at the Mayor's office where Governor Holden himself appeared in a rage that almost precipitated a riot. Littlefield's only part in the affair was in the news report in his *Standard,* ridiculing Turner for cowardice, which the assailed *Sentinel* editor declared in much longer space contained 39 falsehoods in 31½ lines. Turner called the engagement a bold attempt to assassinate him in broad daylight and two weeks later reported an attempt to shoot him in his room at night through the blinds. In addition, Turner wrote that Governor Holden (about whose personal habits in connection with the bottle the *Sentinel* made constant references) had told General Estes that he would pardon anyone who killed the *Sentinel's* editor.

No such furies were attributed to Littlefield. Indeed, on the day Turner reported the pistol shot into his room from the dark, the *Sentinel* noted "Judge Settle of the Supreme Court walking with Littlefield arm in arm on Fayetteville Street." They were, the item said, just about "the best looking men of the party. Settle looks a good deal like Littlefield and Littlefield a good deal like Settle."

Arm-in-arm in the spring of 1869 Settle and Littlefield were approximately the same age and much alike in mind as well as appearance. Dr. Hamilton, whose sympathies in the Reconstruction story were definitely with the Conservatives, wrote of Judge Thomas Settle as "a superbly handsome man with a magnetic personality." And he added: "He was genial, witty, and affectionate in personal intercourse, and courageous and tolerant in his public relationships. His mind was quick and acute, and he was a well-informed and persuasive debater. He was best fitted for the political arena, but made an excellent though in no sense a great judge. He was impartial, humane, and just, and his judicial opinions were terse, concise and clear." Settle's family was as good as any in North Carolina. His father had been a prominent man before him. He was highly esteemed by President Grant who made him not only Minister to Peru but the permanent president of the Republican National Convention which renominated him in 1872. All in all, Settle was the kind of man who made absurd Turner's suggestion that the entire Republican Party in North Carolina was disreputable. Littlefield in Settle's friendship was obviously not ostracized (as the tradition about all carpetbaggers is) by all the nice people of the state.

That vignette of Littlefield, gay in the company of Settle on Raleigh's principal street that spring, is clearly a better picture of Milton's situation in the southern town than those generally given by the *Sentinel* at the time, or in stiffly slanted history since. April in the little capital was always lovely. And though in 1869 the *Sentinel* complained that the weather was a little cool for the season, that paper was aware of the spring though it noticed even nature sadly in a brief observation that "the old landmarks around Raleigh are slowly, but surely, disappearing."

Even that sad fact apparently was attributable to local Republican government: "We were mortified a day or two since, to find that the row of walnut trees that had stood for many years in the street south of the residence of Mr. K. P. Battle had been cut down by the order of the city authorities." Undoubtedly, the landmarks in Turner's town must have seemed to be falling more rapidly when he learned that Milton was moving in as a neighbor of the Battles on that part of lower Fayetteville Street of which Mr. Battle spoke only modestly when he said, "the neighborhood was good."

This was Milton's flowering spring. It had been little more than a year since in a trip from freezing winter into southern snow, he had left Anna and the boys on Shoemaker Lane in Philadelphia.

He had lived since in hotels, the Yarborough in Raleigh, the St. Nicholas in New York, the Capitol Hotel in Tallahassee, and on trains and steamers in those days when boosters in Florida advertised rather hopefully that the trip from Manhattan to Jacksonville could be accomplished with several changes, by the cars, steamers and ferries in about three days. Raleigh was not only the center of Milton's influence but mid-point in his operations. He was ready to make it the fixed, comfortable home center of his world.

Times, as Turner told everybody, were hard. "We are the poorest people in the world . . . our very life blood is being sucked out by the insatiate leeches that have floated down from the northern waters and by the vampires that have come from our own creeks and ponds." He undertook to document it. His *Sentinel* printed an item, since stressed by historians, that the sheriff of the county had made distress sales at public auction of twenty-three tracts of land containing 7,782 acres for only $7,718. At a dollar an acre nobody seemed to want any part of the South, but three days later John W. Forney, the publisher-politician-promoter whom Milton had known in Philadelphia, arrived at the Yarborough House.

The Philadelphian was a friend of Thomas A. Scott, the railroad magnate, whose imperial interests turned south as well as west. Forney came with a party of fourteen associates and the declaration that he wanted to invest $5,000,000 in southern lands. The suspicious *Sentinel* noted that Forney "declares his object is not political, yet it appears that the 'trooly loil' here have received some notice of his coming." Milton, of course, was one of the "truly loyal" whose claim to that condition the *Sentinel* regularly put into Negro dialect. Of course, too, as Turner expected, Forney did go back north to say of Holden that though "immeasurably assailed by his enemies, it is beyond controversy that North Carolina is the best reconstructed state in the South."

More startling to Turner was the news which not even the *Sentinel* could disregard: "Charles B. Root, Esq., has sold his residence on Fayetteville Street to General Littlefield for $6,000. The new office for the *Standard* is to be erected near Mr. Root's residence." That was almost as much money as the *Sentinel* had reported nearly eight thousand acres in the vicinity of the town was worth. Battle, though earlier, had paid only $8,000 for his brick house on a much larger lot, which contained not only gardens and great oaks but the reputed ghost of a punished slave girl. Littlefield's was a smaller establishment but one equal to the houses of other prominent citizens in the city.

There was significance besides the price in the sale of the Root residence to Littlefield. Though born in the North, Charles Root had lived in Raleigh since 1837. He had married a daughter of the anciently established Gales family, which had provided the editors of *The Raleigh Register* and *The National Intelligencer* in Washington. Root's wife was a niece of a former editor of the *Sentinel* who a few years before had expressed his unreconstructed contempt for the American flag. Mr. Root was less disdainful of the inevitable. Some complained of the service he provided as president of the Raleigh Gas Company, but nobody questioned the social standing of the Root family in the town. Sale of a house, of course, did not of itself constitute social recognition of a carpetbagger, but it is clear that social barriers bristled more in the *Sentinel* than in society itself.

Milton's house had a pleasant dooryard and side yards containing not only flowers but beds of strawberries like those in Battle's yard in which that gentleman had hidden gold pieces from Yankee bummers at the time of the surrender. The porch across the front resembled the one from which the assembled Battle family, "however regretfully," watched four years before the splendor of the pageant of Sherman's troops. In the rear were stables with a stall in them for the beautiful, dapple gray horse Milton had bought from Allen Howe, of Springfield, Massachusetts. As a Northern creature, much admired on its arrival, the horse remained in Raleigh long after Milton was gone, as hackney, work horse, preacher's plodder, then colored man's plug and finally in 1887, as was noted by the press in that redeemed time, was "traded for a little bull beef worth less than nine dollars."

The house was as handsome as the horse in 1869. Also, even more than Kemp Battle's residence, it was "at a convenient distance from the courthouse, the stores, and the railroad station, and not too far from the Capitol and Christ Church." The *Standard* office near by would be almost as convenient as the law office in the yard in which Battle was then handling, as he wrote later, some strictly legal matters for Mr. Swepson.

The newspaper plant was the proof of Littlefield's exuberant plans for such a fixed residence as he had never had, and long had meant to make for himself and Anna and the boys. Even its design by "J. P. Prarie, Esq., the well-known architect of this city," was impressive. If, as Turner sneered, the *Standard* "really pays expenses with all the pap drawn from State and national sources," the projected plant seemed a civic monument in the little town. It confounded the *Sentinel's* editorial doubts that anybody who amounted to anything read the *Standard*. Turner was even more caustic in his comments on his opposition when he went from his own dingy quarters to Pepper's saloon, though he felt it proper to say editorially of himself, after he had published much about the drinking of others, that "our drinking at Pepper's and O'Connor's has been not exceeding three glasses a week, and that only ale."

Governor Holden did give Milton the position of State Printer, which in those days was a party organ's expected plum. Not even the profits from that political appointment, however, could justify the new plant unless, as sometimes even Turner recognized though only as a horrible possibility, people were reading the *Standard* and advertisers were finding it effective. Under such circumstances, probably no more enthusiastic comment could have been expected from the *Sentinel* than that the new plant "presents a handsome appearance outwardly."

Milton himself made no such limited and exterior comments on his building. It was, his paper pronounced, "a model building, and we have no hesitation in saying that it is the most complete newspaper building in the Southern States." It was of "brick mixed with granite," two stories high, with a half basement story, and was "built in a shorter time than any building of its size in the State."

"The front," said the proud editor, "is forty feet wide by twenty deep, and contains the editor's room, the counting room, local editor's room, proofreader's room and private office. The ell is fifty feet long by twenty wide and is two stories high with a half basement story. In the basement story are three presses,—a Campbell cylinder press, an Adams press, and a Gordon 'half medium' press, all run by steam, rather caloric power." On the next floor was the composing room and job printing office where eight first-class printers in addition to the foreman "get up two papers per day with a speed that would make country printers open their eyes." On the top story was the book bindery.

"The entire office," the exuberant report went on, "is lighted with gas, and can be so illuminated as to almost rival daylight. Water pipes run throughout the building and into every room. The water is supplied from a reservoir at the top of the building into which water is forced by a force pump from below, which obtains water from a large cistern holding some 20,000 gallons."

And finally: "The *sanctum* is adorned by the presence of the editor who will be happy to welcome his brethren of the press whenever they may call upon him, and whose Castalian fount is never out of order." Mr. Turner, whose Parnassian spring generally produced bitter waters, added to the description of the editor's office when he reacted to Milton's always evident good humor, "Oh, yes, you are laughing, jesting, only jesting, while you quietly smoke a fine cigar, and lounge on one of your fine sofas the people paid for!"

Milton paid more attention to the praise of his building from other sources. He reprinted with satisfaction an item from *The New York Tribune* which emphasized his continuing concern for the welfare of freedmen. There is no evidence to support the *Sentinel's* often-repeated charge that the *Tribune* and Wall Street brokers owned the *Standard,* but that great Republican organ showed a paternalistic—or political—interest in Milton's concern for the colored man as well as for his new plant. Obviously, the information which it passed on to other interested Republicans came from Milton himself.

"The job of digging the cellar," said Horace Greeley's paper which had rejoiced with Littlefield in Grant's election the year before, "was done by a colored man in three days. The contract for laying the brick was also given to a colored man, who did the job in 18 days and a half. The job for carpenter work was given to a white man, but colored men worked with them side by side. The building was completed in less than 60 days. These facts argue well, not only for the Raleigh *Standard*, but for Negro labor in the South as well as elsewhere."

Though some Democrats paid more attention to the report that Milton at the time had, as president of the Union League, bailed out two Negro burglars who belonged to the League, his attitude toward the freedmen helped make him the obvious choice as orator on National Memorial Day, then regarded almost as a day of enmity by ex-Confederates. (Indeed, that year the *Sentinel* ridiculed what it described as the Negro and Republican celebration of the Fourth of July.) Apparently beside the graves of Union soldiers in the Federal cemetery, the General in peaceful mood stirred no old furies, addressing himself only to the thesis that "the arms and deeds of civilian soldiers have crowned the nation with unparalleled dignity and power."

Still the occasion was an irritant to Turner who noted that more local merchants—presumably also advertisers—closed their stores than on May tenth, Confederate Memorial Day: "The only reason we can assign for such conduct is that the office-holders and Northern element of our population have far more money to spend than those who tenderly and truly cherish the memory of the Confederate dead." (Some local people had money: Mr. Swepson's bank declared a 7½ per cent dividend, free from U. S. and state taxes.)

With Settle and other friends, or by himself, Milton walked to and from his plant, by the hotels, to the Capitol, speaking to friends, lifting his beaver to ladies not all of whom by any means turned blank eyes to his greeting. Some men bowed with a studied frigidity. Some older women drew their daughters closer to their sides when he passed. They were exceptions. Even some of them after they had passed felt furiously that their stiff manners had been rebuked in burlesque by his assured air of courtesy.

Along Fayetteville Street he moved in a mood of generosity toward the whole town which in so many ways seemed to be becoming his town, too. If Turner charged him with Northern citizenship, when he was made State Printer, Milton walked like a native of the place. He talked with merchants. He knew the children on the streets, and often stopped in Royster's candy store to buy gifts for them. Citizens smelled approvingly the cigars which he offered from his leather case. Young men and women noticed his clothes and the manner in which he took a fine linen handkerchief from his coat pocket and flicked the dust from his sleeve. Nobody ever questioned his appearance, his amiability or his easy giving. Furthermore, it was his Christian charity, possibly attributable among other things to Anna's increasing piety and his plans to bring her "home," which brought upon him Joe Turner's most furious and most frustrated assault.

Like a final welcome in May, Milton received the blessing—or at least the thanks—of the North Carolina Diocese of the Episcopal Church. The Episcopalians then did not constitute the largest religious group in North Carolina. Other churches had far more members—Mrs. Swepson was almost a saint among Baptists. But the Episcopal Church seemed then and later to embody a ritualistic aristocracy holding almost as a possession the traditions of the South. Its pews contained the confident fellow communicants of Jefferson Davis—even Robert E. Lee, who seemed almost to take a place in its apostolic succession. Certainly it was the church of social acceptability. When its diocesan convention met in Raleigh that spring, Littlefield from his sanctum in his fine new plant had generously offered to do its printing free. The offer was graciously accepted. And Turner felt betrayed in the house of his idols. He did not take it on his knees.

"The very marked change in the tone and temper of the Radical press and of the party in this state towards our conservative people," he wrote, "has been observed by some parties and very hastily acquiesced in as an evidence of the return of good feeling and as an unmistakable proof that some of the more respectable among the carpetbaggers and scalawags were coming over."

He pressed his pen harder on the paper.

"The pretended exhibition of liberality on the part of Littlefield of the *Standard* toward the late convention of the Protestant Episcopal Church, held in this city, was construed into kindness, when it is manifest, that no act of his was ever prompted by greater selfishness and more contemptible toadyism, than when he proposed to do the printing for the convention without charge. Littlefield was guilty of a little Yankee trick in that matter, he threw his card well and hit the convention in a tender point.

"They could not in Christian charity decline his offer—even the devil must be allowed to make brick to build the church."

Literally or figuratively he spat before he went on.

"Littlefield, Holden, Dick, Tourgée, Settle, Rodman, Cantwell, Thomas, Watts, Billy Smith, etc.," he wrote, calling a Republican roll, "all cry out, 'Let us have peace.'"

That much-repeated phrase came from Grant's acceptance of the Republican nomination.

"Do they want peace yet?" Turner wrote on. "We think they do. They have got all the offices to be had, the control of 30 or 40 million bonds to be issued by the State, all the fat places for themselves and their friends—the control of the State, of the counties, of the townships, of the Legislature, of the Penitentiary. Littlefield has the public printing for the next four years he thinks. . . ."

It would be unfair to say that Mr. Turner put that which was most precious to him last. His anger was inclusive. But as May turned into June he could not stir the general anger which he was sure was required. Even his *Sentinel* in the days following seemed apathetic in the approach of the summer solstice. There was little political profit in its items: The legislature had already dispersed for six months, flush at its adjournment with "spondulax," said that paper which added its gratification at the departure of the Reconstruction legislators, whom it called "hands," as if all were laborers in Littlefield's vineyard.

"We say, farewell hands: they say farewell, sweet, precious, necessary *per diem—adieu la voîture, adieu la boutique.*"

In the quieter capital the captain of the night police had been bound over to a higher court for getting drunk, going to Kate Dougherty's gay establishment on Vinegar Hill and beating her up when she rejected his amorous advances. The town got a chance to see the famous and beautiful Kate Chase Sprague (whose often drunken husband, the rich Senator from Rhode Island, had recently, with the *Sentinel's* echoing approval, called Senator Abbott a "puppy dog"). She came with her father, Chief Justice Chase, the colored voter's friend, who sat in Raleigh as judge of the U. S. Circuit Court. There was a velocipede race. A public cockfight was held "at the eastern terminus of New Bern Street" with $500 a side. "The noble army of blackberry women" appeared with berries at five cents a quart. Raleigh like the rest of the country was concerned with the "baseball mania." The temperature in the shade was in the high nineties. The dust was so thick on Fayetteville Street before the Yarborough House and the *Standard* office that a buggy ran over a little girl in a cloud of dust which enshrouded them both. And Littlefield, as he so often did, seemed as suddenly and mysteriously gone as if he also had disappeared in a cloud of Fayetteville Street's dust.

Apparently not even the vigilant *Sentinel* knew anything about his whereabouts and his activities until two days before his return when, on June 29, it began reprinting the articles from *The Floridian* of Tallahassee. They reported Littlefield's activities there in a manner which prompted Holden to write Swepson that the time had come to stop nursing Turner and crush him. Uncrushed, Turner added his own comment on a report of the arrival of Littlefield and Senator Abbott in the state which they had visited first as soldiers.

"We think Milton Littlefield and Abbott," Turner wrote, "can administer and sell out that little state in ten days."

Then he added his information that a special session called by the Governor of Florida had passed a bill to pay Swepson's three roads, combined into the Jacksonville, Pensacola and Mobile Railroad (J. P. & M.), $20,000 per mile in state bonds. Littlefield had not only passed out money right and left, the *Sentinel* declared, he had secured alteration of the bill between its passage and enrollment so as to leave the state even without security provided in the bill as the legislature passed it. Turner was no longer nursing Swepson. He stung by quotation from *The Floridian*:

"Whether Mr. Swepson is privy to the fraud or not, he certainly was wise in the selection of an instrument who was equal to any corruption that might be necessary to meet any emergency."

Milton had more than Turner's reprints and charges on his mind when he got back to Raleigh. He returned the same day the *Sentinel* announced that Colonel William Johnston of Charlotte, "one of the most successful railroaders in the country," had arrived in town. Johnston was a power and a personage. He had been the extreme Secessionist candidate for Governor in 1862. Jefferson Davis had been with him in Charlotte in 1865 when the news of Lincoln's assassination came. His closest business associate was Swepson's close relation McAden. Johnston's daughter then was soon to marry Dr. Hawkins' nephew, Captain A. B. Andrews, superintendent of the Raleigh and Gaston Railroad. Through McAden Colonel Johnston had employed Littlefield, at the regular rate of ten per cent of the bonds secured, to lobby for bond legislation for his Atlantic, Tennessee and Ohio Railroad and to secure a compromise in a suit brought, through a dummy and apparently for blackmail, by Congressman Deweese to prevent the issue of the bonds to the road.

More important at the time of Littlefield's return, however, was what Colonel Johnston said later he was told by his old law teacher, Chief Justice Pearson: that the State Supreme Court was about to declare all the special tax railroad bonds invalid. Colonel Johnston in an agitation which he could not contain told Swepson and also Kemp Battle, who wired the news to his friend and client, T. H. Porter, a partner in the brokerage house of Soutter and Company of New York, which handled many matters for Swepson and Littlefield.

The whole edifice of railroad bonds seemed toppling. Whispers spread about the Supreme Court itself. The rumor began about Swepson tapping his pocket and saying he had a decision there which had cost him a lot of money. Holden sent Swepson a wire about the matter which, as Hamilton said later, while not proving improper intervention by the Governor in judicial processes, "casts an unpleasant light upon the general situation of affairs." Out of much wiring, wire-pulling and arranging, however, the case was reargued for the railroads by distinguished Democratic lawyers who received seventy-five railroad bonds (par value $1,000 each) and $21,250 in cash for their services. (Other money put up by the railroads and never accounted for in connection with the hearing amounted to $8,259 and fifteen bonds.) The important event was that the decision of the court handed down July 21 in effect upheld the validity of the bonds of most of the roads, including those in which Swepson and his friends were interested.

"Up! Up!!" said the *Sentinel* on July 24. "Since the decision of the Supreme Court on the Railroad appropriation question, North Carolina State bonds, now, have gone up in New York, from 44½ to which they have fallen to 52, as quoted by last night's telegram. We give the fact without comment: everyone can draw his own inference."

Many did. Rumors were rife. Reports ran from New York to Florida. Swepson, as publicly reticent as always, wrote his friend and lawyer, General Matt Whitaker Ransom, about one of them. Ransom, who was to become a long-time United States senator, had named a son after Swepson. Swepson had helped Ransom in his financial difficulties. In a letter from New York Swepson told him: "So far as this Florida matter is concerned, I know nothing of the fraud if one was committed. It all grows out of their fights in Florida and it is attempted to damage me to prevent my getting hold of the railroad of the State. In this they will fail. I have had much trouble—but all will yet be right & I shall make a good thing, I have every confidence to believe."

The North Carolina situation called for more immediate attention and Swepson arranged with other interested railroad men to advance the money to pay the interest on the special tax bonds which had not been paid in January and April. That both quieted bondholders' loud complaints and helped bond prices. Swepson's activities kept him much on the run, however, between Raleigh, New York and Baltimore where he seemed to conduct many of his operations through a firm called Fels & Company, on South Sharpe Street.

"We miss you very much," Governor Holden wrote him late in July in a letter in which he called Turner "a mean, ungrateful wretch" and sent his "respects" to Littlefield.

Milton clearly then had Swepson's respect. Turner's reprints of charges by *The Floridian* in Tallahassee reflected a real row in Florida, where Swepson's plans and Milton's promotion of them were clamorously criticized. Nevertheless, on July 24, the same day the *Sentinel* skeptically cried, "Up! Up!!" about the North Carolina railroad bonds, General Littlefield was elected, by Swepson and his Florida associates, president of the Jacksonville, Pensacola and Mobile Railroad. Down there *The Floridian* might roar like Turner but there was also the view expressed by *The Jacksonville Union,* a Radical newspaper: "Let us have peace, and railroads and steamships, and let such a costly article as abstract justice take care of itself." Many subscribed to the same doctrine in North Carolina.

Summer was passing pleasantly. The North Carolina bonds were going up. And even in Raleigh, though Joe Turner complained that "Wall Street brokers, with Milton Littlefield to corrupt and buy up the legislature, have put this heavy debt upon us," his paper spoke of "Our Fast Growing City" in describing a drive through "the eastern suburbs." The weather was too hot for any but desultory exchanges of venom between the *Standard* and the *Sentinel*. Indeed, either Joe Turner himself or one of his representatives went with Governor Holden's party on a pleasant expedition on August 6.

They drove up Dix Hill, named after the Yankee woman, Dorothea Dix, who had prevailed upon North Carolinians to build an asylum for the insane there. Times and delusions around it had changed since Sherman's troops camped on its green slopes and Sherman himself there met a demented man who confounded the General with an oracular statement about his power. Power was not quite so clear in 1869 when the non-partisan group went in high spirits up the hill to view the total eclipse of the sun that year. The asylum, the *Sentinel* reported, was "full to its utmost capacity." So was its roof, the highest vantage point around Raleigh, that day. In his palmetto hat Governor Holden on the cupola of the hospital seemed concerned only with natural phenomena.

All present looked at the world through smoked glasses. An expectant silence preceded any sign of change in the sun. Then suddenly the landscape began to darken and, through their glasses, Democrats and Republicans both could see the moon's disk crescent-cutting the sun. Even more remarkable seemed the little disk images on the purpling earth below them. Then, just before the sun was wholly covered, an immense dark shadow swept down from the west with great speed, engulfing the whole area in a darkness like night. In the clear sky there were stars, and on the ground a succession of flitting bands of light and shadow, alternately dark and bright. Around the covered sun irregular streams of light ran out like tongues of flame. Then the changes and the colors reversed themselves. And with the return of normal light the watchers were aware that a chill had disappeared with the darkness.

Negroes were frightened. Chickens went to roost. And even those who smiled in astronomical understanding of the event felt that a portent had filled the skies over the asylum. Such an uneasy feeling passed. The late summer sun was all too naked above the dusty streets. Less awesome spectacles became important again. State bonds were down a little and, as September advanced, the *Sentinel* noted that the Governor and State Treasurer D. A. Jenkins left for New York, in the company of General Littlefield. Almost automatically, it commented: "Next week as the Governor and the Treasurer and Littlefield walk up and down in Wall Street and go in and out at Soutter & Co's, bonds will go up and down, in and out. Littlefield has been buying, it is supposed at these low figures; next week, or within ten days it is supposed he will sell."

The paper counted time on the Governor carefully. Before he returned it noted that he had been absent "for over 20 days." Much happened in that period. On the day following his return the Democratic paper reported that "about nine o'clock last night, the gas failed and left the city in darkness. . . ." Some convivialists at Pepper's were left in the blackness with their glasses still in their hands. And one among them, unidentified, declared, the *Sentinel* reported, that it was a proper illumination of the city for the Governor's return.

CHAPTER XII

Black Friday

I WAS WITH Swepson all the time during the gold panic," Littlefield said. It was the time of the perfection of their partnership.

They could not always be at the same place at the same time. In their train-riding operations, their deals and conferences in Washington and Raleigh, Savannah and Tallahassee, Charleston and Baltimore, separation was often essential and the differences between them were essential, too. One basic aspect of their partnership was that each was able to repudiate in public—and more often in whispered private conversations—the apparent mistakes or misdeeds of the other.

"At that time," said John Preston Arthur in *Western North Carolina: A History 1730-1913,* "no one in North Carolina stood higher in public respect than George W. Swepson." And even the often-critical *Floridian* of Tallahassee said of Littlefield: ". . . not only is he a pleasant enough person to look at, but he has the art of making himself agreeable to everybody, and is never so fascinating as when he is after something. Then his powers of pleasing are remarkable." Neither then nor later in North Carolina did any man have such a genius for deviousness behind a bland exterior as Swepson. As his antithesis in jovial audacity, Littlefield rode to his operations in the best-equipped carriages and seemed not to care at all who saw where he was going. There was laughter always around Milton's jokes; often Swepson gave the impression that he disliked the least noise.

They required each other in New York that late summer which ended explosively on Black Friday, September 24, 1869, though Milton played in the North more of a background rôle than he did in the South. Then greater and more notorious speculators, acting so as to create a panic for the nation, were also bringing on the climax in the first financial phase of Reconstruction in the South. Mr. Swepson undoubtedly watched Mr. Jay Gould with admiration. Both were slight, almost shy, soft-spoken men with all the domestic virtues and singularly free from the familiar vices of their sex. While Milton admired the boldness of Jim Fisk, he regarded with disdain that gambler's flashier clothes and ways. Fisk had seemed blatant in Memphis; in his greater wealth he was only more vulgar in New York. All women looked at Milton; he would have been the last man to flaunt a woman, as Fisk did his glamorous mistress, Josie Mansfield, in the eyes of the world.

In terms of reserve and audacity, however, there were similarities between the four men, though even in the glittering St. Nicholas, Swepson and Littlefield were backcountrymen beside Gould and Fisk in their operations to corner the gold of the world. Gould, who had spent half a million dollars bribing the unreconstructed New York legislature, had stolen millions for his operations from the treasury of the Erie Railroad. The purposes of Swepson and Littlefield were smaller but not much less complex. They were using the funds of one state as a means of robbing another, while seeming to serve both states in patriotic purposes.

Mr. Gould and Mr. Fisk, of course, as Gould told President Grant, were running up the price of gold to help move to world markets the crops of the farmers of the West. The aim of Swepson and Littlefield was to reconstruct the economic fortunes of the poor, ruined South. Such pretensions sagged when the plans behind them crumbled. What was loudly called robbery in the North took the name of Reconstruction in the South, chiefly blamed on Negro governments. Yet despite the lasting impression there were few Negroes involved in the Swepson-Littlefield operations.

Ignorant and venal Negro legislators were available. Some were used for the chores of corruption. Some white men were elected only because of Negro votes. But in North Carolina and Florida there were plenty of white men, most of them native, insisting, as a natural, racial right, upon the first places in line. No Negro politicians or financiers were involved in the Swepson-directed strategy in North Carolina, New York and Florida in the summer of 1869. Littlefield was the only stranger among those Southerners in New York—on this occasion he made himself inconspicuous.

He was, however, not a man to be overlooked. Eyes, male and female, followed him in every hotel lobby. Servants remembered and greeted him. With a salute to familiar clerks, he scrawled "General M. S. Littlefield" on the ledger of the St. Nicholas in mid-September when he accompanied Governor Holden and State Treasurer David Jenkins to the metropolis. He knew that Swepson was awaiting them upstairs in the famous hotel which Judge Rodman said he had patronized before the war and was that summer so crowded with North Carolinians. Many of them had been at a meeting in Swepson's suite a day or two before at which Swepson had outlined a plan for a pool of North Carolina bonds to protect the credit of the state in the threatening condition of the market. All present, said one of the North Carolina legislators whose margins in bond speculations Swepson had been carrying, "seemed actuated by the single desire to arrest the fall of the bonds."

In the interest of that purpose Swepson had sent word to Littlefield to fetch Holden, whose role in so many ways resembled that of Grant for Gould, though Swepson handled Holden with actual assurance, as Gould only pretended to handle Grant. Treasurer Jenkins said later that he only went north with Milton to "settle with the State's funding agent," and "so far as I know, Governor Holden was there on a visit with his family." Behind them in Raleigh the *Sentinel* noted their trip with less charity: "Watch your corks, gentlemen, the eyes of the public are upon you. We say our bonds will go up in a few days to the great gain of Littlefield, Soutter & Co."

Milton delivered his traveling companions to Swepson who then seemed the active partner in the North as Milton sometimes seemed in the South. Milton was insistently inconspicuous in the noisy city. He seemed almost retiring after his ostentatious concern with many matters across the summer. At the St. Nicholas he was often in Swepson's rooms. Swepson came to consult in his. Milton had desk room at Soutter & Company. He was almost casual in his attitude, though he watched all the maneuvers with eyes which kept records as carefully as Rosenthal.

Swepson's chief operating associates then were Andrew Jackson Jones, member of the legislature and president of the Western Railroad (not to be confused with Swepson's own Western Division of the Western North Carolina Railroad) and Dr. William Sloan, new president of the Wilmington, Charlotte and Rutherford Railroad. They were the same two men, who long before Littlefield ever met Swepson, had been involved in the transaction, which Governor Worth called "villainous," in state cotton through the firm of Swepson, Mendenhall & Company in 1866. Worth did not suspect Swepson of complicity, but the two men the Governor did damn were still close to Swepson in 1869.

Sloan afterward claimed to have been a reluctant associate in Swepson's bond pool. Officers of his road had been suspicious earlier in the summer of conditions surrounding the North Carolina Supreme Court decisions as to the validity of the railroad bonds. They had been suddenly told of the first decision in New York by Porter of Soutter & Company, who handled so many matters for Swepson. News that the bonds had been declared invalid seemed to them "a trick, a bogus affair." They were more suspicious "that the whole matter was an intrigue, a scheme for bearing North Carolina bonds on the market for speculative purposes." They noticed that, despite the judicial danger, Swepson and his friends kept buying and selling.

The case was reargued. The bonds went up. Then, Dr. Hamilton wrote, "many accusations were made against the Supreme Court . . . but there is no evidence to show improper conduct on the part of any particular member of it." At the time, North Carolinians in New York knew only that after the decision, holding that most bonds, including Swepson's, were not invalid after all, Swepson put up the margin for a $100,000 speculation in the bonds by Judge Rodman, the North Carolina aristocrat who had been elected to the court by Republicans the year before. That did not convict Rodman; it convinced some of his fellow guests at the St. Nicholas.

Sloan's suspicions grew as Black Friday approached. Swepson insisted that he was not selling his own bonds. He was "vexed and rather put out of humor" even before the Supreme Court decisions by reports that he was. But Sloan could not even get his road's bonds. The excuse he got from Treasurer Jenkins, through Porter of Soutter & Company, who later disavowed it, was that the plate from which his bonds were to be printed had been broken. It seemed to stay broken. And Sloan came to the nagging notion that Swepson was behind the Treasurer and the broker and the broken plate.

The appalling idea occurred to him that Swepson might be keeping other North Carolina bonds off the market while he sold his own, and that in the pool "Swepson might have the controlling influence, and manage them to suit his own interests to the detriment of my company." Feeling so, Sloan said later when others accused him of welshing on his losses, he sought out Governor Holden in the glittering St. Nicholas and told that innocent but not blameless statesman "that the sooner he got rid of Mr. Swepson, the better it would be for the interests of the State."

"The Governor replied," Sloan said, "that he was no financier, and in these matters there might be an honest difference of opinion."

While Littlefield watched, such differences of opinion swirled around Swepson, but the banker remained assured in the midst of them. He could dismiss Sloan's mutterings more easily, however, than more clamorous questions which came up from Florida following Littlefield's visit there early in the summer. In his charming and sometimes almost too persuasive way, the General had aroused suspicions in that state which pained Mr. Swepson when they reached him in New York. He suavely denied any scandal even to his friend and attorney, General Ransom. Also, while he labored, as he said to maintain the credit of North Carolina and the price of its bonds in that summer of 1869, he was happy to reassure visitors from Florida that his purpose was only the development of the railroads of their state, and that if Littlefield had been guilty of any misconduct in Tallahassee he "exceeded his authority."

As he met so many others, he welcomed to his suite in the St. Nicholas one of his Florida agents, Colonel J. P. Sanderson, and a handsome young lawyer, Captain Edward M. L'Engle, who he hoped would become one. Littlefield was definitely not present on that occasion. Young L'Engle was a young man of high repute in Florida, member of one of the best and oldest families in the state, who had served with distinction as a Confederate soldier. He was erect, aware of his honor and, as he himself later discovered, still had much to learn. Swepson greeted them graciously but did not hide a little irritation.

"What have I done? Why are the people of Florida unwilling that I should bring my money into the State and aid them in developing their own resources."

He smiled a little wearily. Nevertheless at the outset of the interview in the richly draped room young L'Engle, as he afterward reported, was reserved in his opinion about his slight, low-toned host. When he went to New York, he said not long after, he "entertained a strong prejudice against Mr. Swepson." Though deferential to the older man as a well-brought-up young Southerner was expected to be, he said candidly to the impressive businessman that "I would have to be satisfied both as to his solvency and as to his integrity before I could be associated with him professionally or in any other way."

Swepson was not disturbed by the young Captain's candor. He met it with some amusement but with an appearance of complete frankness. His shy persuasiveness dominated the room. Swepson had known many such boys before, but L'Engle saw then his first Swepson.

"He took my remarks kindly," young L'Engle reported to fellow Floridians, "and gave me the assurance which I required. . . . I found that his fortune was not counted by thousands or tens of thousands, but by millions. All my prejudices were removed."

In Swepson's golden room in the six-story marble hotel, he seemed a golden man indeed, not merely to a young Florida lawyer but to his own associates from North Carolina. Some, like his old friend Jones of the Western Railroad, were ready to run too fast in his company—for either his liking or Littlefield's. Indeed, Jones more than anybody else at that time seemed to fall into the rôle of Swepson's Jim Fisk. He had not only been in the cotton deal with Sloan—and Swepson. Also, as a member of the legislature, he had received $10,000 from Swepson's funds which Littlefield dispensed. Now he was an enthusiastic partner in the Swepson pool.

His flashy fidelity, however, had its drawbacks. Jones liked high stakes and low women. In the city he satisfied appetites he only dreamed of in North Carolina. Even in glamorous, gaslit New York his activities became notorious. In that metropolis as full of moral causes as market speculators, the representative of "an association established by the businessmen of the city for the suppression of gambling" reported to other North Carolinians at Soutter & Company about his activities. Swepson, who disapproved of such things, knew that he "lost large sums at faro." Dr. Hamilton learned that he gambled away many bonds of his railroad: "On one occasion he sat in a gambling room there, with a pile of bonds on a chair beside him, which he cashed in for chips, one by one, losing in a very short time sixty of them. This method of disposition was prolonged for several weeks with results that can readily be conjectured. Some of the bonds fell into the hands of the notorious Josie Mansfield, and the rumor was general that they circulated largely among the *demi-monde.*"

Jim Fisk's lady friend, as a holder of North Carolina bonds, presented less danger to the state's bonds than that fat speculator himself and the thin and thin-lipped Gould beside him. Perhaps back in North Carolina—maybe even in Florida—Black Friday seemed only as Joe Turner in the *Sentinel* called it "the recent gold flurry." It was clear to the North Carolina railroad presidents gathered in New York, however, that Turner's prediction on September 16, eight days before the crash, that "the bonds will go up" was increasingly improbable. The reverse threatened in roaring terms. Dr. J. J. Mott, president of the Eastern Division of the Western North Carolina Railroad, among those present, might say the bonds were being depressed by "the continual murmuring of dissatisfied demagogues," meaning particularly, of course, Turner. In New

York, however, Mott and all the other railroad presidents from the small-town South could hear the thunder which preceded the smash.

At one of Swepson's bond-pool meetings, even the reluctant Dr. Sloan accepted appointment on a committee with Swepson, the banker's friend Tate, Dr. Mott, and Jones, the faro man, to go to Soutter & Company, to consult with the energetic broker, Mr. Porter, about carrying out an agreement "to buy up bonds to keep up the credit of the state." Sloan, however, always insisted that he never agreed to pay any losses the pool might suffer.

If so, it was well for him. The little North Carolina maneuver was a midge in a maelstrom. By the time Grant released a flood of gold from the Treasury, killing the hopes of those who thought they had cornered all the gold on the market and "fixed" the President, thousands had been ruined. Men went crazy in the Gold Room of the New York Stock Exchange. Mobs threatened Gould and Fisk. The North Carolina bonds, which had been worth from fifty to sixty cents on the dollar before the panic, began a steady decline toward "the neighborhood of 20 odd cents with 7½ cents off," as Sloan put it. Another North Carolina speculator, Colonel William A. Moore, a carpetbag member of the legislature, whose margin Swepson had furnished remembered how "all stocks went down with a crash and these bonds were lost in the general wreck." There was no need for North Carolinians to add their voices to the universal fury with Fisk and Gould. Damnation sought them in droves but Gould escaped. Indeed, Gustavus Myers wrote that Gould got a hint of what was coming and "resolved to betray his partners, and secretly sell gold before the price abruptly dropped." He got out with millions. That required skill as well as duplicity. Also, it was a game apparently which more than one man could play.

At the time it was not necessary to be a speculator to lose. Probably the worst loser, indeed, was Governor Holden who, despite every effort by the Conservatives to prove him otherwise, was apparently an honest man, naïve in his admiration of Swepson. As he was prodded, he was increasingly blind and recklessly violent in his partisanship, but he seems to have been money clean. Undoubtedly, he sometimes took a little spirits to sustain himself when he was most stung. But as homecoming companion of the cynical and dissipated Laflin, he was slandered mercilessly by Turner who said that on his trip home with the Byronesque carpetbagger "things culminated in a big drunk." Also, "the Governor does not dance as does the President, but he 'went home with the gals in the morning.' " His arrival after such a trip home, said Turner, was at night just before gaslights failed in Pepper's saloon. Turner was undoubtedly in the saloon that night, though only having one of the very infrequent glasses of ale which he said was all he ever drank.

The money losers were less hurt than Holden, but Andrew Jackson Jones, who did not much mind losing when it didn't cost him any of his own money, said that the North Carolina pool dropped "from three to four hundred thousand dollars to my knowledge." Of that, $280,000 was to have been divided among himself, Swepson, Littlefield and Sloan. Jones said he paid his losses and had to arrange for the payment of those of Sloan who declined to pay. Swepson, he testified, "paid his part and part of Littlefield's, and gave his draft on Littlefield for the remaining portion."

Swepson himself said that he sustained "enormous losses" in the effort to "keep the bonds from being sold under the decline of the panic." He lost, he said, not only more than a million dollars (par value) of the bonds of the railroad, but "hundreds of thousands of dollars besides." He repeated in emphasis: "I not only lost the bonds as stated, and all the money realized on them, but to meet my losses there on that account principally and on other accounts, it became necessary to realize on all my bank stock in North and South Carolina, and most of my available securities; besides I have called largely on my particular friends for loans in these troubles."

Those losses Swepson reported had been sustained, as he was at pains to point out later, in an effort to keep North Carolina bonds afloat in a storm and so serve the credit of the state. They helped explain what had happened to the bonds he had received. But Littlefield later told a story which did not jibe with his partner's tale. Before the market crash, Milton said later, "he knew that

Mr. Swepson had sold all or most of the bonds, and had sold the greater part of them well. He did not sustain any loss, but made a considerable amount in buying and selling gold."

Yet Milton at the time seemed to be sweeping up Swepson's wreckage, even though the banker said that Littlefield came to him and told him that he was to be dropped as president of the Western Division. "The party" wanted a Republican as president of the railroad, Swepson said he was informed, namely Littlefield himself.

"I told him very well," the banker said, "but that they must settle with me . . . and let me out with whole bones."

To others at the time Swepson gave a different story.

"I am complained of on all sides," he said irritably of those who criticized the lagging construction, "and I mean to resign and have some one else do the work."

Undoubtedly, Swepson dictated the election of Littlefield at a meeting of the road's stockholders less than a month after Black Friday. And after the election he and Littlefield went off together to make the settlement between the old president and the new one in Taylor's Hotel in Jersey City. If that seemed a strange place to account for the affairs of a North Carolina railroad, there was a certain fitting symbolism in their choice of the hostelry to which Gould and Fisk had repaired in haste in March 1868 to get out of the jurisdiction of a Vanderbilt judge in the Erie War. Mr. Swepson did not want to be disturbed, but both he and Milton moved like men with whole bones so far as their North Carolina operations were concerned—and those in Florida, too.

Even before the Western Division meeting in mid-October, a sort of civic convocation, sponsored by Swepson's agents in Florida, Colonel Sanderson and young L'Engle, was held in Jacksonville. Its purpose was to reassure the Florida public about Swepson's railroad plans there. The only extant report of the meeting is from *The Florida Union*, a Republican-carpetbag paper edited by J. K. Stickney, brother of Lyman D. Stickney, who as a tax commissioner had pressed so hard for the abortive Florida redemption expedition in which Milton took part in 1864. Colonel Sanderson denied that Swepson had been involved in frauds in the purchase of the Florida railroads the previous March; he disassociated Swepson from Littlefield. Sanderson and L'Engle were so persuasive that L. I. Fleming, a prominent Jacksonville lawyer and member of a distinguished Florida family, summed up the feeling of the gathered citizens: "We have no money and must depend on foreign capital to assist us . . . let us . . . unite together and join with the person who will spend the money and do the work."

Swepson crowned such confidence with immediate orders for work to begin on extension of the road to Pensacola, thus toward New Orleans, in the direction of the fulfillment of the Southern dream—by no means limited to Florida—of a railroad across the South to the imperial Pacific. Even the often-furious *Floridian* practically sang its enthusiasm.

"Go on Mr. Swepson in your noble enterprise," that Democratic paper said, ". . . let us have the happy assurance that the iron horse will carry us all the way to Pensacola."

Milton moved that autumn from New York to Asheville to Jersey City to Raleigh to Tallahassee to Washington. He maintained a house at the national capital that winter and during the following year, conveniently located at 1106 F Street, just a few blocks from the convivial bars and lobbies of the Ebbitt House and Willard's. Later generations can better understand its location as just across the street from the big store built subsequently by Woodward and Lothrop. Then, Thomas Walsh had a restaurant at the corner. A druggist and a grocer were in the block, but solid residences stood on the street there, too. It is not clear whether the remote and religious Anna brought the children there to live, though one child later had a vague memory of a house in Washington from which the family for some reason departed in a hurry. That could have been an 1870 memory. Certainly in Washington in 1869 Milton could help and be helped by his national Republican associates.

There also he talked with a director of his Western Division who later said that he was in Washington at the request of the road "to assist in getting an appropriation for the Southern Pacific Railroad." (Such a reference to the Southern Pacific could hold great implications in relation to American railroading and railroad financing then. Joe Turner in the *Sentinel* that fall was relating Milton in some transportation matters in North Carolina, through

Alexander K. McClure, journalist and politician of Philadelphia, to Tom Scott, president of the Pennsylvania and later of the Texas and Pacific as well.)

Milton was in high spirits at the time. He told the director of his company that he had bought out all Swepson's rights in the Florida railroads "several months previously" and expected soon to get enough money out of the Florida investments to prosecute vigorously the work on the railroad in North Carolina. But at the same time he was less exuberant toward Swepson though clearly in partnership with him still.

"Dear Swepson," he wrote in his almost indecipherable scrawl. "I have read and digested and tried to see the way out of the Jones matter but I cannot sell bonds and pay Jones. That must be arranged outside the collateral I have. Just look for one moment. All I have is 400 N. C.s, 100,000 Floridas and 130,000 (or in that neighborhood) R.R. bonds. I must go vigorously at work on the road or show my hand, which would be s——."

If that last indecipherable word was "suicide," Milton had no predilection for it. Whatever else Black Friday may have depreciated in value, the collapse of the prices of North Carolina bonds had skyrocketed North Carolina suspicions about them and those who had received them. In Raleigh, Milton knew, more attention was paid to Turner when he spoke of "President Littlefield, of New York . . . the man who has the legislature in his pocket" and control of $7,000,000 in North Carolina bonds. Suddenly, as it turned out, though Republicans still remained in a majority, the legislature definitely was not entirely in Littlefield's hands. On the twenty-sixth of November the House resolved itself into a Committee of the Whole for the purpose of investigating frauds in regard to certain railroad bonds. The event did not come wholly as a surprise. It was not surprising either that the legislature wanted as witness the General then in Raleigh attending to his many North Carolina affairs.

An elated Joe Turner promised his readers that the General would not be on hand as a witness before the Assembly. He was right. Milton seemed to disappear as Mrs. Cavarly had disappeared before. He sent no one before him this time. Ann Cavarly was not in his van or train. Even without a lady to give a romantic air to flight, Turner had another year's end tale into which he put all his literary powers. On the day the House began its investigation, the *Sentinel* emphasized the fulfillment of its prediction of Milton's absence. Like a cock crowing, Turner quoted Scripture.

" 'The prudent man foreseeth the evil and hideth himself,' says the Good Book," his report ran, "accordingly the General went to Mr. J. Lewis' hardware store to buy a large tin box to put deeds, etc., in, and, on Friday night, he had a straight coat-tail sticking out behind him towards the city of Raleigh, while he was making tracks towards the Depot, to take the train for Florida, or some other point outside the State."

This time the *Sentinel* offered its $50,000 reward in invalidated special tax bonds. It described the General as a wanted man in handsome terms and reported with some exaggeration that he had in his possession as he departed $4,000,000 in state bonds, "the unsquandered portion of $7,000,000." The paper's witnesses followed Milton on his ride. They reported that State Treasurer Jenkins was with him and "ate fat roast chicken leg and biscuit" furnished by General Littlefield. Milton, in his light trousers and black coat, a white shirt and bright cravat "did not look as if he had done anything mean or was running away" and "men and boys went into the smoking car to look at him," none with intent to stay him, some with admiration. Finally, it reported that he had arrived in Tallahassee, "the capital of the land of flowers." It added mystifyingly, however, that Milton "is or will soon be in Montgomery, Alabama." Actually he went to attend a session of the Florida legislature which at that time was much more important to him than any clamor behind in North Carolina.

No air of flight was left behind by the General. His *Standard,* sticking its tongue out, offered one cent reward for Joe Turner. Friends in the legislature rose to call him an "honorable and respected gentleman," much maligned. The tumult against him was sounding cymbal and nothing else. One of Milton's strong vocal supporters was A. H. Galloway, a Negro who had had even the *Sentinel's* reluctant praise on occasion. He had been active in efforts to make it possible for Negroes to buy land. Now he declared in the legislature that "there are Senators here who have been fed and clothed" by the General "who now vote for this resolution to have him turned out of office." Galloway spoke on a motion to remove Littlefield as State Printer which the Senate refused to pass. Not all by any means were ready to agree that Littlefield *et al.* "have swindled the State of its last dollar and left the Treasury as clear of funds as a coal scuttle; there is not enough left to pay Friday Jones for guarding the oaks and rose bushes in Capitol Square. . . ."

Turner and the increasing number of articulate politicians on his side did not neglect small matters in corruption including the cost of the care of Capitol Square. Indeed, the cost of cleaning a privy on the grounds was made a resounding issue against a Negro representative, Cuffee Mayo, of Granville County, by his political opponent and former master, Colonel Leonidas Edwards. The indignant and immaculate Colonel reported the cost of that job from the stump in amazement: "Two-thousand-four-hundred-and-fifty-six-dollars-and-twenty-five-cents!" But Cuffee, whom the *Sentinel* used much as a clown, asked and received the Colonel's permission to put a question.

"Marse Lee, what would you have done it for?"

There was more humor in history then than afterward appeared, but it was a time of much tension attended by little levity. Early in February the *Sentinel* reported that "Laughing Laflin" had arrived in town with the report that Littlefield was on his way back to Raleigh "to silence Joe Turner." However his readers may have taken that report, Turner took it seriously. "We tell the Governor that when his State Printer comes, we are not to be 'handled' by him, nor by his detectives, nor his militia." But Turner concluded that "you may bet your bottom dollar they [Swepson and Littlefield] will not both be in Raleigh at the same time, yet awhile, if they can help it."

Milton returned to Raleigh, without fanfare or apology, for a meeting of the stockholders of his Western Division to which he and Swepson were expected to account. He did not molest or even seem to notice Turner. But he indicated that, in the possible event any testimony from him was desired, he would be happy to appear as a witness before the legislature. Then a day or two later Swepson came, too, from his country place sixty miles west of Raleigh on the North Carolina Railroad. Even after his business had grown in Raleigh, New York and elsewhere, the banker preferred to live there with his protective wife, Virginia. The house seemed big and lonely for the childless couple. It did not seem ill-omened then. Though as a consort of carpetbaggers Swepson was distasteful to some of his night-riding neighbors, he did not seem a target of the Ku-Klux who Holden said were so active in the neighborhood. The Haw River place provided a garden-like seclusion and a domestic refuge.

Swepson came to Raleigh with obvious reluctance, quietly but in a scarcely concealed state of agitation. There all one day, early in March 1870, he urged flight on Littlefield: the General to go to Florida, himself to Canada. Also he sought out Nicholas W. Woodfin, chairman of a commission named to settle matters for the railroad. He was suddenly full of promises. "He desired," that official said later, "to make a compromise of the whole matter with the company. . . ." He said that he and General Littlefield "had a very wealthy and experienced railroad contractor" who "would make a first class railroad, stock it well, for assets in his and General Littlefield's hands." But when the commissioner went to talk to him further about the matter, he found only McAden and Rosenthal in Swepson's hotel room. There was a supper for one or more men upon the table. McAden asked him to wait, "as Mr. Swepson had just stepped out."

"He did not return," the commissioner said.

Then next morning at the stockholders' meeting Littlefield was called out by a colored man and told the news. Swepson was gone but not all the facts came out until years later. Holden and W. A. Smith ("Blow-your-horn-Billy Smith," to Turner), president of the North Carolina Railroad which the banker had first desired, had arranged for a special train which slipped out of Raleigh in the dark without lights. Not even the train's young engineer knew who his passenger was but when he stopped the train as directed at Haw River, he held his lantern in curiosity to look, seeing a man with "a pleasant face with features nevertheless sharp and pronounced beneath a head of white hair." He wore a dark traveling coat and carried a small trunk and a valise. "Then the man disappeared down the steps and toward a carriage waiting by the station platform."

In Raleigh Swepson left a note for Littlefield saying "that his wife was sick, and that he was going to Haw River."

Virginia Yancey Swepson was sick, but unlike her husband, sick with fury, not fear. She was the aristocrat assailed. "I am a proud woman. Pride is my birthright," she wrote General Ransom, still her husband's attorney though soon also to be dramatic defender of Democrats against Holden's alleged tyranny. She was grateful to Ransom for confessing himself "the friend of a man who is slandered and abused." This was "our dark day" but she had "unwavering trust in my husband's integrity."

At forty-three, Virginia Swepson, as people commented, had already begun to look like Queen Victoria. She was imperial in defense of her slight, shy husband.

"Had his business plans succeeded," she told Ransom, "as he reasonably hoped . . . he would have been flattered & called the greatest financier in the State. There will still be a great deal of prejudice—envy & lies. . . ." But she added the time will come when no one could say "you are dishonored by being the warm friend of G. W. Swepson."

Swepson himself wrote Ransom more briefly that spring.

"You can manage Woodfin better than anyone I know," he wrote him of the chairman of the railroad's settlement commission.

Littlefield remained in Raleigh. He gave, the *Sentinel* reported indignantly, a sumptuous oyster supper for Republican legislators on the evening preceding his appearance as a witness before the legislature. At that supper, said Turner who still insisted he had only an infrequent glass of ale, "over a hundred dollars' worth of champagne [was] drunk at, as it is said, Littlefield's expense." Turner described it as "a drunken revel assembled at the National Hotel" though one who was present said Littlefield only came into the room late and drank a glass of wine with the company. Undoubtedly, at the party Republicans pledged themselves to put a stop to the investigation.

Littlefield was never in better form than when he appeared as witness, smiling, in high spirits, confident and friendly. The impression created by Swepson's flight had not hurt him. Though Turner was insisting that Swepson had been made a scapegoat for him, Republicans smirked at the suggestion by one of their own that "the Democrat [alluding to Swepson] had run away from the investigation and the Republican [Littlefield] had held his ground." The point seemed still effective though an angry Democrat insisted that he was not aware before that Swepson was a Democrat—"if he voted it was for Grant."

In such an atmosphere the General took the stand. He readily admitted making small loans to his friends, one he smilingly recalled particularly because Senator W. M. Robbins, a Democrat, in repaying him twenty dollars in the Capitol yard remarked that he wanted them to witness that he paid Littlefield twenty dollars loaned, but it had not been received for corruption.

"It was the circumstance and the mirth created," Littlefield said that "impressed it upon my mind."

One stern member wanted to know if he had given railroad passes to members of the General Assembly.

The General smiled audaciously about his still-unconstructed road: "I am not president or any other officer of any railroad that has anything but carts, and I have given no transportation over them."

Then, before any serious questioning had begun or any serious answers given, a Republican member moved that the Committee of the Whole rise and be discharged. It was done by a vote of forty-eight to forty-one. Littlefield walked out slowly taking plenty of time to chat with old friends. Some Conservatives cursed in the hall. But Milton walked down the chief street, bowing to many, to his handsome newspaper plant. He read the proofs—if he did not write the comment in his *Standard.* It emphasized a question from Plato Durham, reported to be a Ku-Klux chief as well as a Conservative legislative leader, "that called forth the reply from General Littlefield that he had loaned Gen. Robbins from Rowan *twenty dollars!* We regret very much that this declaration drew forth great laughter from the committee, but such is history and we are not responsible for it. . . ."

Robbins was the same Conservative leader who had been embarrassed the year before when it was discovered by Senator Sweet's committee that he had taken a small fee in connection with a legislative matter. Apparently he was a good man but fated to serve Republican laughter at times of tension.

Littlefield's paper was serious as well as amused: "The cost to the people for this worse than a farce amounts to over $1,500 per day, and the only discovery made is the loan of $20 to Senator Robbins, and $75 to Mr. Harris of Franklin, and these loans merely of a business character, and in no wise connected with the legislation of the General Assembly.

"Such folly, such nonsense, such a reckless waste of time and money has never been witnessed in any civilized community. . . .

"The honor and integrity of the Republicans of the Legislature are fully vindicated. . . ."

General Littlefield, the papers coming from his fine building said, "comes out of the ordeal with honor to himself and the Republican Party."

For the moment, even the *Sentinel* could only sputter in fury:

"The brazen effrontery, the unparalleled impudence of the man are construed by many into evidence of conscious innocence and honesty . . . the cool audacity and effrontery . . ."

Almost, admiration overtook Joe Turner. But not quite.

"Rejoice, O ye Rascals, and be exceeding glad, for you have escaped if only for a little while!"

The struggle was far from over. As the mounting cry from the Conservatives was "Thief!" the Republicans responded with the shout of "Murder!" Violence had been riding the roads at night. Conservatives insisted that the Union Leagues of which Milton had been the president in North Carolina created the situation which called for the Ku-Klux Klan. There can be no doubt that the Leagues were guilty of grave excesses. Murders of white people were attributed to the Leagues. Barns were burned but, says Dr. Hamilton, the fact that the Leagues usually met in a schoolhouse or church "explains the burning of so many schools and churches by white people."

Basically the white objection to the Leagues was their effectiveness in organizing the Negro vote. "At first," says Hamilton, "some attempt was made by white Conservatives to check the growth and activity of the organization by refusal of employment to all its members. But it soon became evident that this meant refusal to employ colored labor at all, and the time came when the employing class became suppliants, so sharply was the need of laborers felt." Therefore the Klan. Yet as Hamilton also reported, "It was essentially a movement of the Piedmont region of the State and was never very successful in spreading in the eastern counties where there was a large Negro population." By no means all white Conservatives approved the Klan and former Chief Justice Thomas Ruffin, perhaps the most respected man in the state, sharply condemned it.

Important to Littlefield, in March 1870, the Republican fury against the Klan reached its height at the same time Democratic indignation mounted against the railroad manipulations. He did not spend all his time in Raleigh deftly dodging his enemies. He was not running away. A week after Littlefield appeared before the investigating committee, Governor Holden wrote to Senator Abbott demanding, "What is being done to protect the good citizens of Alamance?" (It was only a coincidence that that happened to be Swepson's county.) In his letter Holden added: "We have federal troops, but we want power to act. Is it possible the Government will abandon its loyal people to be whipped and hanged? The *habeas corpus* should be at once suspended."

Before Holden wrote that letter Milton had already gone to Washington to carry similar word for the Governor. Indeed, the *Sentinel* reprinted from the Washington correspondence of *The New York Herald* an item which appeared less than a week after Milton smilingly terminated his testimony. The *Herald*'s report said: "Tomorrow General M. S. Littlefield who has arrived in this city will present to the President a communication from Gov. Holden of North Carolina requesting a force of United States troops to assist in preserving order in that State."

That was Milton's last arrival in the national capital from Raleigh after his final stay in the North Carolina city. He had departed with dignity. But before he left he wrote his farewell with his flags still flying as high as his men had held them at Shiloh.

"To the Patrons of the *Standard*," he wrote in an editorial which appeared on March 11, 1870.

"With this issue we close our connection with the *Standard*. It has been our sole aim, since we became proprietor, to publish a paper devoted to the advancement of the great Republican Party, and to serve the best interests of the people of the State; how well this has been accomplished, we will let our numerous friends say for themselves. The proprietor of the *Standard* has been most wilfully, maliciously and falsely assailed by the rebel press of the State, and their orators have joined in the chorus, but not one word has been said in defense for the reason that it has been in the interest of no clique or faction. It has been, what it will continue to be, we are confident, the PEOPLE'S ORGAN."

Its new proprietors, he said, were "tried and true Republicans." More than that, though Milton did not mention it, the new publisher was the president of the North Carolina Railroad who had provided the special train on which Swepson fled in the night to the bosom of his Virginia.

"Readers," Milton said in final farewell, "remember defeat has not been written on our banner. Let our successors be able to repeat the same words, from the mountains to the sea. VICTORY!"

And that editorial he signed, "M. S. Littlefield."

Friends saw him off at the depot. Some accompanied him in departure. Others followed. When florid Byron Laflin took the bus at the hotel the day the legislature adjourned a bystander asked him, "You are coming back, General?" And Laflin replied, "What is there to come back for?" Joe Turner liked and reprinted that wry joke. The *Sentinel's* editor still needed antidotes to Littlefield's successful final scenes. Some Democrats were saying that his editorial excesses had served the Republicans rather than hurt them. *The Charlotte Democrat,* which felt that strongly, had also intimated that Turner's tirades might well have been tempered in view of the fact that he had received funds from Swepson. But Turner sharply replied, "I have had no presents, gifts, fees, or rewards from Swepson, directly or indirectly."

There he stuck to the very literal truth. Perhaps he did also when he wrote of Joe Holden, the poet who should never have gone into politics. After young Holden succeeded to the editorship of the *Standard,* Turner printed almost as a welcome to him that "we must relate how he lay on the front porch of a house occupied by a colored lady, in East Ward in this city, an hour after sunrise, sans culottes, and sans everything else but a shirt, with the end the feet grow on pointing to the street." Furthermore, as Turner piously pointed out, the *Standard* worked its printers on the Sabbath Day.

On the benign other hand, the *Sentinel* described the excursion of the Oak City Council, Friends of Temperance and the special "efforts of Capt. A. B. Andrews, of the Chatham Road, to render the trip comfortable, safe and delightful." Andrews' train took them to an "old village, handsomely located at the junction of the Haw and Deep Rivers." Swepson lived on the Haw, and the Deep had been the stream of promise at the conjunction of Littlefield and Captain Andrews' associates just two years and a half before. Much water had run in North Carolina streams in that time.

Littlefield was well out of those waters. The collision of the Ku-Klux and a nondescript, ruffian militia which Holden mobilized to suppress it occurred after he was gone. After he was gone, too, the body of a prominent Republican, Representative John W. Stephens, dubbed "Chicken" Stephens by Turner, was found with his throat cut, mysteriously murdered in a room in the courthouse of Caswell County where Swepson had begun his North Carolina career. Much else was ahead—and behind him the legislature had repudiated the bonds which, as lobbyist, Milton had persuaded legislatures to issue. He went from Raleigh to his home in Washington where his boys were and Anna, who left no letters like Virginia Swepson's to show either fury or fear. Some North Carolina friends came to see him there.

He was in Washington a gentleman of such position, as *The New York Herald* indicated, as might confer with President Grant on disturbing conditions in the South. Washington then was not a place in which ostracism attended unproved suspicions of railroad corruption. Oakes Ames of the Crédit Mobilier was still a respected member of the House. Statesmen only hoped they would be among those considered when he was putting the lush Crédit Mobilier shares "where they will do the most good. . . ." Among Southerners in Washington the chief complaint was that the South had not received its share in the dispensing of Federal favors to railroads and other such projects. No one yet was complaining of the corruption of "The Big Barbecue." Envy not indignation attended those who had found their place at the public table—or the public trough.

In Washington, that spring of 1870, Milton moved as a confident man. No one ever saw him—though Turner sometimes imagined it—in a state of agitation. He walked on F Street and the Avenue in Washington with the same handsome assurance even Turner had begrudgingly noted in Raleigh. But Swepson seemed suddenly naked in cowardice. He continued his flight from Raleigh to Haw River to Taylor's Hotel in Jersey City. From there late in March he sent a wire like a cry of anguish to Senator Abbott in Washington.

"Why can't I hear from Littlefield. Have written, telegraphed and sent special messages & hear nothing."

Swepson would hear in time. But Milton did not seem in a hurry. There was a lull everywhere. The spring was slow in coming that year. And behind them in Raleigh Joe Turner, who was in the approaching summer to be arrested by Holden's militia, seemed momentarily out of ammunition for his indignation. In the streets where no legislators strolled or any lobbyists offered them drinks or bonds, the *Sentinel* turned its attention to its conviction that Raleigh beat any city of its size in creation for fice dogs, and also for an "overcrop of juvenile beggars," largely white and "mostly girls."

CHAPTER XIII

Old Friends in Florida

IN CONNECTION WITH Littlefield's operations in North Carolina, Joe Turner, in his *Sentinel,* tried to keep up with the General's Florida story which was taking place on another stage at the same time. He presented it through clippings from papers in that state with the same purposeful use of his scissors which he exercised with his pen. Turner clipped to cut and, if possible, to draw blood. The General's position in Florida, therefore, had not been altogether objectively presented late in 1869 when Turner, describing him as a man in flight, reported his arrival in "the capital of the land of flowers." For Milton it was a return to a state in which he had friends, admirers and many eager sharers of his munificence. Indeed, even the *Sentinel*'s collection of clippings and reports from Florida exchanges showed that the General had a wide range of relationships.

Milton had begun his activities in the old tadpole state of Secession in the summer of 1869, the *Sentinel* had reported with a sneer, "by an inflammatory appeal to the Negroes on the occasion of the dedication of a freedman's schoolhouse." But in the balmy midwinter of 1869-70, Turner clipped and reported the news that soon after the General's arrival the Episcopalians of old St. John's

Church in Tallahassee had accepted a gift of $500 from him "as a subscription for paying off a debt hanging over the church."

All classes and kinds of people knew Littlefield well in Tallahassee. Even in comparison with Raleigh that capital was a very small town—almost a frontier village. It was no longer, as another Yankee, Ralph Waldo Emerson, had pictured it, "a grotesque place . . . settled by public officers, land speculators, and desperadoes." Still, it was the capital of a sparsely inhabited state not yet provided with the guidebook soon to be written by Sidney Lanier as poet on the payroll of the Atlantic Coast Line Railroad. Some Alabama, Georgia and Carolina families had moved to Tallahassee after the war. Harriet Beecher Stowe had bought her orange grove on the "lapis lazuli blue colored" St. Johns River, farther up the stream than the Jacksonville house, which, in addition to a Tallahassee mansion, Littlefield later maintained.

Many other Northern people, including both consumptives and carpetbaggers, had come into the state. Colored people had moved into the towns. Also, then, said Dr. Paul E. Fenlon in the *Florida Historical Quarterly*, "an opportunity to combine political power and economic gain enticed hundreds of get-rich-quick devotees to Florida's war-shattered economy." What was lacking, however, was "the longed-for immigration of monied men." Nobody looked more like that genuine article than Milton—particularly with George W. Swepson behind him. Or, as happened to be the case in timing, with Swepson before him.

Milton, in Florida, was himself returning to familiar ground and familiar faces. There is the possibility that the potentialities of the battered Florida railroads had caught and held his imagination when and after he camped beside them in 1864. It is certain that he found in Florida, returning as a charming civilian, people he had seen when he went there first as a soldier. Indeed, the Reconstruction government of Florida after 1868 seemed to contain many of the same characters involved in the feuds between the Northern politicians Secretary Chase had put there as Treasury agents in 1862.

The Governor was Harrison Reed, whom Milton had known in his Sea Island service. On the thinly held Southern shore then Reed had been the properly critical antagonist of his associate in Federal tax gathering, Lyman D. Stickney, who had arrived in Florida as a slave smuggler and had become a perambulatory politician for freedom. Stickney had not fooled Reed though he had apparently fooled Milton almost as much as he had Lincoln—or John Hay—in the early Reconstruction fiasco in 1864. Now in Florida politics, Reed had outlasted Stickney who earlier had complained that Reed "hangs around like the itch."

When Milton first returned in 1869, Stickney men or men like Stickney had already formed almost a habit of trying to impeach Reed—a process in which Littlefield was sometimes supposed to participate. Worse, so Reed's friends said, they tried to scare him out of office with the threat of mobs composed of political bums and black razor-carrying prostitutes. Rumors spread of plans to assassinate him and then blame it on the Ku-Klux Klan. It is possible that other Republicans hated him, as William Watson Davis said in *The Civil War and Reconstruction in Florida,* because of his refusal "to aid them in certain financial undertakings which smacked of graft."

Some historians have not placed Reed in such clear opposition to graft. Claude Bowers, who wrote of every Reconstruction figure with almost apocalyptic certainty, said that Reed "was something of a hypocrite and everything of a scamp." Reed, who came to Florida at fifty after his career as editor and politician in Wisconsin, was one of the few of the carpetbaggers who remained long after Reconstruction. He was acceptable as postmaster at Tallahassee as late as the 1890s. During his term as Governor he often seemed besieged in his Capitol on a little knoll in the center of the town. He sometimes needed Milton, sometimes distrusted him. Milton needed Reed and, in his most difficult situations, found him his protector. Yet sometimes Milton was made to appear the epitome of perfidy toward the Governor. Reed was certainly monstrously fooled if that was true.

It would be difficult to think of two more different men. North Carolina was accustomed to Milton's good looks, but Hamilton Jay, a young carpetbagger who later described most of his comrades without too much charity in *The New York Sun,* saw Milton first in Florida as a man "in the full flush of a magnificent manhood, the handsomest man in the State, and of wonderful magnetic power. He was tall, well-proportioned, with dark hair and dark, close-cropped beard, rosy cheeks and genial laughing eyes. His personal magnetism was very great and few could resist the charm of his address. As a manipulator of legislatures he had no superior. He got desired legislation with scarcely any trouble. With money he was as free as water, and when he had no money was just as free with checks."

Harrison Reed, as described by Dr. Davis in his history of the period, was, at fifty-six then, "a little man, slightly built, with a big bald head and a bushy beard—almost goat-like—the upper lip clean shaven. A full fringe of hair on three sides of the bald spot, a high forehead and heavy spectacles gave to him an owl-like appearance which accentuated his calm moderation and well-poised address." He did not look afraid of his enemies. He had friends. Also, improbable as it may seem from his description, at that time Reed was involved not only in feuding but romance as well.

Milton's approach to him was facilitated, as so often seemed to be the case in his operations in the South, by old upstate New York ties. Reed's young private secretary was Charles Kinne, son of Professor A. E. Kinne, of Syracuse. Reed was engaged to be married, soon after the legislature adjourned, to Chloe Merrick from Syracuse, daughter of a gentleman with the unusual name of Susbanus Merrick. She was the schoolteacher whom young John Hay, with his alert eye for pretty ladies, had particularly noticed in 1863. Also, she had been Milton's friend at Fernandina who provided him and his soldiers with the fine flag upon which "Liberty" was emblazoned.

Littlefield, of course, went to Tallahassee on no romantic mission. Reed undoubtedly greeted him as an old acquaintance but Milton's business and the Governor's related to the basic fact that when Reed arrived in office in Florida at about the time Holden took over in North Carolina, on July 4, 1868, he found not a fat job but an impoverished state. The treasury was empty; taxpayers were broke; and the state was holding a number of bankrupt railroad systems built before the war with state aid. Reed had gone to work to develop them. Hopefully, at a time when Northern companies and communities were grabbing great grants from the

Federal Treasury, he memorialized the Congress for aid in completing the railroad lines from the Atlantic to Pensacola on the Gulf, as an "eastern link" from New Orleans in the line of a southern railroad to the Pacific.

Instead of Federal aid, Reed got Milton's friend Swepson. And Swepson early in 1869 got railroads in a fantastically complex transaction, involving natives and strangers, and including Florida railroad bonds Swepson bought for thirty cents on the market and presented at par in the purchase, a $472,065 bad check, and $726,281.89 which he took from the receipts of the bond sales of the Western Division of the Western North Carolina Railroad. In the transaction the State of Florida, Dr. Fenlon estimated, was defrauded of over three-quarters of a million dollars while Swepson secured control not only of two hundred miles of railroad, with its rolling stock, equipment, depots and warehouses, but also of over a million acres of land included in the assets of the railroad companies.

That required conspicuous sharpness even in economic chaos. Littlefield's more difficult assignment was assuring immediate profit from the fraud. He used, according to Florida accounts, $117,351.50 more of North Carolina funds to "protect" Swepson's investment in the control of the Florida Central, the Pensacola and Georgia, and the Tallahassee railroads after Swepson sent him to Tallahassee to start "protecting" in June 1869.

No secrecy attended Swepson's and Littlefield's general plans. Though he was by no means the only lobbyist attending the special session, Littlefield's arrival received the attention of a parade. John Wallace, the ex-slave who became a state senator and left the best eyewitness account of the period in his *Carpetbag Rule in Florida,* wrote that it was apparent "'from the presence of an unusual lobby" that "some great catastrophe was to take place in the shape of a law." The little capital seemed to be contemplating celebration rather than catastrophe, however. Wallace noted that "the carpetbag element seemed to be elated and the hotels and boarding houses in the city were filled with strangers. The poorest and most shabby carpetbagger could be seen drinking the sparkling champagne and wearing fine beavers." And with top billing: "The famous Littlefield was too much engaged to walk, and his carriage was kept at the hotel in readiness to convey him to any part of the city to see the different members of the Legislature."

Wallace did not exaggerate. Dr. Davis in his researches found that Tallahassee then was a rendezvous of men seeking favors. The more prosperous lobbyists, including, of course, Milton, lived at the Capitol Hotel. Champagne, oyster suppers, cigars, liquor, and "well-equipped carriages were the vulgar physical evidences of these promoters of legislation." Davis also towered Milton above the others as a gentleman who with a clear eye, an agile brain, "a supply of money and a lordly air . . . made the more humble among those who smoked his cigars and drank his whiskey feel honored if he deigned even to bribe them."

Littlefield's progress, however, was no prodigal procession to his purposes. He was not merely dealing with a capital which at the time seemed ready to make a carnival of corruption. Apparently, he also had to operate with a government which, below the beaver hats and around the champagne, was torn by blood feud between Republican factions headed by Reed and United States Senator Thomas W. Osborn. Osborn, who in his relation to Reed inherited all Stickney's bitterness about him, had come to Florida in 1865 as an official of the Freedmen's Bureau. A native of New Jersey, he had graduated from what is now Colgate University at Hamilton, New York (irrelevantly perhaps but interestingly, in the same tier of upstate New York counties from which Chloe Merrick and so many others in Milton's Southern story came). He had been elected to the United States Senate from Florida in the same year in which Reed was chosen as Governor. And at thirty-two, a young man in a hurry, he had Stickney's old feeling that Reed "hangs around like the itch."

So Littlefield had to seek his aims in a situation in which his fellow Republicans and carpetbaggers hated each other more than the Conservative Democrats hated them. He had no such dependable assistant as "Laughing Laflin" in Florida. Abbott, French and Estes made no effective "Ring" of his own on the legislative floor. Osborn headed the organization Floridians called The Ring. And some thought Governor Reed was a sort of "Ring," too. Milton had to deal, largely alone, not only with cupidity but a political competition in it and legislative confusion around it.

His course was not smooth. Obviously, Governor Reed had expected his arrival in the summer of 1869. Then the Governor called upon the legislators for railroad development "in accordance with the spirit of the age and the progress of modern civilization" which would assure Florida of "her full share of the immigration and the capital now flowing southward." That was what Milton had come to provide. Before the legislature had been in session many days, however, Reed was "alarmed at the prospect of corrupt legislation," as Wallace put it, and even more alarmed by Littlefield's apparent generosity to his enemies. The Governor, not missing the fact that Littlefield's bill was introduced by a legislative lieutenant of Senator Osborn, telegraphed Swepson to come to Tallahassee.

Instead, Swepson dispatched Senator Abbott as the agent of his responsibility. Abbott came down to Florida, where he and Littlefield had served together in the war. This time he had no raw substitutes to break and run. Littlefield met him like a comrade of old times. With them it was a meeting like that which had brought Littlefield, representing the upstate New Yorkers, to Raleigh to work with Abbott and his friends in the North Carolina Constitutional Convention.

Senator Abbott might be called a "puppy dog" by Kate Chase's husband in the Senate. In North Carolina, Turner with impunity might refer to him as a coward. He was impressive in Tallahassee. In his company Littlefield seemed almost imperially penitent. For Swepson, Abbott assured Governor Reed no more money would be used, and "no legislation but what was legitimate would be sought." He called in Littlefield to witness the pledge. The General not only agreed, but added that the money he had given Osborn's lieutenant had only been a contribution to a reception at the hotel. Abbott departed full of assurances. Yet, said Wallace, who was there, "within ten days $22,000 more were distributed by Littlefield as a corruption fund for the Osborn Ring" and Wallace thought the funds were to be used "to control the Legislature against Gov. Reed with a view of ultimately disposing of him."

Neither corruption nor playing a double game with the Reed and Osborn forces in corruption, nor even perhaps the more complex dissimulation of a double game where none existed, quite sufficed to secure the requirements of Swepson and Littlefield that summer. Beyond all such, apparently, legislative forgery was required. After much bargaining and compromising, daytime persuasiveness and night rides in his ever-waiting carriage to secret talks and private deals, Milton succeeded in securing the passage of a bill. It consolidated the Tallahassee Railroad and the Pensacola and Georgia Railroad into one company, the Jacksonville, Pensacola and Mobile Railroad Company. The legislation also gave that company authority to extend its line from Quincy, just northwest of Tallahassee, to the Florida-Alabama border, and provided state bond aid at the rate of $14,000 a mile.

Still Littlefield was not satisfied. After the passage of the bill and before it was enrolled, so the always waspishly Democratic *Floridian* reported, he bribed state employees to omit two passages requiring that the state be given a first lien on the already-completed part of the road from Jacksonville to Quincy and that the company prove its clear title to that property before it got any bonds. Littlefield's arrangement of this matter was denounced as a "cunning fraud, boldly and adroitly perpetrated." How Milton got away with it was never proved. Apparently no one suggested seriously that he be punished for it. He was by no means universally denounced.

Governor Reed still "was on rather good terms" with Milton, according to Wallace, the witness and historian. It is even possible that after the session ended they headed toward North Carolina together. There in Wilmington—Senator Abbott's town—on August 10, 1869, Reed, though long a "fussy old granny" to his enemies, became the husband of Chloe Merrick, who was still operating a Yankee school in the Carolina port. Milton may very well have been at the wedding. It can be assumed that he sent a present. The event made it certain that in Florida he would be even more welcome for old association's sake when Chloe moved as first lady into the "very pleasant house" which was the Governor's mansion in Tallahassee, conveniently located across the street from the Capitol. The General undoubtedly talked to Reed about bonds there. There, too, he and Chloe had much to talk about of the "earlier movements for the improvement and education of the

Freedmen," in which as a visiting reporter from Syracuse said later, she—and Milton—"sustained a prominent and efficient part."

Not all that late summer went merry as a marriage bell. After the session, efforts were made to indict Littlefield for bribery. A grand jury called for Milton's accounts in the Freedmen's Bank of Tallahassee, in which he seems to have had an operating interest as well as deposits. The investigators decided, however, that since Milton's payments to legislators (up to $2,000 and $6,000; Wallace said only two Negro members got any, they a cut-rate of $500 each) did not indicate what they were for, a charge of bribery could not be sustained. Still, not all suspicions were quieted. That was the period in which Swepson, busy trying to save North Carolina's credit in advance of Black Friday, had to reassure Floridians important to his plans. The Raleigh banker, of course, as he told even General Ransom, knew of no frauds in the Peninsula State. There, in an atmosphere in which the jungle of suspicion grew rank to the door of the Governor's mansion which Chloe kept with Yankee neatness, no charges about anybody could safely be believed—or dismissed. Clearly, however, after the grand jury dropped its charges against him, Milton went back to Tallahassee at the end of 1869 exonerated, as he used that word in the *Standard,* and even more welcome than before in the "capital of the land of flowers."

It was then that his money was welcomed by St. John's Episcopal Church, of which one of Thomas Jefferson's grandsons had been a vestryman. On that trip, too, he looked at the mansion built by Territorial Governor Richard Keith Call (far more impressive than the Root house in Raleigh) as a possible establishment for a railroad magnate engaged in building at least a fraction of a possible southern road to the Pacific. His carriage stood at his hotel door as before but less vulgar tumult seemed in prospect at the regular session of the legislature to which he had come. All his plans seemed in good order. But it was then that he had to arrange escape from a more precarious situation than any he ever faced in North Carolina.

In that session in which Swepson and Littlefield finally secured the Florida legislation they required, Senator Osborn and his friends brought new impeachment charges against Reed, and this time produced a letter, said to have been written by Swepson and brought to Tallahassee the summer before by Littlefield. It damned Reed as accepting a bribe, Swepson as giving one, and put Littlefield in the position of serving as a messenger to betray his friend and Chloe Merrick's husband, Governor Reed.

When the legislature convened in January 1870, Reed in his message referred to "conspiracies formed to secure control of the financial policy of the State in the interest of corrupt men." If he was talking about the Osborn men, they retaliated quickly with a motion to investigate the Governor. And soon thereafter the committee named for that purpose produced the purported letter from Swepson to Governor Reed. It ran:

> (Confidential)
>
> Raleigh, N. C., May 31, 1869.
>
> HON. HARRISON REED, Tallahassee, Fla.:
>
> DEAR SIR—I regret my inability to be in your city during the extra session of the legislature. Had it been convened on the first of June, as at first contemplated, I could have come. As it is, I cannot. General Littlefield has the bill, etc., and will fully explain everything to you; we expect him to prevent any difficulty being made with you by Osborn's friends. I write hastily and to the point. You remember, when in New York, our agreement was this: You were to call the Legislature together, and use your influence to have our bills passed as drawn by us, and if you were successful in this you were to be paid twelve thousand five hundred dollars in cash, out of which amount was to be deducted the seventy-five hundred (7500) dollars you have heretofore received, leaving a balance of five thousand dollars to be paid at an early day.
>
> Should our bills as drawn pass, we want you to go to New York and sign and issue to us the State bonds, and receive the bonds of our road in exchange for them.
>
> Any arrangement General Littlefield may make in this matter, will be carried out in good faith.
>
> Very truly,
>
> GEORGE W. SWEPSON.

Wallace stated that the letter was a forged document. Davis felt that "on its face and coupled with the success of Littlefield in dealing with the Governor it constitutes a damaging piece of evidence against Reed." Obviously, however, it put Littlefield as the old friend of both Reed and Chloe in an acutely embarrassing position. According to a version passed on by Wallace, Osborn, who knew of Swepson's railroad plans, visited Raleigh in advance of the session the summer before to which Littlefield came. Osborn did not care to be disregarded in those plans. Indeed, they seemed to provide the very instrument he needed for work on Reed.

"I control two-thirds of the members," the Senator said to Swepson, of the Florida legislature, "and unless you sign this letter you shall have nothing."

So, the story goes, Swepson signed and gave Littlefield a copy of the letter to take to Florida for use by Reed's enemies. They contended that Milton blandly delivered the original to the Governor a day or two before the summer session of 1869 began. Also, at the same time Swepson was supposed to have given Osborn several thousand dollars to assure the success of the legislation he required. Whatever the facts, as presented at the session in the winter of 1870, the letter was a malignant document. Yet though Milton often appeared with members of the Florida Ring which presented it, the certainty is that it did not interrupt—and may have strengthened—his lasting friendship with the Reeds.

In this matter, it seems just possible that moral scruples, with which historians have seldom credited him, moved Littlefield and served his friends. He had few compunctions but much sentiment. He could rob a state but never pass a beggar. Betrayal was not his business. Obviously, as a lobby lawyer, his conscience did not plague him in the bribery of legislative bodies. Greater figures than he were untroubled by that procedure in legislatures, North and South, even in the Congress, in that period. Like some other men Littlefield may have even taken pride in a slick trick by which a bill as enrolled differed in important particulars from one which was passed. Still the General's greatest triumph was that he earned and kept—and may well have deserved—the lasting, even fierce and protective friendship of old Governor Reed and of the Governor's lady, too.

It is, of course, possible that Littlefield bought that friendship.

The documents leave no doubt about the fact that he loaned Reed money. Reed was listed as receiving later $223,750 from bond-sale money Littlefield secured. Perhaps neither he nor Reed ever contemplated any repayment of such sums, but if Swepson proposed that with his letter Milton blackmail Reed to serve Osborn, nothing is more evident than that Reed, who knew of the charge, was confident that Littlefield did not betray him. Indeed, the greater likelihood is that the true target of the blackmail was Littlefield himself. He was not unaccustomed to phony documents. In his scrapbook he pasted a clipping of an obviously fabricated letter he was supposed to have written to Governor Holden not "about State bonds and railroads" but sanctimoniously about "the indispensable duties of religion."

"Bogus," Milton scrawled beside it. "This letter purporting to have been written by myself, is pasted herein to show to what depths of villainy the rebel democracy will go to work upon the passions of the people to overthrow the Reconstruction government of the South."

While less obviously bogus, the letter from Swepson to Reed is intrinsically incredible. Osborn would have undoubtedly liked to have had such a letter incriminating Reed. Swepson might conceivably have written it if it was a price he had to pay. An Osborn henchman swore that the signature was the same as one he had seen on a deed signed by the North Carolina banker. But it is fantastic to suppose that Littlefield, who had at best a difficult job to do in Florida, would have carried there a letter which provided proof that he was involved in corruption with his oldest friend in Florida. Undoubtedly he needed the help of Osborn men. He would have been helpless without Reed. In the session at which the letter was produced, he evidently had the aid of both.

At that regular session Milton submitted a new railroad bill to end legal protests and ensure the issue of the state aid bonds. He had much less trouble and got much more than he had been able to secure the summer before. The Act as passed provided that $16,000 of bonds (up from $14,000) could be issued for each mile of road built west of Quincy. Furthermore, by its terms the $16,000-a-mile bond grant was made to apply for each mile of a hundred-mile stretch of road already in existence to the east of Quincy.

Littlefield's action in the impeachment proceedings is much less clear. His success with the bond bill, however, indicated that he had influence in the legislature where the House voted to drop the charges against Reed by a vote of twenty-seven to twenty-two, with all Democrats voting for impeachment. And after the effort to impeach Reed had failed, Milton appeared, Wallace reported, at a conference of leading Republicans, seeking to patch up a party peace. At that meeting in the Senate chamber, Milton made a speech congratulating the Governor in which he made the cryptic remark that he felt like the old woman who sang, "Hey, daddy's diddle, the cat's in the fiddle, and her tail flew out."

Just exactly what he meant by that nursery rhyme parody Wallace did not make clear. It served Littlefield on the occasion. Not only had his friend Reed been acquitted but he in effect had been acquitted, too, of participation in bribery and blackmail. He had his bond legislation. It was a time when he could happily participate in a celebration of party peace. Undoubtedly such success in Florida in February served Milton's assurance when he appeared before the North Carolina legislature in March as a witness—and, in effect, as the accused. Good Florida fortune was behind his mood which was so frivolous that Joe Turner regarded it as sheer effrontery.

Nevertheless, Littlefield and Swepson still had their troubles. Milton's friends could protect him as witness. They could not, however, after his farewell editorial as he departed forever, prevent legislative action. Measures were passed repealing all North Carolina laws making appropriations to railroad companies and requiring them to return all bonds still unsold to the State Treasurer. Littlefield's presidency of the Western Division was terminated. The commission appointed to investigate and settle all Swepson's railroad affairs was anxious to get on with its business. It had enough to do. It was named to salvage what could be saved, pay the debts of the Western Division of the Western North Carolina Railroad and—hopefully—apply the rest to the completion of the road. Its chairman, Nicholas W. Woodfin, was a man from the mountains in which the railroad was still a myth. Archaic-appearing, voluble, implacable and impractical, he became one of the most unusual man hunters in the history of pursuit.

Woodfin was not a new figure in North Carolina affairs. In 1866, Governor Worth, in urging a Federal pardon for Woodfin, who had been a member of the North Carolina Secession Convention, had referred to him as "an aged man," though at fifty-six then he was eight years younger than Worth himself. Before the war, as successful lawyer and legislator, Woodfin had been lamenting the loss of old-fashioned, independent ways in his mountain country about the village of Asheville.

"Twenty years ago," he lamented in 1860, "there were looms to be found in every farm house—now it is hard to get a good piece of home-made jeans."

He was no mountain reversionary, however. Active Episcopal layman and ardent Whig, before the war he had been one of those anxious for the establishment of a penitentiary for humanity, not profit. Above all, he had sought railroad connections for his isolated mountains, and had been about ready to secede and seek South Carolina railroad connections when dominant Eastern North Carolina politicians in prewar legislatures declined to provide state aid for a railroad to climb the mountains. Swepson and Littlefield had found him almost too eager in co-operation when they set up the Western Division with a promise to do just that.

In determination to control the road themselves they found means to reject a million dollars in bona fide stock subscriptions he said he had secured. That was while they were accepting Littlefield's ephemeral proposal to take more than that amount. Woodfin was suspicious as the road remained unbuilt. He was a furious mountaineer defrauded again by the outlanders when he set out in pursuit of Swepson—and Littlefield—in the spring of 1870. With a mane of white hair, a carefully combed white beard and a curling white moustache above it, Nicholas Woodfin looked like an immaculate, indignant, determined St. Nicholas ready to chase his quarry to the ends of the world. Almost, in the case of Littlefield, he had to do that.

In the first phase of pursuit, however, he found them fairly quickly. Swepson's brother, Robert, was counseling him against stubbornness in trouble and not finding that easy. In indignation and disgust Robert Swepson, on March 19, 1870, wrote General Ransom from the St. Nicholas where the brothers had argued.

"I may know more than you think I do," he told Ransom. "You know that he is a self-willed, money-loving man & I intend to deal firmly with him.

"He tells me that if he were to give up every cent, some people would still say he had a million. I tell him to do *right* & let them talk so if they will."

Perhaps Robert Swepson was effective in pushing his nervous brother toward a settlement, but George Swepson was not ready to be firmly handled for the "right." From Jersey City, less than a week later, the "money-loving" Swepson also wrote Ransom calling for that soldier-statesman as the man who could "manage Woodfin better than anyone I know." From the same place he impatiently wired Senator Abbott for help in communicating with Littlefield. It was important, he told Abbott, "to Gen'l Littlefield & his friends that we get together & arrange our statements & see the committee together as he has made some errors in his report which he ought to correct—much trouble might thus be averted."

The record is clear that Littlefield did not fail him. Soon after Swepson's frantic wire to Abbott, Milton was conferring with the beleaguered banker. On April 9, Milton was seeking Governor Holden's aid, too. From Washington he wrote the Governor "at the request of our mutual friend Swepson & this is sent by the hands of General Ransom."

"The condition of things," he wrote, "is far better than we had [undecipherable word] by the enemies of us all. Mr. Swepson will make a good showing. He will return the bonds that he was short, and pay up. This I know of my own knowledge. I will not go into figures but I hold in my hands an offer to build the road from Paint Rock to Waynesville. The point now is to keep the case without further embarrassment. The court meets on Monday and an effort will be made to indict Swepson and perhaps others. This ought to be stopped as it will not accomplish anything and [undecipherable word] may do us harm. We can get a good settlement and I think it will be a good thing for us . . . all depends upon our getting a good and final settlement."

How much Governor Holden, urged by Littlefield, could or did help is unknown. But, after Robert Swepson's castigation of him at the St. Nicholas, after he began telegraphing like a man at bay from Taylor's Hotel in Jersey City, George Swepson's associates, friends, relatives and lawyers rallied to him. Robert apparently was not as firm as he intended to be. He was ready with financial help. So was McAden, who was deep in the railroad-bond business, too. His chief attorney and first friend Ransom was less rigid than Robert Swepson had first seemed and as thrifty in his own money matters as George Swepson himself. Ransom's character as a Southern Christian gentleman was perhaps epitomized in a creed which, before the war, he was said to have piously prepared for his own slaves: "Love Jesus. Obey the Master. And don't steal Mr. Ransom's corn." That ex-Confederate General rushed to Swepson's rescue though he became that summer a popular leader in the redemption of the state from Reconstruction as attorney for Josiah Turner when Holden, who had the editor arrested, declined to honor a writ of habeas corpus.

Swepson also had as his attorney Augustus Summerfield Merrimon, who had drawn so much of his bond legislation but was also to be one of the attorneys employed by the North Carolina House of Representatives a year later when it moved to impeach Holden for his high-handed efforts to suppress what he called "insurrection." Interesting in that connection is the fact that in the articles of impeachment then adopted by the House was one alleging that Holden conspired with Swepson to defraud the state by the wrongful issue of bonds to the Western Division of the Western North Carolina Railroad. Of it Dr. Hamilton noted: "It was adopted by a vote of 74 to 9 and disappears from view, neither the journal nor the press ever mentioning it again. Why it was never presented cannot be ascertained." Merrimon, who was soon to be Democratic candidate for Governor and later United States Senator and Chief Justice of the State Supreme Court, might have known.

The result, however, was that Holden in his impeachment was not even charged with financial corruption. Littlefield and Swepson were not involved in the trial. Swepson came into the proceedings only for the purpose of identifying the scene at Haw River where one of the night whippings occurred which, along with some murder, Holden's lawyers tried to show justified the force he used. One of Holden's witnesses swore that in the nighttime disguised men "tied me and took me the way they came. They took me down towards the hill out in the big road between the depot and where Mr. Swepson lives, and they passed by the gate, and when they got beyond the gate under the culvert they halted and mumbled something I could not tell what." It did not concern Mr. Swepson. The furies of the Ku-Klux and Holden's rough retaliators were all around him but he was carefully, insistently, not involved.

Such violent matters were for other men. Mr. Swepson, with all the help he could get, attended to financial matters and did very well in arranging and reducing his debts to the state. In the document he signed for Woodfin on April 15, 1870, he spoke much of his efforts to sustain the credit of North Carolina bonds on Black Friday. Then, like a man professing too much, he put great emphasis on the large losses he insisted he had had. As a gentleman, Swepson declared, he felt he should not reveal the names of parties on whose margins he had gone with railroad bonds unless they relieved him from the obligation of confidence.

"It is a matter of regret to me," he avowed, "that the persons who know many of the facts stated here, and who participated in the events that resulted in their ruinous losses, do not allow me to give the fullest information without a breach of confidence. But I have done all in my power to comply with my whole responsibility in this matter."

In addition to such pious protests, Woodfin got a supposed settlement from Swepson for the 6,367 state bonds of denominations of $1,000 each which he had received. In the settlement an error in addition of $10,001 in Swepson's favor was made. Woodfin overlooked $87,000 paid to Swepson in bond coupons. But he got $50,000 in cash from Swepson and a four-month $100,000 draft on Littlefield for 1,278 bonds for which Swepson could not account. Swepson assumed responsibility for $164,000 in cash which he had received from bonds for which he also could not account. For this he gave a draft on Littlefield at twelve months and as security gave a deed of trust on certain lands he owned in western North Carolina, with Robert Swepson and McAden guaranteeing his title.

There remained expenditures of the Western Division of $1,287,436.03, most of which had gone to the Florida railroad speculations. Littlefield as president then of the Jacksonville, Pensacola and Mobile Railroad and Swepson as president of the Florida Central Railroad agreed to pay this with half the proceeds of bonds they expected to be issued soon for the J.P. & M. for the purpose of building roads in Florida. They chose the firm of S. W. Hopkins & Company of New York and London, dealers in railroad iron and securities, to handle the Florida bonds and pay the North Carolina railroad its share. It took Mr. Woodfin some time to discover that the Hopkins firm had been, as he said, "well selected to finish up the work that had been so skillfully inaugurated by Swepson and Littlefield."

Mr. Woodfin had his document. And five days later Swepson called on the effective Ransom to meet him at the Planters Hotel in Augusta, Georgia, on the way to Florida. The truth was, he told Ransom, that "I cannot get along with my business in Florida without you." Swepson went down from Haw River to Raleigh to see Merrimon, too. Then toward the end of the month he wrote again to Ransom calling him to Florida again, this time to meet on the way in Savannah. Milton, of course, was already there. He already had full authority under the act of the Florida legislature to issue bonds of the J.P. & M., but new questions arose in the mind of Governor Reed about the acquisition of the road by Swepson. Reed said that he would issue no bonds until Swepson cleared up the detail of the bad check for $472,000 used in the purchase.

Reed wavered. Littlefield persuaded. Toward the end of May the Governor said he understood that the state had "in no case" promised aid before the completion of the parts of the road for which bonds were to be issued. He added, however, that "the falsehoods which have been so widely circulated of loose legislation and lavish issue of bonds have no further basis than the malice and vindictive hatred of disappointed corruptionists."

He was clearly not referring to Swepson and Littlefield. They were not the disappointed. Indeed, ten days later, early in June 1870, the Governor issued to General Littlefield's agents $4,000,-000 of state bonds, $3,000,000 to be exchanged for J.P. & M. bonds and a million for the bonds of Swepson's Florida Central Railroad which was not even mentioned in the act authorizing the issue. Swepson, fearing he could not get the road's treasurer to sign these bonds, got an acquaintance to put his name on them. Leaving a million in Florida to secure a debt, Littlefield sent $3,000,000 to Hopkins & Company to market.

Mr. Swepson did not linger in Tallahassee. Soon after the bonds were issued he was back at his farm place near Haw River, which he cared for like a garden. Once in a letter to Ransom about his tangled affairs, he asked that lawyer-soldier-farmer about getting "one or two tons of bone dust" and "a few tons of the best manure." Now back in North Carolina he was carefully tending his home scene. Clearly then he was withdrawing from his friend Governor Holden, who had begun his fatal course of suppressing with an irregular militia what he called a state of "insurrection." He charged the conditions to the Ku-Klux and as it seemed the Democrats in Swepson's old county of Caswell, then in Alamance where Swepson lived. Soon Swepson was writing that he wanted to help release some of his friends arrested by Holden, and, characteristically, also that he wanted to collect the debt Turner owed him on the *Sentinel* because he feared that he would "be killed & if so I fear it will then be too late to get the matter made safe."

Most significantly for himself, plans had already been made in June for a quiet meeting of Swepson with his two attorneys, Ransom and Merrimon, and former Governor Thomas Bragg, who in the January before had been named chairman of a first commission to investigate frauds. Swepson did not mention the purpose of the meeting about which he wrote Ransom from Charlotte, where McAden's wife was desperately ill. He told Ransom that in Raleigh he would find "a check for all the money that can be had." He wanted Ransom to be sure to "give immediate and particular attention to my matters—*regardless of all other business.*" And he added that he "would greatly prefer seeing Gov. Bragg, yourself and

Judge M. at my house" in Haw River, midway and remote from such cities as Raleigh and Charlotte. This time Littlefield was gone from North Carolina and Swepson meant to stay there.

Milton had remained in Tallahassee to clear up the details of the issue of the bonds. The little town was hot and empty in June. A few Negroes sat in the shade of the Monroe Street side of the Capitol. Even a panting dog made hot dust as he crossed the street in the sun. Few carriages moved. Most verandahs were empty. Only a few inert men sat in rockers, not rocking, before the Capitol Hotel. No breeze anywhere moved in the live oaks or the magnolias and oleanders planted beside them. In such heat Milton relaxed after his labors, often with his friends, Governor and Mrs. Reed. Undoubtedly he was sympathetic with the good works Chloe planned in the state over which her husband ruled, not always comfortably, sometimes still under siege. Littlefield seemed the embodiment of reassurance. When he stood smiling in the Governor's mansion even old Reed grinned behind his spectacles and Chloe smiled as if she leaned on his strength. Unfortunately, he could not linger long in Tallahassee. One day from an envelope marked S. W. Hopkins & Company, he took a clipping from *The New York World* of June sixteenth.

"We have received a telegram dated Tallahassee, June 13, and signed by five respectable names," that Democratic journal bluntly stated, "warning capitalists against purchasing the Florida State bonds which have just been issued for railroad purposes."

From his office at 71 Broadway, Sidney Hopkins wrote Milton that he proposed to see what could be done "in the way of fixing that paper." Apparently, however, the *World* was not as subject to pressure or persuasion as some Southern politicians were. The report spread in New York. Thus, almost before they were offered, the market for Milton's bonds in the United States was seriously damaged. Milton headed north to see what arrangements could be made.

CHAPTER XIV

The Grand Tour

THAT SUMMER OF 1870, the third year of Congressional Reconstruction and the second year of the first term of President Grant, General Littlefield presided, as Dr. Hamilton noted in his North Carolina story, over the meeting of the National Council of the Union Leagues at Long Branch, New Jersey. Such activity may have seemed remote from his efforts to protect the bonds of Florida from the damaging reports of the Democratic *New York World*. Actually at a time when the Ku-Klux in the South seemed to the Union League chiefs to be everywhere riding with blood on their hoods, it was the appropriate place for the General to be. It gave him special opportunity to show, where it mattered, the eminence of his position in the North as a dependable Republican in the South.

Long Branch was a pleasant place to be. He was more welcome there than in Raleigh. And New York, to which he hastened on receipt of the threat to his bonds, seemed hotter than Florida. Not even legislative tumult in Tallahassee matched the normal, incessant noises of hoof and rim on stone in its streets. When he arrived in the great city, he came from Broadway as from a furnace into the cool and shadowed lobby of the St. Nicholas. Clerks and servants greeted him there as familiar, always flush and generous patron. But not enough breeze came over the city even to stir the curtains in his heavily furnished rooms. Outside, the drays and trams clattered all night long. Long Branch was respite and parade ground, too.

That was the same summer Jim Fisk took to Long Branch the 9th Regiment of the New York National Guard, of which he had been elected the Colonel to help meet its bills. The financier arranged no grim bivouac at his "Camp Gould." In a uniform loaded with gold lace, Fisk daily drilled his troops for the ladies. He concluded the encampment with a ball. The Jersey resort was particularly gay that summer. The Monmouth Park race track was opened. Carpetbaggers were not unpopular there and then.

The council of the Union Leagues over which Milton presided represented the command of the field forces in the purpose embodied in acts Grant had recently signed to compel observance of the Fourteenth and Fifteenth Amendments and to strengthen Reconstruction governments against the Ku-Klux Klan. President Grant was at Long Branch in the summer of 1870, too.

The President came to the resort soon after seeing other North Carolina Republicans on a mission similar to the one on which, as *The New York Herald* reported, Holden had sent Littlefield to Grant in March. The President seemed prepared for their visit. Colonel William J. Clarke, a colonel of the state militia, who saw him with the state's two Republican senators, Abbott and John Pool, wrote Holden that those who knew the President observed that "they never knew him so talkative, or to talk so well." He "warmly approved" their purpose. With his own hand he wrote a letter to General Sherman, then acting Secretary of War, directing him to provide the military equipment needed, as the President put it, "for State militia which is about being organized to restore order in their State." Grant spoke of sending Federal troops and declared he would support Holden with "the full power of the nation." Sherman promptly agreed, adding only that while Holden would "have to sign a bond as Gov. to pay for the supplies . . . it will, in effect, be payable at the Day of Judgment."

"Heaven seems to smile on us," Colonel Clarke told Holden, "and I trust that the undertaking will end as auspiciously as it has begun."

It was in such an auspicious atmosphere that both Milton and President Grant went to Long Branch that summer. Soon after talking with the North Carolina Republicans, wrote Claude Bowers as both historian and Democratic partisan, Grant escaped to the shore from the miasmic Washington heat. There Grant, said Bowers, bowed to smiling ladies without lifting his hat. Only once did the President join in the lancers and then he "cut a sorry figure," as was duly reported by *The New York World.* The description of the place that summer by Democratic reporters and historians belied its popularity: "It was a place of much dancing and heavy drinking and billiard playing, and, strangely enough, not so much given to bathing; albeit the ladies daily dressed with elaborate care to stand demurely, or flirtatiously, on the sands of the beach and look on discreetly." Though Milton's position as presiding officer of the National Council of the Union League marked his relationship with other prominent politicians who followed the President to the shore, he received less publicity than some other statesmen, celebrities, ladies and millionaires. Undoubtedly there as elsewhere, however, people noticed General Littlefield. Eyes followed him when he moved through the carpeted halls of the Stetson House and the Continental Hotel.

He could not linger as President Grant did on the shore. That summer he had more than politics and pleasure on his mind. Certainly he was in hot New York on June 27, when Ann Cavarly met him again there. That lady of the bonnet box and Saratoga trunk always gave the exact and proper places of her meetings with Milton. This time, she said, she saw him in the law offices of Cross, Rice and Holt at 176 Broadway. There was nothing unusual about Milton's being in a lawyer's office, however odd that may seem as a place for a meeting with Ann.

Though the bands were playing loudly at Long Branch that summer and some gaiety offset the heat in New York, too, from this time on much of Milton's life was spent with lawyers and in courts. Ann did not explain her presence. But in telling about it she disclosed a certain eagerness to bring bad news. Once, she said, he "waived" a question which she asked him as if in relinquishment without explanation. She was, by her own testimony, tenacious in her questioning. Yet Milton, as she publicly remembered the occasion later in testimony before the North Carolina Fraud Commission, was as amazingly frank with her as he always seemed to be in her recollections. Apparently, however, he mentioned no Florida matters with which he was most concerned then.

"In conversation with him," she said, "I asked him if he knew they were going to sell the *Standard* office."

Undoubtedly she knew that the building had been to Milton a symbol of high hopes. Gone forever as he was from North Carolina, perhaps the question pricked his pride.

"He replied that Holden would not sell it.

"I asked him why; he waived the question."

Then: "In the course of the conversation he said he had not paid Holden in full for that office, and said he did not intend to do so, and that Holden would not let it be sold."

Mrs. Cavarly was persistent.

"Upon my again asking why, he said that Holden knew that he [Littlefield] knew that Swepson had paid him [Holden] $30,000 for his [Holden's] action in one matter. The conversation was interrupted and he did not say in what matter."

Mrs. Cavarly did not report how the conversation was interrupted. A lady may sometimes be reticent about such things even when telling all or much. But if Ann Cavarly, who so often appeared as the self-confessed confidante in Milton's life, can be believed, something sharper than annoyance may already have developed between old associates in North Carolina. If Littlefield had urged Grant to give Holden military aid in rounding up his political enemies as the enemies of the state, General Littlefield was not then preparing to take any part in the business. Swepson, after working on the bond issue in Florida, was at home in North Carolina conferring with local lawyers and friends not all of whom were friends of Holden or Littlefield. And Milton in New York had $3,000,000 in Florida bonds which he could not sell. Less than a month after he saw Ann Cavarly in the summer of his political prominence at Long Branch, Woodfin wrote to Senator Ransom about a $50,000 check which Milton had given him as a part of the Swepson settlement he had agreed to in April.

"I am sorry to say that I was hoaxed & the check of $50,000 drawn by General Littlefield was protested."

He did not ask Ransom to get the money out of Swepson. He was looking for Littlefield, who, with the heat behind him and hope ahead, was already on a fast and fashionable liner on his way to London. The impression was given later by North Carolinians that Littlefield fled to Europe with the hoaxed Woodfin hot on his heels. That picture of Littlefield in flight became a cliché of hope —and history.

It would have been a good time for flight from the South. Littlefield's journey took him from that region at the time when mutterings had advanced to proportions of explosion. Even if exaggerated in remembrance, violence had increased in North Carolina and Florida and other Southern States. That was the summer from which the melodramatic memory of Reconstruction takes its material. In Florida the homicide rate was doubled even in the deaths which reached the statistics, not counting forgotten corpses in the swamps. The standard historian of the period in that state declared that the election of 1870 "clearly marks the beginning of Republican decline in Florida," though Republican feuding did not abate with the improvement of Democratic hopes.

In North Carolina, while Littlefield sailed to England, Holden began in little towns and rural areas the operations which had seemed so auspicious in the office of President Grant. As it turned out he laid the groundwork for Democratic advances in North Carolina when he turned his militia on the Ku-Klux Klan—and on such personal enemies as Turner, too. Though uniformed by Sherman at Grant's direction, that military force has been pictured in history as a dangerous and disreputable mob-in-arms. It was led by a Civil War Union guerrilla from Tennessee who operated in the Carolina mountains. His name was George W. Kirk, and Joe Turner, even before Kirk had him manacled, described Kirk as "notorious and bloodthirsty." He undoubtedly was. In the war, his raids as a Union irregular had been marked by atrocities. So had those of his Confederate guerrilla counterpart in the same area, Colonel James A. Keith, whose bloody behavior on the Confederate side brought protest from Governor Vance that if half the charges against him were true, he would be "a disgrace to the service and to North Carolina." Such men proved that fighting between partisans at home can be fiercer than formal warfare.

From his offices where Milton had so often conferred with him, Holden, driven to hysteria by the denunciation and defiance of men who listened to Turner (whether or not the editor was the King of the Ku-Klux), was preparing the basis for his own impeachment. If he had started to catch the Ku-Klux, he lost the state election in August. Grant was not then talking so much or so well as he had been in June. Even the Federal courts upon which Holden depended rebuked his course. Some of Swepson's lawyers took their places as Holden's prosecutors. Swepson himself carefully gave no sign that he returned Holden's pledge that "I am your friend and will never desert you." He was not as comfortable in his Haw River house, and perhaps began then to plan the move to a residence in Raleigh two years later. None of Holden's "standing army," as Turner termed it, molested Swepson. Neither did the Ku-Klux which the armed band sought. But at least one of the men Kirk caught as a Ku-Kluxer, Swepson's neighbor, Adolphus G. Moore, began then to taunt the banker as they passed each other on the streets.

Though he might well have been, Littlefield was not in flight from such events or from Woodfin. Actually his European tour was planned as a necessity before Woodfin learned his check was bad or Governor Holden's troops marched to the arrest of Turner. When *The New York World* published the item from Florida destroying the American market for Littlefield's bonds, his European tour became a necessity. Obviously his next move was to try to sell the bonds in Europe through the Hopkins & Company house there, though that firm's London officers knew even more about the quality of the bonds than *The New York World.*

He sailed just as the Franco-Prussian War was beginning. He was not alone in his difficulties. Dr. Mott, one of the railroad presidents who worked with Swepson before Black Friday, described the time as one marked by "the increased distrust which had obtained during the summer with regard to all Southern railroad enterprises, and the breaking out of the European war which unsettled capital to a very great extent, and destroyed for the time the German market for American railroad securities." All had troubles. Not all dealers in securities, however, had to deal with Woodfin as well as the war.

Bright young men in the Old Broad Street offices of the Hopkins firm in the same building as the Bank of New Zealand regarded that elderly North Carolina mountain man as a comic character when he first arrived in London in August. Littlefield had already left London for the Continent where he was to make the grand tour in truly grand style, trying to sell the bonds in St. Petersburg, Berlin, Paris and on the Riviera before he returned to England. At the time of Woodfin's arrival he was carrying on his operations from the Hôtel de Flandre in Brussels. He was by no means an innocent abroad, and he worked with English and European brokers who definitely proved that not all abroad were innocents.

In gay mood the Hopkins London office wrote Milton that Woodfin "called yesterday in a full new suit of broadcloth. He said little—nothing for or against the Florida bonds. He talked mainly of the railroad in North Carolina and stated he came over to arrange for iron as they wanted rails immediately. He is very anxious to secure possession of the money due from sale of Florida bonds or in some way to raise money at once. . . . We informed him you had gone to Berlin and St. Petersburg, that the moment you found the war had placed a damper on securing funds here you started for those places determined on realizing as you were bound to send out rails to your Florida road."

Woodfin seemed content. He was then enjoying his expense account, too, as a North Carolina legislature in a new mood of moralistic economy noted later. He wrote Swepson's lawyer, Ransom, who seemed to hear from him more regularly than anyone else back home, that a Hopkins partner had told him that Littlefield "had gone into France following the Prussian army and especially to see Metz bombarded so he might or might not be here in a fortnight." Unfortunately a legend which grew among some of Milton's distant relatives later that he watched the bombardment with General Sherman does not jibe with Sherman's schedule that summer. Undoubtedly, having left Sherman in Lincoln's service too soon to see the siege of Vicksburg, Milton did not mean to miss as spectator the military event of that year.

There were evident similarities in the war he watched to that one in which he had served. Here again in the onslaught of Prussian power on French pride, a North fought a South. Milton evidently associated himself with the German efficiency. He kept items about their railroad iron. Yet he himself looked then a little as Napoleon III had when he had been forty, too, and on his way to absolute monarchy in France. Certainly, in 1870, as an American, Milton had little sympathy with Napoleon's recent American adventure in which he had sent to Mexico Maximilian, now dead at Queretaro. Even in Carlota's company, Maximilian had not seemed like another Cortes. But Milton would not have admitted to himself that Napoleon's puppet in Mexico had been a man in the character of an imperial carpetbagger, and one deserted at the last and in disaster by practical men—or at least men who could no longer afford adventures which did not pay. Milton watched the bombardment of Metz as a spectacle, not a parable.

Woodfin made the most of his opportunities, too. In London, as Milton was informed by the Hopkins office, the old gentleman in his new tailored broadcloth was "seeing the town, attends service daily at St. Paul's and seems in no hurry, only to let us know what are his expectations." Indeed, he was momentarily "so quiet and manifests so little anxiety we do not know what to make of him." Prospects for the sale of the bonds seemed pretty good, they told Milton. Then suddenly it turned out that Woodfin had not been merely seeing the sights or remaining as quiet as a North Carolina senior warden in St. Paul's.

"We have had news in the shape of a bomb which has been thrown into the camp of our London bankers," Hopkins' London manager wrote Milton in a scrawl with the characteristics of a scream. ". . . Woodfin called at the Oriental Bank to which he had letters of introduction & laid before them his whole project stating the North Carolina railroad had been defrauded and that the parties now holding the bonds had no right to them . . . desired their assistance in attaching as soon as offered for sale. . . ."

The London dealer was flabbergasted: "You have been entirely in error and have misled us as regards this man Woodfin. Had we known this it would have been an easy matter to have fixed him in time. The other evening he dined at the writer's house where he said Gov. Reed received $30,000 for signing the bonds and pronounced him a great fraud."

Such talk was frightening in London.

"Our first impulse," the English operators wrote Milton, "was that you should go to Berlin and we would send Woodfin to meet you in order that you might keep him away from London but upon reflection we fear this will not do as he would doubtless leave orders with the Oriental Bank who have correspondents all over Germany and Holland to attach during his absence. The obvious necessity is now to have him retrace his steps and undo what he has done. With this view the writer will meet him tonight and have a distinct understanding with him and make any arrangements possible to again place matters where they were. Even if we arrange *him* you see the difficulty there will be in healing the damage already done with our friends so alarmed."

Woodfin, he added, was "so operating as to ruin the whole enterprise if we cannot repress him." He had "evidently been talking incessantly & telling to the parties he had met all and every item of his business. He is the most consummate blockhead on some points that one would meet in a year's travel."

One to whom Woodfin had been talking was Henry Clews, who in later years became the most moralistic memoir writer out of Wall Street, but had been like so many other prominent brokers out to make all he could from the Southern bond issues. Clews had been an early member of the Union League. He was one of the chief money raisers of the Republican Party, a friend of Grant, and reported himself that he had been twice offered and turned down the position of Secretary of the Treasury. Perhaps in politics he was, as Donald Barr Chidsey said in his biography of the highly professional Roscoe Conkling, only a dabbler, "very proud of his little accomplishments and delighted to think of himself as an insider." As a banker, however, his firm was sufficiently important to signal, when it failed three years later, the dimensions of the panic of 1873. He did not like to be outsmarted in finance. It is possible that his distaste for carpetbaggers stemmed from a claim that he had lost $50,000 on bonds, guaranteed by Swepson, sold him by Byron Laflin. He had had, Clews wrote later, the "purest motives . . . to aid the South in the work of Reconstruction." But he added that, though his office became a meeting place "of Southern generals and Southern people generally, almost as soon as the war was over," that experience was a sad one.

"For these kindly offices," he said in his memoirs, *Fifty Years of Wall Street,* "I was treated with the basest ingratitude by some of the Southern States."

Clews, of course, was only one of many insistently respectable Northern bankers involved in Reconstruction finance. Few historians have crossed the Mason-Dixon line in an effort to show the connection between the carpetbaggers and the brokers, though throughout Reconstruction in the South the commonest cry was that Wall Street was leading the looting. Much bigger steals and more extensive corruption outside the South have preoccupied national historians. Southern writers have devoted themselves largely to the more dramatic black and white materials on the Southern scene. And, of course, the transatlantic aspects of Reconstruction finance has received even less attention. Some sympathy has been spent upon poor European investors in Southern bonds, more perhaps than they deserve when it is noted that they expected to get eight per cent in gold on the par value of bonds for which they paid only a fraction of par. Their tragedy was that the pound of flesh turned out to be just a piece of paper.

At home and abroad, Henry Clews was one of the least offensive of those ready to profit as much as they could on the securities of bankrupt states, and who only began to be highly indignant with the carpetbaggers when they did not seem to be bringing in the profits any more. But in London in the early fall of 1870, Clews wanted his money. He listened to the voluble Woodfin and he let it be known that he would do all he could to injure the Florida bonds unless he got his money.

The Hopkins people reassured Milton about Clews. Rather remarkably, in view of that banker's prestige at home, they wrote him of Clews & Company: "We care nothing about them in this market. They have no weight here." Woodfin had noted, however, that Clews' London firm had an office just opposite the Bank of England. Perhaps then he began to be a little disturbed about his own talk. What worried the Hopkins officers, as they wrote in daily reports to Littlefield, was Woodfin's general garrulousness at a time when "this market would not stand an attack on any security, a doubt was enough," to prevent the sale of the bonds. That would end the hopes for Hopkins' commissions, Littlefield's share, or any money for the North Carolina railroad.

"Until past midnight and all to no purpose," the British dealers talked to Woodfin one evening. He seemed as stubborn as he was garrulous. Therefore, solemnly next morning they told him (as they informed Littlefield) that they had decided to announce that they were dropping the business, selling no bonds.

"He at once came to his senses . . . and stated if we would only show him how he could protect himself, he would go to the continent to see you or go to America or anything we wished."

In effect, then, the solemn mountaineer agreed as North Carolina's agent to let what he believed to be a fraud proceed so that he might get the money he sought. And, without stressing the difference, Hopkins agreed, in order "to protect ourselves against this fool," to accept his draft on Littlefield, signed "not as President hence not official," if he would "sail tomorrow in the *City of Brussels* for America and assist us there."

"But," Hopkins added, "he flies off so we do not count on its fulfillment until we get him on the steamer . . . His tongue is a most unruly member. . . . We have been airing him out at Windsor. . . . In case he kicks out at going to America we shall send him to see you as we must get him out of London."

Apparently Woodfin did kick out of going to America but he stopped talking in England. Furthermore, a secondary plan to send him to meet Littlefield in Berlin while the General was en route from Brussels to Cologne was abandoned. An entirely cooperative Woodfin was waiting for Littlefield when he returned to London a month later. Woodfin noted that the General was living in almost regal splendor. Apparently, he had lived on a similar scale on the Continent. Hopkins regularly enclosed travel funds of fifty pounds in each letter to him. His expense account for the trip was later shown to be about $24,000, as one commentator noted, "a round sum for a little tour of a few months."

In his splendor, Milton greeted Woodfin, that worthy wrote home, "with every proposition of fairness." He even talked, so Woodfin said later, with the kind of candor which Mrs. Cavarly suggested he usually reserved for her. In their talks Woodfin indicated that he thought Littlefield and Swepson had secured the bond issue for the Western Division to get the money rather than build a railroad. It was then that Littlefield told him that he was mistaken, that he and Swepson had meant to build a railroad but to do so in such a way that they could get it for themselves. The General also told Woodfin how Swepson had determined to squeeze him out as a stockholder because he was "stubborn and self-willed, and could not be managed, but would ruin everything."

Apparently Littlefield managed Woodfin very well. The General had to go off to the country for a day or two with friends. Woodfin wanted time to think. There were more interruptions. Finally, more than a month after Littlefield returned they made another agreement on November 10. The General paid Woodfin two hundred pounds sterling, agreed to place eight hundred of the Florida bonds to the old man's credit with, of course, Hopkins & Company. Also Milton agreed to furnish enough iron for laying the Western Division from Asheville sixty-five miles to a connection with the Cincinnati, Cumberland Gap and Charleston Railroad. He threw in another thousand tons of iron for good measure. Woodfin got the promises but little else. He came home, however, very proud of his appearance in his London clothes.

The State of Florida did little better. The bonds were sold. Under the terms, $2,800,000 of the three millions were sold to a Dutch syndicate, headed by the brother-in-law of one of Hopkins & Company's chief agents, by Littlefield for $1,358,000. From that sum was subtracted $340,000 to pay the first three interest installments and a commission to Hopkins of a little over $40 per bond. That left a million which he brought home. Out of it Milton gave $50,000 to Swepson and $20,000 more to "a Tennessee bank," probably the First National Bank of Knoxville of which Robert Swepson was president. Other items included large sums to Milton's relatives from Jefferson County, New York, J. B. Clarke and Calvin Littlefield. Another $350,000 was supposed to go to the North Carolina road. Woodfin's commission took $48,600. Apparently Milton also invested money in the stock of the Florida railroads. More went to legal expenses and "advances designed to placate some individuals and reward others for their co-operation" —including presumably Governor Reed. Less than a third of the million he got in London was left for the construction and operation of Jacksonville, Pensacola and Mobile Railroad facilities.

Even so Milton returned from London with the air and the appearance of an imperial builder. He took passage on the gleaming white *Russia* of the Cunard Line, then the most luxurious and fashionable of the transatlantic liners. She was the ship on which the President's daughter, Nellie Grant, was to begin the romance which led to her White House marriage to Algernon Sartoris, nephew of Fanny Kemble whose path Littlefield had followed to the South Carolina Sea Islands. Such people sailed on the *Russia,* and aboard her in December 1870, Milton was distinguished-appearing among her elegant passengers. Perhaps he was not surprised when the *Russia* slipped into her berth in New York to find Swepson standing on the cold dock.

The banker had gone to New York three weeks before, expecting to return to Haw River in a week, but had decided to wait for Littlefield due on December 21. Swepson was then in no expansive mood. He was cold and lonely in New York and he knew that behind him in North Carolina, as his proud and indignant wife put it, "the wolves" were howling for his blood. Mrs. Swepson used that phrase in a letter to Ransom which she wrote the day after a Christmas spent alone in the big house at Haw River. Two days before, on Christmas Eve, Governor Tod R. Caldwell, who had taken Holden's place while the Governor stood trial, had issued extradition papers to the Governor of New York for both Swepson and Littlefield on an indictment for conspiracy and embezzlement returned in Asheville which had waited so long for the railroad they had promised to build.

No officers found them at the dock. Apparently they had time for talk in New York. Littlefield went on to Florida. Swepson returned to North Carolina. Mrs. Swepson told the news in more dramatic terms than the *Sentinel,* even in this day of triumph for Turner who was out of jail and about to destroy Holden, could have done.

"I see from this morning's paper," she wrote in the first week of the New Year, "that my husband has been arrested & held to bail in so large an amount that I do not know how possibly he can give it.

"I am ready to go with him to prison or to death—a thousand fold more dear to my heart in this dark hour of misfortune than in his most prosperous & popular days. When he was courted & flattered I could see his faults, now they are all hid, covered by his misfortunes."

Mr. Swepson, with the aid of McAden and his brother Robert, furnished the $200,000 bond. He was not repining. He consulted Ransom about a suit in Florida affecting the bonds there. He wrote that he thought the additional item, involving himself, in the articles of impeachment against Holden were "drawn for the purpose of getting some testimony against me." Very definitely "the wolves" were still going to have trouble getting his blood—or his money. It was then that he put a significant passage into a letter to the romantic, thrifty, ever-ready Ransom.

"If Littlefield writes to you to appear for him as his attorney," he wrote, "please write me forthwith and hear from me before you reply to him."

There was no doubt that Ransom would. Like many others still, he was George Swepson's man.

CHAPTER XV

The Game Is Open

GENERAL MILTON SMITH LITTLEFIELD, or the Honorable M. S. Littlefield, president of the Jacksonville, Pensacola and Mobile Railroad, as his name began to appear in the papers, stood in 1871 before the changeless façade of the Southern dream. He possessed the classic columned image of Southern dignity and beauty. His house in Tallahassee was the traditional stage set of enchantment: "a beautiful mansion . . . connected with many historical associations of Florida."

"It was built," a man who stood in awe before it then said, "by Governor Call and long occupied by him in the palmiest days of Southern glory. Gov. Call was an ardent admirer of General Jackson and not infrequently entertained him in his splendid mansion. The house is situated in a magnificent park of twenty acres or more, filled with moss-draped oaks and beautiful evergreens. The broad portico with its lofty columns trimmed with ivy—the wide aristocratic hall with spacious parlors on either side—a smoking verandah in the rear, and balconies on the upper stories, giving splendid outlooks upon the distant landscape are prominent features in these Southern mansions, built for luxurious enjoyment and wide extended hospitality."

That estate was only one of Milton's residences then. In Jacksonville to which he had brought Anna and the boys, he had a "fine residence about a mile up the river." That was in the direction of Mandarin on the St. Johns. There Harriet Beecher Stowe, where tourists could see her under a great live oak, was then writing in enchantment of the South she had damned before. Even Mrs. Stowe did not become disenchanted with Northern politicians and promoters in the South until her brother ceased to be the Reconstruction superintendent of public education in Florida. In 1871, those who came for shorter visits than Mrs. Stowe saw only the approximation of perfection.

Such a visitor was the one who described General Littlefield's house, a young correspondent from *The Syracuse Journal* in the General's native land. He wrote an almost rhapsodic article, headlined, *A Trip to Tallahassee,* about the South he found in Florida. It was a long trip, though one often made, in those days for reporters looking at the emerging South which had not yet quite become the New South of its prophet, Henry W. Grady, but was eagerly hoping to be. The journey had been a long one for Milton, too, but it had brought him in the ephemeral winter and hurrying spring of 1871 to the success and the South he had sought. Both were flowering and sunlit and imposing, though occasionally there were in the success and the South around him vague apprehensions like the fears of frost in the orange groves. Men like Littlefield publicly dismissed them.

"He is confident," the reporter told his readers, "that the gloomy outlook of political affairs in the South will give way to brighter prospects in the future, and that the desperate efforts of the Democratic rebel leaders to secure political control will be signally and effectually thwarted."

With such assurances the General sent the young man off "with special facilities for learning all that was possible, in so brief a visit, respecting the condition and resources of Central and Western Florida." He provided him with passes on his trains. And above all he sent him to the mansion in Tallahassee where Governor Richard Keith Call while territorial Governor had provided feast, music and Florida weather for Andrew Jackson. As the guest of the president "and, if I am rightly informed, sole owner" of the Jacksonville, Pensacola and Mobile, the reporter felt that he had been equally entertained.

Later, perhaps then, the place was called The Groves. In Littlefield's absence it was presided over by "Mr. Allen, formerly from Jefferson County, New York," and his two pretty daughters. The young ladies fed the enthusiastic reporter on "garden luxuries found only in the greenhouses of the North." Yet he discovered himself home with home people. He called at the Governor's mansion to pay his "respects as a Syracusan" on Mrs. Reed, but did not find her at home.

As Littlefield's guest he would have been welcomed there. The ties between Milton and the Reeds were clearly documented then. Obviously, no one had told the reporter, but, not long before he arrived, Governor Caldwell of North Carolina had issued another writ of requisition for Littlefield this time to the Governor of Florida. The North Carolina executive asked Governor Reed to deliver Milton to the authorities of that state where he had been indicted in Raleigh on charges of conspiracy and embezzlement. There Swepson had been arrested, Holden impeached.

Reed refused. Then the North Carolina Governor offered a $5,000 reward to anyone who would deliver Littlefield to him. There followed reports of kidnapers foiled, once, according to Hamilton Jay, at Live Oak, a central point on his railroad, "by a timely warning and the pluck of a conductor on the railroad," once in a night chase only by a confusion of carriages in the dark. Reed met such incitement to the kidnaping of his friend by offering a $5,000 reward himself for the apprehension of anybody who tried to capture Littlefield and collect the North Carolina reward. Perhaps, as the indignant *Floridian* said, Reed was "Littlefield's tool." The certain fact is that the Governor's mansion was the house of Milton's friends.

Milton was not hiding. He did not look hunted. Indeed, the inescapable impression is that he wanted to become the railroad magnate he seemed. Boldly, he operated as if that had been what he had sought always. He could have followed the plan of flight which Swepson had in panic proposed for both of them the year before. Instead, he made himself more ostentatious on the face of

Florida, brought his family to share the hazards on the scene. No one, of course, knew the limits of his resources better than he. In retrospect he seems to have assumed an unnecessarily precarious rôle. But he played it in such a way that even the *Floridian* felt "compelled to express ourselves gratified with the prospect" of the extension of the road across the Chattahoochee River in West Florida and a hundred miles beyond: "The iron has been purchased. . . . The road will be completed to the river by September next . . . bonds have been sold in London at a very flattering figure." That was not all. In March 1871, Littlefield advertised for the bids on the construction. Also, he headed the list of those setting up a new company, the Florida Seaboard Railroad Company, to provide better service from Jacksonville to Fernandina. He seemed to work smoothly in confusion. The second man on the list proposing the new road was William H. Gleason, who had come, like Reed, from Wisconsin to grow tropical fruits but had later as Lieutenant Governor tried to take the governorship from Reed.

Between Jacksonville and Tallahassee—as well as to Syracuse in New York—Milton expansively spread the story of his road and its plans. Clearly he believed it himself for with some of the money he had brought back from London he began to buy stocks in both the J.P. & M., and the Florida Central. Furthermore he undertook to make passengers happy. In the sun and the dark his railroads seemed vividly alive, not only going to new places but serving old ones. Indeed, the Syracuse correspondent was hardly less impressed by the possibilities of West Florida and the mansion in Tallahassee than with the quality of a supper served him at midnight at Live Oak on the line where some passengers changed for Savannah.

"The moon was shining with great brightness," he wrote, "and stepping out upon the platform between the tracks, I saw a sight not easily forgotten. Three tables were spread with every appurtenance for a full dinner, coffee, meats, vegetables, etc., etc., and Negro waiters stood around to take the orders of the guests. The tables were full of hungry travelers, porters were hurrying to and fro with baggage, the locomotives on each side of the platform were hissing and smoking all under 'the clear silver light of the moon.' "

Milton's situation seemed like that scene, opulent, active, vividly lit, yet surrounded by a dark wilderness, too. He was not quite the "sole owner" of the railroad. There were others greedily claiming a share of the money he had brought back from London. They included other politicians, lawyers, promoters in Florida. There would be clamorous, disappointed Dutchmen soon. And at just this time Ann Cavarly served as very feminine reminder of the demands of the North Carolina railroad and of Swepson who then, escaping punishment, had taken an oath that he was insolvent.

Mrs. Cavarly never explained what took her to Jacksonville and to Littlefield. She was so often in so many places where he was that perhaps no explanation is needed, though of course many reasons might have brought her there. That town was becoming a popular place in the winter and spring. Sidney Lanier's Florida guidebook, written with the feeling "that God meant this land for people to rest in—not to work in," had not appeared. But Walt Whitman had seemed as prophetic as usual in his invocation of "O magnet-South! O glistening, perfumed South." Others came to see the transparent lakes, the hummock-land, the blossoming titi and the parrots in the woods about which Whitman had written before he wrote of lilacs in the dooryard.

More and more ladies and gentlemen were arriving in such a poetic Florida every year. Jacksonville, which Milton had seen first as a frightened and deserted village, had reached a population of nearly seven thousand. The St. James, described with not too much exaggeration as the Fifth Avenue Hotel of Florida, had opened two years before Ann Cavarly arrived. Many Northerners came for the mild climate, not any political advantages. A Philadelphia physician had written a guidebook in which he noted that "a warm climate promises aid . . . in marriages not blessed with offspring. Heat stimulates powerfully the faculty of reproduction." The annual migration to the sun, which Olmsted had predicted before the war, grew in the lengthening peace.

Mrs. Cavarly required no excuse to go to Florida. In April 1871, when Milton's hospitalities were most extensive, it seems natural that she should be in Florida. She did not mention being entertained at Milton's "fine residence in Jacksonville, about a mile up the river," where Anna Littlefield and the boys were happily established. But there as always, as she reported it, he told her about his confidential business affairs. This time without any show of bitterness he repeated to her, she said, that neither Swepson nor Hawkins in North Carolina had sent him all the bonds they had "agreed to give him." He also repeated there, she said, that Swepson had bribed Holden. Then he said that Swepson had not paid all of the $240,000 which Littlefield was said to have dispensed through him to North Carolina legislators. Some Swepson had used, he told her, for "outside influence . . . a large amount to John T. Deweese for outside matters." If he was more specific about the matters for which Swepson paid that disreputable Congressman, Mrs. Cavarly did not indicate it.

Perhaps Ann Cavarly's meeting with Milton in Florida was no different from any of their other meetings. She reported him as being just as candid. A difference followed it, however. From that conversation she went to Raleigh and three weeks later—on May 23—she took the witness stand of the Commission to Investigate Charges of Fraud and Corruption, headed by William M. Shipp. That commission, wrote Dr. Hamilton, collected "most of the material relating to North Carolina financial history during the period," but he added, "the investigation might have been made more exhaustive with profit to history, though the results would doubtless have been disastrous to certain members of the Conservative [Democratic] party."

Mrs. Cavarly, "being duly sworn," on May 23 did not seem engaged in preventing disaster to anybody. No description of her on the witness stand is available. Joe Turner's *Sentinel* seemed less interested in her disclosures than he had been interested a year and a half before in her flight when she left even her bonnet box behind. Perhaps some idea of her appearance can be gained from a description of a stylish bonnet of the year which the *Sentinel* published at the time Ann testified: "one very beautiful white chip gipsey, bound with a delicate shade of pink velvet, trimmed with rich black lace, crushed roses, and falling low over the crown a graceful ostrich plume."

Mrs. Cavarly was in Raleigh at least ten days in May 1871. She was still accompanied by her unimpressive husband who testified that the first time he had speculated in North Carolina bonds he had invested $60,000 in the bonds selling at sixty cents on the dollar and sold them at seventy-nine. Profit $11,600. But the next time he bought $100,000. He could not recall the purchase or sales price but remembered very clearly that he lost.

Ann talked of no such transactions. The commission did not ask her a single question. She took the stand and told. As early as the late spring of 1868 Littlefield had been the friend to whom she turned in reporting Swepson's risky proposition to her husband about helping him get the North Carolina Railroad. She had gone north with Milton in the fall, fled at his request to Richmond in the winter. They were together in Washington at Grant's inauguration, and again in New York just before he sailed for Europe. Only touching upon pertinent conversations, she recited the procession of their meetings through the recent one in Florida. Now their private meetings became a public story. But in telling it in an uninterrupted flow of accusations she still made Littlefield emerge as a man whom both Swepson and Dr. Hawkins had short-changed in North Carolina.

No members of the commission prolonged Ann's testimony or sought to develop it in greater detail. The absence of any questions seems almost eloquent testimony to their willingness to let the lady leave. She came down from the stand and, so far as the record goes, moved gracefully into oblivion. But she left as she departed the clear impression that even then Swepson and Littlefield had passed the breaking point in their partnership.

Swepson himself, confidentially at the time, verified that impression a month later in a letter to Ransom. He had just returned to Haw River, he wrote his lawyer who was soon to be a Democratic senator, from New York where he found old man Woodfin angrier than ever because he had not been able to get any of the bonds promised him in London the fall before. Indeed, instead, Swepson reported, "Hopkins went to Florida and one of Littlefield's friends had an injunction served on him to prevent his paying anything to the Western Division of the Western North Carolina Railroad or myself. . . ."

Swepson continued in the kind of indignation which led a lawyer in the complex litigation about the matter to refer to him as "the virtuous, innocent, upright and injured Swepson." His report on the injunction to prevent Hopkins from paying him anything from the Florida bonds led him to the first contemptuous use in his extant papers of the word, "Carpetbagger."

"This was done," he wrote, "after all the Carpetbaggers, Clarke, Col. Littlefield, and the Florida people were paid. Gleason, ex-lieutenant-governor of Florida, Carpetbagger, was in New York and told Rollins [a member of Woodfin's commission] that they never intended paying the road or myself a dollar."

It is difficult to understand Swepson's evident sense that he was being robbed. He had never had any investment in the Florida railroads except with funds he had taken from the Western Division of the Western North Carolina Railroad. In his settlement with Littlefield as the road's new president, he had presumably transferred that road's rights in the Florida roads to Littlefield as its new president. Just what was actually transferred at that time late in 1869 in Jersey City when Swepson was determined to get out with "whole bones" is not clear; neither is what Littlefield kept. Certainly, though Woodfin found that his checks bounced, Littlefield must have been undertaking to pay for something when he put up part of Swepson's settlement with Woodfin also in Jersey City some months later. The certain thing is that Swepson was not happy. His characteristics as the "money-loving man" his brother called him were showing themselves beyond his timidity when caught with somebody else's money.

Beyond the oath of insolvency, which he took when he came home after meeting Milton on the *Russia,* his affairs were improving. Dr. Hamilton described the process by which he said Swepson's "account with the State, skillfully handled by his lawyers, Merrimon and Ransom, steadily grew less. . . ." Even when he complained of "Carpetbaggers," he reported to Ranson that he had "made sale of 215,000 acres of my wild land in the trust for $100,000." Also, it was about that time, according to an article later in *The News and Observer* of Raleigh, that he quietly bought the Virginia Cotton Mills (named after his wife and perhaps acquired in her name), which were to contain 4,000 spindles and 175 looms. Mr. Swepson no longer required the carpetbaggers but he did not mean to let them or anybody else take anything to which he could stake a claim.

Other claimants and associates hung around Littlefield. In Florida, as Hamilton Jay later wrote in *The New York Sun*, after Milton returned from London "the carpetbaggers pounced upon him, blackmailed him right and left, and it is said that some of them even now are enjoying property acquired with his money." Thieves in the South, native and Northern, were falling out. And in the process, Milton seemed certainly not the most guilty. This was a time, too late, when apparently he wanted to build and run the railroad and not merely steal its bonds.

It is possible, of course, that his purchase of the stock of the roads he had looted had a further sinister purpose behind it. It might have been a process of postponing the evil day. Jay thought he was an artist at that. "A certain gentleman," he wrote, "followed Littlefield to collect a sum of money alleged to be due. He swore he intended to have that money or a fight. He met the handsome General, took dinner with him, and, before night, loaned him about the same amount he was so determined to collect." Undoubtedly, however, Milton appeared to array, not only the bond money, but other outside capital in his operations through Colonel Calvin Littlefield and Clarke of his native New York country who had been associated with him since the 1864 draft deal. Undoubtedly also they took money away.

Clarke, who was credited with receiving the most money in the Florida accountings, is the more nebulous figure of the two. Colonel Littlefield gave evidence of being a substantial character. Old deeds show that he bought business property in Raleigh while Milton was operating there. He maintained a pleasant estate, The Maples, in Jefferson County, New York. At this period of Milton's Florida career Calvin had offices in the Drexel Building at 3 Broad Street in New York. He was an officer of both the St. Louis and San Francisco and the Atlantic and Pacific railroads. Apparently this was the same Atlantic and Pacific Railroad about that time headed by Thomas A. Scott, president of the Pennsylvania Railroad, who was planning a transcontinental railroad across the South.

In 1871 Scott put the Pennsylvania behind the Southern Railroad and Security Company to control tottering railroads in the Southeast below Richmond and make them traffic feeders for the Pennsylvania. And in March of that year his Texas and Pacific Railroad Company was chartered by Congress to build a road to the Pacific from the South, through Texas, New Mexico, Arizona and California to San Diego. That was Scott's project but he had no monopoly on the dream. Before Milton arrived in Florida Governor Reed had petitioned Congress for aid in completing the railroad, of which Littlefield became president, as an eastern link in a road through New Orleans to the Pacific. Later Reed's bitter enemy Senator Osborn was, according to George R. Foster, an official of the Florida Central, "making a dust about building the Great Southern Railroad." That may have been the same Great Southern Railway Company with "assets exclusively political" which Dr. Vann Woodward reports was sponsored by Swepson's lawyer, Senator Ransom.

Milton was not denied a part in the dream if he had no central part in the grand design. He had been accused of bringing A. K. McClure, as Tom Scott's great friend and agent, to Raleigh to try to lease the North Carolina Railroad in 1869. Another of Scott's friends, John W. Forney had consulted with Littlefield when he came south earlier to talk of Southern investments. Milton had apparently known Forney and McClure, perhaps Scott, in Philadelphia. He was not a great frog in their pond, however. And whatever may have been Colonel Calvin Littlefield's relationships with national railroad magnates, he had also been engaged with his cousin, Milton, in so many small deals that their association in the 1870s was not necessarily in a great enterprise.

It was an increasingly precarious enterprise. The Florida legislature in January 1872, put increasing rumors about Milton's operations into resolutions. Even his friend Governor Reed, while in somewise excusing him, told the legislators that the bonds had fallen into the hands of "one of the firms of swindlers who abound in New York." Perhaps, as John Wallace wrote, a resolution calling for Milton's arrest for failure to appear before an investigating committee "was undoubtedly passed to extort money from him." He was not arrested but lawsuits grew like a sawgrass and cypress swamp around him. Milton put off claimants with declarations that "Col. Littlefield is expected daily as he left New York Friday . . . everything will be settled when Col. Littlefield gets here. . . ."

Perhaps Calvin Littlefield came, but in July 1873, a Florida attorney, Colonel Daniel P. Holland, who had once been Littlefield's lawyer, got possession of the J. P. & M. railroad. This course of proceedings, Aaron Marvin, of Jacksonville, wrote Captain L'Engle in a letter, "does not seem to be very agreeable to the General." And the same man wrote that same month: "General Littlefield's residence was sold on last Monday by the sheriff." That was the Jacksonville house. Undoubtedly, the Tallahassee mansion already had other tenants.

"No news of importance here," said the man who wrote of the sale.

Other news of much more importance was soon to come. That was the summer which ended with another Black Friday, on September 19, 1873, which created a depression in the country and not merely a panic in Wall Street. The firm of the great Jay Cooke, who had been promoting railroads as well as Republicans, closed its doors. More important, the doors of shops and factories closed, too, all over the country. Farms began to go under the hammers of auctioneers. Eight years after triumphant Union victory a new and apparently permanent army of the jobless began to grow. Thousands of men were out of jobs for months, some for years as a part of a homeless, wandering population, composed not merely of bums, hoboes, tramps but hungry, desperate, potentially dangerous men. Suddenly Negroes, who had slaved without freedom, seemed less significant socially and politically than men unable to work for bread. And to them in 1873 were added nearly half a million immigrants, most of them men without skills. It was set down only as a detail in a recounting of the situation that "some Southern states, desperately in debt, bitter about the carpetbag governments . . . were threatening to repudiate their bonds." Some had already done so. Now Conservatives in the North felt as beset as those in the South. The Bloody Shirt of Union war memories seemed a less effective political argument for Northern Republicans. The march by political torchlight procession from John Brown's body had become under Grant a parade encumbered by bribery and incompetence, nepotism and scandal, all of which are most shocking in hard times.

The Big Barbecue of Federal railroad subsidy and Congressional corruption was ended. Oakes Ames, of the Crédit Mobilier, had died in disgrace in May—two months before Littlefield's house was sold. Now an era was inaugurated of "reform, remorse and morality —moods characteristically reserved by Americans for hard times," as Vann Woodward put it. Florida, of course, was not too remote to share it. A Negro legislator, John W. Wyatt, there rose to declare, "We want no Tom Scotts, Jim Fisks or Vanderbilts in this state. . . ."

Littlefield gave no public appearance of depression. His beard was clipped as neatly as ever. His boots shone. He moved in a carriage. Apparently his house was bought in for him at the sheriff's sale by a friend. He fought the seizure of his railroad to the United States Supreme Court and got it back by High Court order. In May 1874, he was writing Swepson's lawyers, Ransom and Merrimon, both then members of the United States Senate, about a bill fostered by his enemies to grab the railroad by Congressional Act after it had been restored to him by court order. Such an Act, he told the senators and lawyers, would put an end to negotiations by which "Mr. Swepson or the W.D.W.N.C.R.R. Co., can get any money claimed by them to have been by Mr. Swepson invested in the Florida railroads." Undoubtedly, the senators noticed that phrase "claimed by them." Their answers are not available. Perhaps the most important item in the correspondence was Littlefield's uncharacteristic lament.

"When I think of the hangers on and blackmailers," he wrote, "that have been sucking money blood from myself and the interests I represent I feel like exclaiming 'Oh! Lord How Long!!' "

Apparently, however, it was not an altogether unhappy time in the Littlefield family. A month after the General wrote the senators, his son and namesake, then not quite ten, wrote to his aunt, Mrs. Martha Harbert, in Philadelphia. In a big scrawl the boy, who was to become one of the country's leading compilers of hymn books, said:

> DEAR AUNT MATTIE:
>
> Mama says this is your birthday, & that as I had no present I could give, perhaps my first letter would be an acceptable remembrance—Auntie May—Alfred and I wish you many Happy Returns. I wish you were here—we would have

something good to eat watermelons and peaches are ripe. I wish you were here to eat some. Papa discharged Mike because he got drunk & Peter Goss is now the coachman and we all like him very much. He gave me a nice little goat, & made me a nice little harness for it. But . . . just as it was commencing to work nicely in the harness it died, and the harness was stolen from me. There is a nice school here kept by a Miss Painter from Ohio. — was the last day before our vacation. (I should have put down in Brockland after Ohio) which I go to and as I said today was the last day before our vacation. You must excuse this writing because it is the first letter I ever wrote in my life. Serving Maggie is going to Philadelphia and she says if she was going anywhere near you she would come see you. She sends her love to you. So does Papa and Mama and Alfred and I.

Your Affetionate
Nephew MILTON S. LITTLEFIELD JR.

Below the letter Anna Littlefield added a note:

I send this uncorrected, as it is his own & I tho't you would prize it the more. He thinks it is not fit to go, but I tell him it is. Baby has honored you also & if you can't interpret let me know & I will translate. I think it will be employment for your leisure hours. Time is up & I with Milton wish much love and a good bye.

The goat was dead and the harness was stolen. But Anna spoke of no troubles. There was a coachman still and a serving woman. There were lawsuits and lawsuits and lawsuits. And Florida did not escape the national "Democratic Tidal Wave of '74," as the newspapers termed it. Samuel J. Tilden was elected Governor of New York. In the country the Democrats carried the national House of Representatives where Congressional Reconstruction had begun. In the Florida legislature, where Milton had worked so well, the Democrats and Republicans split the Senate 12 to 12, and the Republicans had a majority of only three, 28 to 25, in the House.

Gradually—perhaps the proper word should be desperately—Milton found himself working to save and reorganize the railroad with the young ex-Confederate Captain Edward M. L'Engle, who before the first Black Friday had been so much impressed by Swepson. That young lawyer had later opposed Littlefield and Swepson, helped secure the repudiation of the bonds on the Florida Central, and taken from Littlefield the authority to dispose of any bond of that company, which Milton had controlled as well as the J. P. & M. Yet as a man trying to save the road and settle its problems L'Engle was the person to whom Milton turned as his troubles increased.

"I am ready to [go to] Tallahassee tonight," he wrote L'Engle in a letter marked "personal" in June 1875, "but I have not the money to pay my expenses—wish you would loan me $100. I have no security to place in your hands but I will return it during the month of July and this is all I can say. If you can give me this accommodation I will esteem it a great personal favor. I must leave some with my wife as well as to pay my expenses."

That was a month before Milton's forty-fifth birthday. He no longer had the Call mansion behind him. Any lodging in Tallahassee was a problem. Obviously, he received no help from Swepson in North Carolina though that gentleman had moved to Raleigh from Haw River in 1872 and taken a spacious, white house across the street from the Capitol and next door to the First Baptist Church of which Mrs. Swepson was the chief contributor and patron. (The house was purchased for him by his brother Robert and immediately put in Mrs. Swepson's name, though the deed to her was not recorded until 1885.) Perhaps the reason for his move was indicated by a statement about the charges against him in a letter to a Raleigh lawyer from another out of town: "I have understood that the State cannot try this case in the county of Wake—that Swepson and his friends had more influence in your county than the State had. . . ." The better reason was pointed by homicide in Haw River. It marked the beginning of 1876 which is generally dated both as the year in which the South was redeemed from Reconstruction and the Presidential election was stolen in Florida in what some have angrily called the crime of 1876.

Even when he moved to Raleigh Swepson kept his place in

Haw River, though there were in that neighborhood some hotheads and ex-Ku-Kluxers who declined to accept the distinction Swepson austerely drew between himself and the carpetbaggers. The Ku-Kluxers still had losses to lament in the Kirk-Holden war. When one of their number had confessed at the time, Hamilton noted that "several hundred young men hastily left the State for the Southwest, many of them never to return." One who had held his ground was Adolphus Moore. He taunted the banker whenever he saw him. That was not considered very wise by some others.

"'Dolph," said Thomas M. Holt, afterward Governor of the state, "Swepson's going to kill you."

"No," said Moore. "He's too big a coward."

And Holt told him: "Cowards are the most dangerous people in the world."

Moore, on his way home from hunting, came by Swepson's house a January day. Apparently as he passed he spoke to the banker. There was conflicting testimony as to what happened then. But a correspondent of the *Sentinel* reported: "The big road passes within a few steps of the door. Capt. Moore was in the big road a little past the front gate when the fatal bullet passed out of Mr. Swepson's window from his Sharpe's rifle. The ball passed through a plank paling about one inch thick before it struck Moore." A telegram to Raleigh said, "Captain Moore . . . a brave and fearless man . . . had many warm friends in Alamance and feeling runs high on his side." However, "Swepson was held for trial in a bond of $10,000 which he promptly gave."

Mr. Swepson was, of course, acquitted. Ransom and Merrimon were in the Senate and could not join his battery of lawyers but Merrimon's partner, Colonel Thomas Fuller, was available, so was McAden, though he had become much more a banker than attorney. There were others. They convinced the jury that in this as in so many other things Mr. Swepson was an innocent only defending himself, his rights and his home. Mr. Swepson himself was at the same time proving that he was one of those standing in defense of his state. Quietly he made it clear that there should be no confusion about his politics. He was a Democrat standing with those who labored to redeem the South from Reconstruction.

Even in that he expected a quick return. He wrote to Ransom

immediately after the election in November in which a Democratic governor was chosen in North Carolina and Samuel J. Tilden seemed certainly the victor over Rutherford B. Hayes for the Presidency. His letter was on the stationery of the Falls of Neuse Manufacturing Company—R. Y. McAden, president; G. Rosenthal, secretary and treasurer.

"Remember if Tilden is elected," Swepson said, "Rosenthal is to be pension agent at Raleigh. Merrimon has promised to go for him."

Littlefield had not changed his politics in Florida. He cast his vote for Hayes and was caught up with other Floridians in the excitement of the national doubt which centered on the Florida returns. The "smallest tadpole in the dirty pool of Secession," as *The New York Herald* had described Florida in the war, had become something very different to *The New York Times* in 1876. Early in the morning after the election, that strong Republican paper, after accounting politically for every state in the Union but Florida, announced: "This leaves Florida alone still in doubt. If the Republicans have carried that State, as they claim, they will have 185 votes, a majority of one."

The situation was not quite that simple, but Florida's vote was that important. "Visiting statesmen" of both parties hastened to Tallahassee. Local partisans were active, too. There is no evidence that Littlefield played any leading rôle in the Florida situation in which one writer has said "dishonors were even," between the parties. He kept in his scrapbook batches of clippings largely from *The New York Tribune* suggestive of dishonorable Democratic activities. Some of the Republicans who came were old acquaintances of his. Governor Edward F. Noyes, of Ohio, who presented the Republican case and was said to have made some remarkable Republican promises, had served with the Union Army in Missouri, Tennessee, and Mississippi when Milton did. Lew Wallace, the politician and novelist, had come down the Tennessee to the battle of Shiloh in the same armada in which Milton sailed. Wallace described the Florida situation in a letter to his wife: "It is terrible to see the extent to which all classes go in their determination to win. Conscience offers no restraint. Nothing is so common as the resort to perjury. . . . Money and intimidation can obtain the oath of white men as well as black to any required statement. . . . If we win, our methods are subject to impeachment for possible fraud. If the enemy win, it is the same thing. . . ."

Apparently, after American fashion, however, the operations in Florida were often pleasant as well as dishonorable. Young, gay Henry W. Grady, who was to become the prophet of the New South, was there as a reporter for *The New York Herald* and his own *Atlanta Constitution.* He and Lew Wallace, said Raymond B. Nixon in *Henry W. Grady—Spokesman of the New South,* did not care for "the diversions of the bar and the gaming table" which occupied many visiting statesmen in the midst of political skulduggery. There were balls with a noisy brass band in the Tallahassee Hotel. Much gaiety attended the counting—or miscounting of the votes.

Fraud was national. It applied to the Presidency as well as railroad bonds. "Visiting statesmen" who came late showed no more scruples than carpetbaggers who came early or the scalawags whom they found. The Republicans secured the vote of Florida, Louisiana and South Carolina. But the Florida vote remains more significant in view of Dr. Vann Woodward's statement that the consensus of recent historical scholarship is "that Hayes was probably entitled to the electoral votes of South Carolina and Louisiana, and that Tilden was entitled to the four votes of Florida, and that Tilden was therefore elected by a vote of 188 to 181."

Littlefield did not crown his career by that theft. Other greater, more eminent and presumably more honorable men did that. Indeed, the only suggestion of his prominence at the time comes from a strange, probably politically naïve source, John Greenleaf Whittier. That radical abolitionist poet had written a special song for little Negro children on the Sea Islands. Now an aging reactionary, he rejoiced in the election of Hayes because he was safer than Tilden. While Hayes' inauguration was still in doubt, he wrote a letter.

"If he is President," he said, "he will need the wisest counsels of the best men of the party. Coming in as he will, he must not be a mere partisan. He must conciliate in some way the best men of the Democratic party in the South. It is folly to rely any longer upon such 'carpet-baggers' as Littlefield and Purman. An honest, fair-minded, intelligent democrat put in office at the South by President Hayes would do more to perpetuate the party, than a knavish, unprincipled & low minded republican."

The Purman of whom the Quaker poet spoke had been defeated for Congress in the same election in which at last Hayes was given the victory. He had been in the legislature which had approved Milton's bonds. After the Hayes-Tilden election he served four years on the Republican National Committee, though he left Florida in 1878 to go back to his native Pennsylvania. It is not clear how he or Milton came to Whittier's mind as those who had been relied upon, unless some whispers of special gratitude to them in the Florida situation had come to the poet. If he was politically naïve in mentioning them his letter practically reflects the alignment in securing the compromise of Conservative Southerners, many of them old line Whigs, with Northern Republicans, both heirs to the Hamiltonian tradition of Federalism.

Milton was not politically rewarded. Apparently he was not called upon in the energetic maneuvering of sound businessmen, North and South, to find a basis for compromise in connection with the election. The removal of Federal troops from the South was not all. They undertook to secure for the South some assurance of Federal aid in railroad and other projects, notably Tom Scott's road from the South to the Pacific, in return for the South's peaceful acquiescence in the inauguration of Hayes. The election was hardly over, however, and its outcome had not been determined when Mr. Swepson in Raleigh stirred himself with regard to his Florida claims and reasserted his partnership with Littlefield.

Swepson had been too sick to attend to business, he wrote to Colonel C. B. Fenwick, a lawyer concerned with Florida railroad matters, just before Christmas in 1876. But he was stirring mightily. Apparently the lawyer had written Swepson in the hope that he might help in rehabilitating the Florida roads. What Swepson proposed, instead, was to break up a settlement of the debts of the Florida roads which Captain L'Engle had been negotiating with the Western Division of the Western North Carolina Railroad and other claimants. The claim of the Western Division (from which Swepson had gotten the money he invested) could, he said, be broken down "on several grounds—first the bonds were unconstitutional—second—the settlement in Europe where they actually received 800 bonds & the guarantee of Hopkins & Co., for iron. The iron contract they released Hopkins & Co. from without the consent of Gen. Littlefield or myself and agreeing to compromise with Hopkins & Co., and receive from them a claim against certain state bonds releasing everything else. I want you . . . to come right to my House just as soon as you get this & bring from the General all the papers & points about the various settlements etc., in Europe & in N. York so we will have all the facts."

Swepson then spoke of L'Engle and General Joseph B. Stewart, a New York attorney who had been working with L'Engle on a settlement.

"It seems the parties represented by General Stewart and Mr. L'Engle think General Littlefield and myself powerless or afraid to interfere with their plans. We now have to show fight—if we can then compromise on fair terms all right—if not we can whip them out. . . .

"Show this to Gen. Littlefield & you come here forthwith."

Somehow within ten days the letter was in the hands of Stewart and L'Engle. Littlefield was not joining Swepson this time. It was, Stewart said, through Milton's "non-acquiescence" that he was informed of the plans of Swepson to put a $2,000,000 mortgage on the road of which "about $1,400,000 were to belong to George W. Swepson who has *no* claim on the property and about $600,000 was to be divided between those who have *good* and *valid liens*. . . ."

"By this letter," wrote Stewart, almost incoherently, "we see a man who has but recently escaped from the grip of the penal code of North Carolina because of the embezzlement of funds of a railroad of that State of which he was president and who is afraid to come into the State of Florida for fear he may be held to account for a like depredation upon the railroads of the latter State. A man who has wrecked and ruined the railroads of both states by the fraudulent appropriation of their assets whereby he had put millions into his pockets and now seeing one of the Florida roads about being resuscitated by escaping a bogus $2,000,000 bonded debt of his own concoction and for his own benefit." Swepson, he added, was "blackmailing those whom he has already swindled."

Littlefield left no such strong language about his old partner. Indeed, the only report of his action in the matter is in a letter Stewart wrote from New York to L'Engle months later.

Swepson and Colonel Thomas C. Fuller, a law partner of Merrimon's, Stewart said, "followed Littlefield here to try to control his actions: And to induce, if not force him to sign certain papers. But to the credit of Littlefield I am pleased to say he refused and Swepson left in a great rage, after both of them had received a castigation from me that neither of them will soon forget."

It certainly cannot be said with certainty that Littlefield was at last taking his place on the side of the angels. There were some real questions as to the rights of all the parties in the efforts to resuscitate the Florida railroads. General Stewart was a proud and partisan as well as an indignant man. Also in L'Engle's efforts to arrange a settlement Milton often led him to the offices of Calvin Littlefield on Broad Street in New York. That process did not enrich Milton. It seems evident that he might have done better by himself if he had joined Swepson again and required the price of his partnership.

He had been broke before he saw Swepson in New York. Indeed, as the term of President Hayes began and Swepson moved in the reassertion of his amazing claims, Milton was writing L'Engle asking for another loan of "$100 or $150."

"Please do the best you can," he wrote in an unusual, cramped scrawl. "I am in a bad condition. . . . I am in great need of some money for my board, washing, etc."

And less than two weeks later he wrote again to L'Engle who apparently had given him a small position.

"I must have $125 today. As you must know my situation has been such that sundry bills for my family have accumulated. The $150 went far towards paying."

His bill for room and board for forty dollars a week was some months behind. There was a bill to a "Mrs. Dr. Mitchel . . . which is very pressing upon me today because she is going North upon the Dictator tomorrow and I last evening made the promise that she should have it." He owed a note for $150 at the bank.

In New York and Florida he was still much harassed by debts, honest claims and perhaps by blackmail. *The New York Tribune* said that in the summer of 1877 "a Mrs. Hayes, of Boston, while a guest at the Metropolitan Hotel, made a sensation by alleging that detectives under General Littlefield's direction had tried to enter her room to secure papers in her possession, which she claimed were damaging to General Littlefield." Not all the facts about that incident, including the identification of the lady, are made clear by the *Tribune*'s statement that "it was the general impression then that Mrs. Hayes was suffering from monomania."

Anxieties and depressions were crowding around Milton, too. Finally, on July 22, 1878, he wrote L'Engle a letter which seems his farewell to Florida and the whole South above it. It was brief and unmarked by emotion. He would appreciate it if L'Engle would "pay my wife $200 and give her tickets to New York." And he added still with some show of assurance, "Let the tickets be charged to me." Where Anna went when she reached New York is not known. Probably she went as to a familiar refuge to visit Aunt Mattie in Philadelphia. She did not stay with Milton in New York. He continued to work there with L'Engle in his railroad rehabilitation plans. He made engagements for the Captain to see his cousin Calvin, at his impressive-seeming offices in the Drexel Building. He had to make one appointment at an odd time because Calvin and his associates had to attend the board meetings of other railroads in which they were interested. In 1879 he arranged for them to meet again in July, the month in which the Florida courts rejected another requisition for Littlefield by North Carolina on a charge that he had stolen $4,000,000. Then in November he made another appointment for L'Engle with Calvin.

Perhaps it was the last. That was the month in which "General Milton S. Littlefield, of Jacksonville, Florida, who is said to be connected with a railroad in that State" was arrested for failing to pay a bill of $94 at the Park Avenue Hotel. The hotel's manager, Henry Clair, said the General told him "that he was called out of town suddenly and would soon return. This he failed to do, being sometime afterwards found at the Astor House. He had acted so contrary to ordinary usage that Mr. Clair was moved to proceed against the General with stringent measures." Littlefield spent the night in a cell in the Ninth Precinct station house. Even then apparently he had not lost his persuasiveness: "He had intended to return to the hotel but had been prevented by circumstances."

The story ends: "On his promise to pay the bill, Mr. Clair withdrew his complaint and the prisoner was discharged."

CHAPTER XVI

At the Last, No Stone

MILTON LITTLEFIELD DID not leave only a poor and looted land behind him in the South. Indeed, before he departed, the states in which he had operated had already announced their purpose not to pay the bonds they had issued and he had helped to squander. Other later, honored Northern capitalists and their highly respectable Southern assistants got most of the railroads at a bargain—and often with a blessing. Soon after Milton ended his career in that redeemed region, the South's well-loved Henry W. Grady was describing a land in which the golden thread of continuity was easy to see.

Henry Grady gave special attention to the new riches required by a New South. Much poverty, of course, remained which did not seem then to require much prose. Much poverty had always marked the South. The conditions existed which later put landless Negroes and poor white men briefly and desperately together in radical Populism, and then in frustration drove them farther and more angrily apart. But, always optimistic, Grady wrote as the 1880s began of the "millionaires" he found in North Carolina who seemed glittering even beside their counterparts in his own flourishing Atlanta. One of the chief of them, he said, was George W. Swepson.

Grady was a harbinger of change. And times were changing swiftly. Reconstruction was over—and there was momentarily among important people a substantial demand that much of it be forgotten. In no golden mood, Grady's fellow editor, Josiah Turner of the *Sentinel,* had found it that way. Grady, already then emerging as the apostle of the New South, on his trip to North Carolina apparently did not see or talk with Turner, who regarded himself as the defender of ancient Southern ways. Few other people did, if they could help it. The day was long passed on which Turner had come home as a hero to the State Capitol he was saving from the carpetbaggers, after his release by court order from Holden's Reconstruction militia. Then a tumultuous, grateful crowd had taken the horse from the shafts of Turner's carriage and pulled him to the ceremony where he was praised as the man redeeming the state from Reconstruction. No reward was too great for him then. He was, of course, given the position of public printer which Littlefield had held. There was a quick proposal to send him to Congress.

But Turner apparently expected too much appreciation. Evidently he thought he ought to go to the Senate, but Ransom had to be served first, then Merrimon. Enthusiasm had died somewhat when the next Congressional election came around in 1874; he was defeated for the Democratic nomination. He was turned down a second time in 1878. Also, "his paper was sold to pay the purchase money still due on it." Sensible men obviously could not blame McAden for seeking the judgment to cover sums he had advanced to help Swepson, who had lent Turner the "purchase money."

And after all, men were saying, Joe Turner was "good to pull down, but not to build up." Finally he was elected to the lower house of the state legislature. Then two years before Henry Grady arrived, he was expelled in 1879. He had talked much and sharply. He had, his fellow Democrats said, been "persistently disorderly." Undoubtedly he seemed insulting, too, when he shouted that he had fought the rascals as Reconstructionists and now found them leading the Democrats. Sensible men, of course, dismissed Turner as a crank. Such a man was of little interest in the New South.

Actually, soon after Littlefield left the state, Turner had seemed eager to serve the New Southerners. They were not exactly new. But, with Governor Holden impeached and Littlefield gone forever, the *Sentinel* seemed to pay only half-hearted attention to the hearings of the Fraud Commission. Instead, as those hearings began in 1871, Turner's paper ran a glowing leading article about the development of the Chatham Railroad and the Deep River Manufacturing Company which had brought the Whig capitalists and Milton Littlefield together a few years before. The pattern of fraud had become a dream again without any suggestion of interruption.

"The road is in fine condition," the *Sentinel* said, "and managed with Dr. Hawkins' and Captain Andrews' well-known ability."

The article went on as if it might have been written by Grady afterward or Littlefield before: "The locks are rapidly being repaired by the Deep River Manufacturing Co., by which boats will be enabled to pass between Fayetteville and the Chatham coal fields, thus giving an outlet and a market for the vast coal deposits in this section. The water power here is immense, there being a fall of forty feet in about two miles, and always water in the greatest abundance. . . . Thousands upon thousands of spindles can find full force here. . . . Then immediately surrounding this place, the earth teems with the deposits of the richest copper and iron ore—inexhaustible in quantity, and unsurpassed, so said to be by assayists, in quality. Here foundries and rolling mills without number can find constant and most profitable labor. There are lead mines, gold and silver in more or less quantities, and other valuable minerals. Then come the immense coal-beds which can supply all the workshops that can be erected within the State and all the people with fuel for years and years to come. Here within a scope of twelve miles square, is contained resources inexhaustible, centering at Lockville which could furnish wealth and prosperity for a nation."

Turner's reporter ended in a final burst of enthusiasm: "Within a month this iron horse will traverse all this region, and then we may look for the erection of all such works as are conducive to the wealth and prosperity of a people. Under the management of such truly live men as Col. Heck, Dr. Hawkins, Captain Andrews . . . it cannot be long before those who have the money and the energy to develop these immense resources will be brought in."

Littlefield had been brought in. He was gone. And though Turner was at the moment helping keep alight the fatuous fire with its tendency to mislead travelers, north- or southbound, the foundries were never built; the rolling mills never appeared. More mills grew on the shores of other streams. But the Southern men who had first fashioned the Deep River dream did very well. Under the heading, "Some Carolina Millionaires," Henry Grady listed several, then added: "The richest man in the State, though, I am assured by General Roberts, the comptroller-general, is George W. Swepson. . . . Swepson operated with Littlefield in this State, and the firm handled over $16,000,000 in bonds. Both of them were enormously wealthy and lived in princely style. In the Democratic revival Swepson went to cover and back with his money. Littlefield went to Florida, lived like a Monte Cristo for a time, operated largely in Florida railroads, and is now bankrupt and extremely poor."

Some estimated Swepson's fortune, Grady said, at $1,000,000, some at $2,000,000, and he added: "Everything is in the name of agents or his wife, and a judgment of $10 against him could not be collected, but he conducts large operations. He has little or no social recognition and lives quietly with his childless wife."

Mr. Swepson lived quietly but well. People remembered him for favors. W. Plummer Batchelor, son of one of the gentlemen who had served on the Fraud Commission, recalled in a speech years later that he "incurred a heavy debt" to Swepson when he acquired the *Sentinel* which Turner was not able to hold. Batchelor said that when he resold the paper he managed so that Swepson got satisfactory security for this debt, but that "the kindness, the patience with which Mr. Swepson treated me in this time of trouble I have never forgotten and will never forget." Others remembered that in those years, in addition to the mortgage on the newspaper that had saved the state, cotton mills, real estate, timber and securities, Swepson owned in this period more "undeveloped water power than any man in the State."

Undoubtedly the financier lived quietly in his big house by the

Capitol and the Baptist church with his wife who, travelers abroad came back to report, looked even more and more like Queen Victoria as the years went by. Mr. Grady's notion that Swepson had "no social recognition" was certainly in error and nothing proves that better than the pallbearers at his funeral, when he died in Raleigh on March 7, 1883. Mrs. Swepson, of course, made up that list of mourning and assisting gentlemen as she also arranged for the preparation by her pastor of the obituary which appeared in *The News and Observer* of Raleigh.

That article recited little of Swepson's story except in metaphorical or scriptural form. It stressed his marriage: "Without issue, this marriage was marked by eventfulness seldom surpassed, leaving the wife a widow with a single aspiration—the love and honor of her husband." The article which the editor of the paper carefully labeled "Communicated" continued a poetic tribute to the deceased:

> Mr. Swepson was a person of remarkable kindness of disposition. Toward the poor and friendless he held an open hand, and wherever his prejudices were not aroused almost anyone would meet with success in appeals to him for aid to any public charity or private sufferer. His strongly marked character brought him into collision with his fellows, and all through life it was God he was stuggling with when he thought it was only a man. And this is true with most of us. God touched his thigh and made him realize his own utter powerlessness. This was his supreme soul-struggle, in which Christ was conqueror, and the server was saved, strong in his weakness. As Noah stretched out his hand to the dove, so the infinite love grasped him and drew him in. The sympathies of the public are extended to his afflicted widow and friends.

The pallbearers in themselves marked no such mystical tribute. One of them was another of the Carolina millionaires Grady had mentioned, R. S. Tucker, merchant and railroad stockholder. Fuller, the lawyer Swepson had taken with him on his last Florida foray, was one. Others, along with the corpse, constituted a group from which a quorum could have been called of the stockholders of the

Deep River Manufacturing Company in which Littlefield had been interested when he first came to the state. The well-to-do Colonel J. M. Heck had become the president of the Baptist State Convention. Colonel A. B. Andrews (he was promoted Colonel on a Democratic governor's staff), Doctor Hawkins' nephew, had moved from his position as official of the Raleigh and Gaston, which became the Seaboard, to assume the Carolina suzerainty of the Richmond and Danville Railroad, which became the Southern Railroad. Andrews was on his way at the time of the funeral to the position of economic boss behind the political bosses of the Democratic Party in North Carolina. Later still, his life and his works were memorialized by a fountain throwing an erect stream of clear water into the air beside the railroad into the mountains which Swepson and Littlefield never got around to building. It was ordered by George F. Baker, president of the House of Morgan's First National Bank of New York, which controlled more railroads than even Tom Scott sought.

The funeral was an impressive occasion and afterward Mrs. Swepson, who had received all her husband's property under a one-sentence will, had erected the tallest monument in green Oakwood Cemetery on the crest of the hill above the modestly marked but tenderly remembered graves of the Confederate dead. An obelisk which rose among the oaks toward the sky, the granite memorial over Swepson's bones, bore across its base the legend, "Trusting in Jesus for Salvation."

Milton Littlefield lived longer. In the years after he left North Carolina and Florida, he was able to pay his hotel bills. For a time during the 1880s, he and Anna and the boys lived in Morristown, New Jersey, which Walter S. Dix, a friend of the General's sons, described as then "a town of great wealth, which might prove an advantageous residence for a promoter of business enterprises." Apparently that was still the General's occupation. He had a small office in New York and commuted there every day, Dix remembered. But both his boys became part-time clerks in the Morristown post office. In New Jersey, he was a respected Union General who made a number of addresses about the military campaign in Tennessee. Apparently they were well received, though the reporter for the *True Democratic Banner*, of Morristown, noted that he excused himself "from relating just what his audience most wished to hear, viz: his experiences as an active participant in the bloody battle of Pittsburg Landing [Shiloh] or other army experience."

His youngest boy, called Alfred, however, indicated in an oration at the commencement exercises of the Morristown public schools that, if the General was reticent about lingering over his own war experiences, he had not neglected to pass along to his sons his ardent Republicanism. Alfred spoke on "The Old-Fashioned Man of God," a subject which Anna may have helped him select. The General's influence showed in the speech. When the young scholar declared that some of the descendants of the Puritans had degenerated enough to "vote the Democratic ticket and march with Tammany Hall," the reporter assigned to cover the juvenile occasion was amused. Apparently as there were serpents in Eden, not even Morristown was free of Democrats. And young Littlefield's remarks, the reporter said, "seemed to have a depressing effect upon some members of the school board who were seated on the platform."

The South was a long, safe way off. The North had its dangers. On March 11, 1888, Anna with hundreds of others in the area was caught on a train in the great blizzard of that year. She was marooned for three days. Anna and Milton began to realize that they were no longer young. She was fifty-two, he fifty-eight. They had been married for twenty-six years. Alfred was twenty-one and young Milton, at twenty-four, was an over-aged sophomore, who had to earn his own way at Johns Hopkins University in Baltimore. He transferred the following year to Union Theological Seminary. Alfred got a job as a clerk in New York. And Milton and Anna moved to the Hotel Albert on University Place there.

Younger Littlefields remembered the grace with which at the Albert the General arranged dinners of epicurean preciseness in terms of dishes and wines. One was for a girl from little, familiar Ellisburgh in Jefferson County, New York, to whom young Milton was engaged. However elegant, that became in memory a mournful celebration of an engagement broken, apparently by the girl's family, because even in the North carpetbagger had become a fixed label for ill repute. Perhaps more than rumors about the past entered into that, however. There was another incident which may prove that General Littlefield, impeccable still at sixty-two, when his eldest son was ordained, was still incorrigible, too. Research does not indicate that any attention was paid to the occasion by the press. But there was the case, recorded only in recollections, of an unknown lady with $7,500 to invest who raised some clamor about the manner in which General Littlefield had handled or mishandled it. It would be romantic but historically outrageous to suppose that she was a final Mrs. Cavarly.

Apparently the old man was incorrigible, but by no means unloved. Anna, growing old and retreating into a religious faith which after Milton's death kept her away from doctors when she knew she was dying of cancer of the breast, was, according to her granddaughter, "very proud (outwardly anyway) of the 'General.'" Anna was the one who argued theology with young Milton; she was a fundamentalist and he a modern of that time. But the General joined heartily in the singing of the hymns as a compiler of which his son was to make a reputation. He did not ever become a sanctimonious hymn singer. His pretenses were in the flower he wore in his buttonhole, the beard trimmed as precisely as a banker's, his erect stature, and his still-springing stride. If perfidy marked him, he left piety for others. But he kept among his papers a letter which Milton, Jr., wrote him just before Easter in March 1895—the twenty-fifth March after he had paid his farewells to investigating North Carolina legislators with what Joe Turner called "brazen effrontery" and "unparalleled impudence."

Young Milton, then as an assistant minister of the Central Presbyterian Church in New York, had as his first charge Mizpah Chapel in Hell's Kitchen (now, in a changed city and time, Trinity Presbyterian Church at 422 West Fifty-seventh Street). He prepared an Easter letter for his congregation and sent a copy to his father, though he was living in the house with him. Within the folder on which it was printed he wrote a letter.

"Dear Papa," he said.

> I send you a letter that I have prepared for my congregation.
>
> It has been my earnest hope and prayer that you might be with us Sunday. You have a right to go to the Lord's Table. Dr. Hastings said so distinctly. The Table is not for the Church

members only, but for all who love the Lord Jesus and wait for his appearing.

I have been thinking about you a great deal and praying earnestly for you. Whatever the burdens may be you may be sure that your boys believe in you, and their only desire is to bear whatever part of the burdens they can. If you can't be with us Easter we will be together in spirit. You will pray for me that I may have the power to preach and we will remember you, asking that God will give you his peace that passeth understanding.

Your loving son,
M.S.L.Jr.

From the tone of young Milton's letter, it is doubtful that he expected his father to come. As a young clergyman he presented his most persuasive witness in Dr. Thomas Samuel Hastings under whom he had studied at Union Theological Seminary. Dr. Hastings was of the General's generation and had come from the same up-state New York area from which the elder Littlefield and so many of his associates had come. There is no record that the General went then. Later, quietly, he joined the church of his son.

He walked erect until the day when he fell, stricken with "cerebral apoplexy" on March 7, 1899, in the apartment where the family then lived together on the top floor at 1184 Madison Avenue at Eighty-sixth Street. The younger brother Alfred paid the rent, which members of the family recall was fifty dollars a month. Street car barns were located just a block away in those days. The Deaconess' Home of the Reformed Church was near by. There was a Cushman Bakery close at hand and, near too, a drugstore with large colored jars in the window.

His death was not important news. The funerals of too many greater Civil War generals had passed. Even most of the carpet-baggers had gone, as North and South seemed to agree, to hell or into hiding. Not many attended Milton Littlefield's funeral, few followed to the grave, at Kensico Cemetery in Westchester County, which remained unmarked more than half a century later. All he left apparently was a deed to some not then much sought-after lands in Brevard County, Florida, which his sons in amusement referred to as their Florida fortune. He left also in North Carolina an enduring item of comedy in the grim recollections of Reconstruction.

It is a story of uncertain date. The incident is not documented. Perhaps it belongs rightly only to the folklore of history, but certainly no history has been so much written out of folklore as that of Reconstruction. It was told by one whose memories deserve respect, even though he did not wish to vouch for the story with his name. He told of a time when North Carolina officials, still seeking Littlefield, decided that persuasion might serve better than writs of extradition, rewards to kidnapers or any other means in getting the General to come back to North Carolina and stand trial. With such a purpose in view, the much-respected, elderly William T. Dortch, who had served in the Confederate Senate, was chosen as emissary. He found Littlefield in a modest house in the North, probably Morristown. At the door he was greeted with cordiality by the General.

"I have been expecting you, Colonel Dortch," he said, with a bow. "Of course, I still read the Raleigh papers. And I have about made up my mind to do what you want me to do."

The North Carolinian showed his surprise.

"Yes, I'm tired of all this and I'm ready to come back. I have only one condition."

Littlefield pointed to a desk covered with documents.

"Only one condition. Here are the papers. I'm going to leave you undisturbed with them. I have complete faith in any promise you will make me. Read the papers. Read them, and afterwards, if you will give me North Carolina's guarantee that all those others involved with me in these matters will be brought to justice with me, I'm ready to go back and stand trial."

Then Littlefield left him. The distinguished attorney read the papers. He re-read some. He checked some against others. He beat a slow tattoo on the desk top with his fingers. When Littlefield came back he was very solemn.

"General Littlefield—" he said. He looked at him quizzically. He appeared duty bound not to smile. "General, I respect your condition. I do not think we will trouble you any more."

With ceremony General Littlefield escorted Colonel Dortch to his hack. Dortch's promise was kept. No writs or rewards for kidnapers followed Littlefield any longer. He spoke without apprehension at public gatherings. And, of course, his most notable oratorical recollection was about the bloody day beside the peach blossoms when young Illinois men first confronted the South at Shiloh. He was never convicted of any crime. That was as it was. Perhaps that is the way it should have been. It is certainly too late to pursue him now. In any judgment out of the era in which he lived—in consideration of all the men North and South with whom he moved and worked and fought and laughed and strutted briefly, too—historical damnation may well take as its own the decision of Colonel Dortch. That old Confederate statesman knew too many sinners to select just one for stoning.

Sources and Acknowledgments

I have the feeling as I try to set down the diverse sources from which this book came that its composition has been less a historical enterprise than a man hunt. And a queer man hunt, too. No culprit remained to bring to justice. Certainly no reward was available for the apprehension of Milton Smith Littlefield for great crimes with which he was charged nearly a century ago. He was still a fugitive and the facts about him were fugitive, too. Nevertheless, I felt it imperative to track down his story and try to apprehend something of his meaning. Perhaps in my case the reason was that he was a part of the folklore of my childhood in an indignant but still romantic South. My ardor was matched by the enthusiasm with which so many people—librarians, newspapermen, historians and others—joined my posse.

When I was young, "Swepson and Littlefield" were the names for giants of wickedness almost as real in our mythology as the chipped stone steps in the State Capitol which many still insist were broken by the barrels of booze the anthropoid Reconstructionists rolled up and down them as a part of the essential fuel of legislative propulsion in the full flight of debauchery. No barrel has been preserved or, as is now the historical fashion, restored. And although Swepson left money and a high monument over his bones, the Yankee Littlefield seemed to have departed into thin air, leaving behind him only a trail of recollections that he was as charming as he was wicked.

I went looking for him. There were the criminal dossiers, politically prepared, in the records of Southern States. The name of his brother briefly appeared in some biographies of Lincoln as a law student in the firm of Lincoln and Herndon. Milton's activities as soldier were records in volumes of the *Official Records of the War of the Rebellion* dealing with campaigns along the Tennessee and Mississippi rivers and on the South Atlantic Coast. The bare bones of his military history were given also in Francis B. Heitman's *Historical Register and Dictionary of the U. S. Army.* And, of course, his larcenous record was outlined in the standard works about Reconstruction in various Southern States. Increasingly, however, his name became little more than a cliché for corruption.

I wanted to know more. Almost by chance I discovered that he had a son, Milton, Jr., a minister who acquired sufficient reputation as a compiler of hymn books to be listed in *Who Was Who.* So, more optimistic than scientific in research, I wrote letters to a group of those for whom my affection grows as the years go on—librarians and particularly librarians in small towns whose eagerness in assistance to searchers seems to have no bounds at all. I wrote to the library in every town in which the younger Littlefield had served a church. One letter went to Corona, Long Island. I never heard directly from the librarian there but she speeded my search.

She passed the letter on and one morning before I was up I got a long distance call from Philadelphia. The caller said she was Helen Littlefield Gursky, and in case I was interested she had a mutilated scrapbook and some other papers which had belonged to her grandfather, General Milton Smith Littlefield. I was promptly in Philadelphia. Mrs. Gursky gave me a good lunch, all the papers she had and all her good wishes in her charming little house on tiny, narrow Arbor Street. She had never heard how bad her well-loved grandfather was supposed to have been until someone, in 1933, called her attention to the description of him in Claude Bowers' *The Tragic Era* as "the notorious General M. S. Littlefield who was to get more than his share of the loot." None of it had come down to Mrs. Gursky. With little of the world's goods and something less than her share of health, Helen Gursky inherited gallantry from somebody. And she was happy that someone was ready to take a whole look at the General. I came away with her papers and since have received her continuing help. Also, she put me in touch with the late Walter S. Dix, of New York, who as a close friend of Milton, Jr., knew the General well.

After that it was as easy as putting together, a hundred years after they were cut, the pieces of an almost continental jig-saw puzzle. Fortunately, I had near at hand a volunteer assistant in another grandchild of the times, Fred G. Mahler, of Raleigh, whose grandfather, Governor W. W. Holden, was impeached by the resurgent Democrats in 1871. Fred Mahler's interest was not merely filial. Though not listed among the professional historians, he is a scholar for scholarship's sake. He lives in libraries. Finding out for himself is sufficient to him. But while I was writing this book he would appear from the recesses of his researches, as he always does with startling suddenness, and deposit a sheet of yellow paper covered with blue typewriting on my desk. Almost always the sheet contained fresh, revealing, significant material about the Littlefield I was seeking.

Others I had never seen before were glad to help. The late Harry E. Pratt, state historian at the Illinois State Historical Library in Springfield, brought to my assistance not only the resources of his collections but his own questing interest. My old schoolmate, David Mearns, head of the Manuscript Division of the Library of Congress and author of *The Lincoln Papers* was, as always, almost a genius in his help, though he sometimes teased me about how long it took me to follow the lost General's trail. I can only begin to thank librarians in various cities and towns from those in the New York Public Library to the Betty Dennis in the library at little Lee, Massachusetts, who labored to get me a detail. Watt P. Marchman, of the Hayes Memorial Library in Fremont, Ohio, dug up a significant letter about the General written by John Greenleaf Whittier. I love all librarians. But there are some special ones. My hope is that all hunters after history can find near them such a biographical Sherlock Holmes as Margaret Birdsong Price, now genealogical reference librarian at the North Carolina State Library.

She not only can find a needle in a haystack. She has given my historical molehills the treatment only deserved by mountains.

Having plagued the librarians I naturally turned also to newspapermen. I hit the jackpot in a letter from Lee M. Woodruff, editor of *The Grand Rapids Press,* who not only dredged up all the published information about Littlefield's youth in Michigan but brought me also the resources and the memories of Mrs. Sarah Littlefield Cornelius, daughter of the General's half-brother, Benjamin Franklin. Similarly, John B. Johnson, editor of *The Watertown News,* aided me with regard to the upstate New York country where the General was born and with which so many of his Reconstruction activities were connected. My thanks go also to Paul R. Coppock, of *The Commerical Appeal* of Memphis, where Littlefield saw or learned many tricks of the times.

There was also a retired businessman, Charles G. Pierie, of Huntingdon Valley, Pennsylvania. He had been on a man hunt himself. Some years ago in a shop in Philadelphia he found and bought an old portrait of Abraham Lincoln. It turned out to be the work of John Harrison Littlefield, who after serving as Lincoln's law clerk became an artist. As possessor of John's picture, Mr. Pierie went after the facts about John who died so penniless and obscure that his widow wrote a still-existing, pitiful, begging letter to John Hay. His findings, which he loaned me, helped much in the quest for facts about the General's brother.

Finally, of course, there were the historians who, far from rebuffing an amateur in their professional field, seemed to get excited about the Littlefield man hunt, too. I leaned, as this book shows, heavily upon the researches and the resources of my old teacher, Dr. J. G. de Roulhac Hamilton, who not only wrote *Reconstruction in North Carolina* but built the great Southern Historical Collection of manuscripts at Chapel Hill. The late Dr. Cecil K. Brown, of Davidson College, helped me much. Dr. E. Merton Coulter, of the University of Georgia, author of *The South During Reconstruction 1865-1877,* gave me advice and assistance. Finally, I should have been lost in the fantastically complicated Florida operations but for the guidance and help of Dr. Paul E. Fenlon, formerly of the University of Florida, now at Holy Cross College in Worcester, Massachusetts.

My thanks also go to Dr. Christopher Crittenden, director of the North Carolina Department of Archives and History; Harry J. Dubester, Grace E. Fuller and Robert H. Land of the Library of Congress; Audrey Braward, of the Jacksonville (Florida) Free Public Library; LeRoy DePuy, archivist of the Illinois State Library, and Clyde C. Walton, of that same fine institution; May B. Leonard, director of the Morristown (New Jersey) Library; Barbara Kell, of the Missouri Historical Society; R. N. Williams II, of the Historical Society of Pennsylvania; R. W. Patrick and Samuel Proctor of the University of Florida; James W. Patton, director of the Southern Historical Collection at Chapel Hill; and James Reese Price, county historian of Jefferson County, New York.

I am not much of a man for footnotes. So far as is possible without cluttering the narrative I have tried to indicate sources in the text. Neither there nor here, however, can I truly state my indebtedness to many who have given great assistance in finding forgotten facts about an almost forgotten man. I have, of course, found invaluable, in putting men and pieces together, the *Dictionary of American Biography*. But I have learned not to scorn the biographical reference books of communities and states which may have been produced in the first place to serve the vanity of their "eminent men" but now provide the only available facts about figures who have passed into historical obscurity. In following the much moving Littlefield, I have found invaluable the *American Guide Series* (if they seemed a boondoggle once they are a treasure now) and the uneven but admirable *Rivers of America* series. Many of the newspapers quoted are from clippings preserved in Littlefield's scrapbook. Files of some of these papers are no longer extant. But nobody can study this period without realizing that we who make newspapers today are providing a first source for history later, though the student may have to read with not only the newspaper but the times, the politics and the prejudices before him. Chiefly in this field I am indebted to the long-gone reporters and editors of the *Sentinel* and the *Standard* of Raleigh, and *The Floridian* of Tallahassee. As a laborer I can only wish they had been indexed as have leading journals in the great cities of the North.

My indebtedness is great. My thanks are unbounded. I say only in sharpness: a pox on microfilm.

Below I have listed the books which it seemed to me were most helpful in a long and satisfying search.

American Guide Series:

Berkshire Hills, The, New York, 1939
Florida, New York, 1939
Georgia, Athens, Georgia, 1940
Illinois, Chicago, 1939
Michigan, New York, 1941
Mississippi, New York, 1938
Missouri, New York, 1941
New Jersey, New York, 1939
New York, New York, 1940
North Carolina, Chapel Hill, 1939
Pennsylvania, New York, 1940
South Carolina, New York, 1941
Tennessee, New York, 1939
Wisconsin, New York, 1941

Andrews, Sidney. *The South Since the War,* Cambridge (Mass.), 1866
Arthur, John Preston. *Western North Carolina—A History,* Raleigh (N. C.), 1914
Ashe, Samuel A., ed. *Biographical History of North Carolina,* Raleigh (N. C.), 1905

Barnard, Harry. *Rutherford B. Hayes and His America,* Indianapolis (Ind.), 1954
Battle, Kemp Plummer. *Memories of an Old-Time Tar Heel,* Chapel Hill (N. C.), 1945
Baxter, Albert. *History of the City of Grand Rapids, Michigan,* New York and Grand Rapids, 1891
Beveridge, Albert J. *Abraham Lincoln 1809-1858,* Boston, 1928
Billington, Ray Allen, ed. *The Journal of Charlotte L. Forten,* New York, 1953
Biographical Dictionary of the American Congress 1774-1949, Washington, D. C., 1950
Bowers, Claude G. *The Tragic Era,* Boston, 1929
Boyd, W. K. *Governor W. W. Holden,* Trinity College Historical Papers, Durham (N. C.), 1899
Brown, Cecil Kenneth. *A State Movement in Railroad Development,* Chapel Hill (N. C.), 1928
Brown, William Wells. *The Black Man,* New York, 1863

Cabell, Branch, and Hanna, A. J. *The St. Johns,* Rivers of America series, New York, 1943
Caldwell, Tod R. Papers, North Carolina Department of Archives and History, Raleigh (N. C.)

Camm, Colonel William. "Diary 1861-1865," compiled by Fritz Haskell, *Journal* of the Illinois State Historical Society, Vol. XVIII, p. 4 (Jan. 1926)

Carter, Hodding. *Lower Mississippi,* Rivers of America series, New York, 1942

Chidsey, Donald Barr. *The Gentleman from New York—A Life of Roscoe Conkling,* New Haven (Conn.), 1935

Claflin, William, and Mary B. Papers, Hayes Memorial Library, Fremont (Ohio)

Clews, Henry. *Fifty Years of Wall Street,* New York, 1908

Coulter, E. Merton. *The South During Reconstruction 1865-1877,* Baton Rouge (La.), 1947

Cowan, Augustus. Papers, Illinois State Historical Library

Cyclopedia of Eminent and Representative Men of the Carolinas of the Nineteenth Century, Madison (Wis.), 1892

Dana, Charles A. *Recollections of the Civil War,* New York, 1898

Davidson, Donald. *The Tennessee: Civil War to TVA,* Rivers of America series, New York, 1948

Davis, Jefferson. *The Rise and Fall of the Confederate Government,* New York, 1881

Davis, William Watson. *The Civil War and Reconstruction in Florida,* New York, 1913

Dayton, Aretas A. "The Raising of Union Forces in Illinois During the Civil War," *Journal* of Illinois State Historical Society, Vol. XXXIV (Dec. 1941)

Dennett, Tyler. *John Hay—From Poetry to Politics,* New York, 1933

———, ed. *Lincoln and the Civil War—In the Diaries and Letters of John Hay,* New York, 1939

Donald, David, ed. *Inside Lincoln's Cabinet—The Civil War Diaries of Salmon P. Chase,* New York, 1954

DuBois, W. E. B. *Black Reconstruction,* New York, 1935

Dugan, James. *History of Hurlbut's Fighting Fourth Division,* Cincinnati (Ohio), 1863

Dykeman, Wilma. *The French Broad,* Rivers of America series, New York, 1955

Emilio, Luis F. *History of the Fifty-Fourth Regiment of Massachusetts Volunteer Infantry,* Boston, 1891

Fenlon, Paul E. "The Notorious Swepson-Littlefield Fraud," *Florida Historical Quarterly,* Vol. XXXII (April 1954)

———. "The Struggle for Control of the Florida Central Railroad 1867-1882," *Florida Historical Quarterly,* Vol. XXXIV (Jan. 1956)

Flick, Alexander C. *Samuel J. Tilden,* New York, 1939

French, Mrs. A. M. *Slavery in South Carolina and the Ex-Slaves, or The Port Royal Mission,* New York, 1862

Fuller, Robert H. *Jubilee Jim—The Life of Colonel James Fisk, Jr.*, New York, 1928

Futch, Ovid L. "Salmon P. Chase and Civil War Politics in Florida," *Florida Historical Quarterly*, Vol. XXXII (Jan. 1954)

Graff, Mary B. *Mandarin on the St. Johns*, Gainsville (Fla.), 1953

Grant, Ulysses S. *Personal Memoirs of U. S. Grant*, 2 vols., New York, 1885

Gray, James. *The Illinois*, Rivers of America series, New York, 1940

Haddock, John A. *The Growth of a Century: As Illustrated in the History of Jefferson County, New York, From 1793-1894*, Albany (N. Y.), 1895

Hamilton, J. G. de Roulhac, ed. *The Correspondence of Jonathan Worth*, Raleigh (N. C.), 1909

———. *Reconstruction in North Carolina*, New York, 1914

Hay, John. Papers, The Library of Congress

Heitman, Francis B. *Historical Register & Dictionary of the U. S. Army, 1789-1903*, Washington, D. C., 1903

Henderson, Archibald. *North Carolina, The Old State and the New*, Chicago, 1941

Herndon, William Henry. *Life of Lincoln*, New York, 1930

Herndon, William H., and Weik, Jesse W. *Abraham Lincoln*, Cleveland (Ohio), 1949

Hertz, Emanuel, ed. *The Hidden Lincoln—from the Letters and Papers of William H. Herndon*, New York, 1938

Higginson, Thomas Wentworth. *Army Life in a Black Regiment*, Boston, 1900

———. *Cheerful Yesterdays*, Boston, 1900

Holden, W. W. *Memoirs*, The John Lawson Monographs of the Trinity College Historical Society, Durham (N. C.), 1911

———. Papers, North Carolina Department of Archives and History, Raleigh

———. Trial of, N. C. Legislative Document 22—Session 1870-71

Irwin, Will. *A History of the Union League Club of New York City*, New York, 1952

Johnson, Guion G. *A Social History of the Sea Islands*, Chapel Hill (N. C.), 1930

Josephson, Matthew. *The Politicos—1865-1896*, New York, 1938

Kent, Frank R. *The Democratic Party*, New York, 1928

Kibler, Lillian Adele. *Benjamin F. Perry—South Carolina Unionist*, Durham (N. C.), 1946

Leech, Margaret. *Reveille in Washington*, New York, 1941

L'Engle, Edward M. Papers, Southern Historical Collection, Chapel Hill (N. C.)

Lewis, Lloyd. *Sherman, Fighting Prophet,* New York, 1932
Littlefield, J. H. "Abraham Lincoln as I Knew Him," *The Beacon Magazine,* Jan. 1892
Littlefield, M. S. *Campaigns in the West in '61 and '62 in War Talks to Morristown Veterans,* Morristown (N. J.), 1887
Lovell, Caroline Couper. *The Golden Isles of Georgia,* Boston, 1932

McLeod, John Angus. *From These Stones,* Mars Hill (N. C.), 1955
McClure, A. K. *Recollections of Half a Century,* Salem (Mass.), 1902
———. *Old Time Notes of Pennsylvania,* Philadelphia, 1905
McKim, J. Miller. *The Freedmen of South Carolina,* Philadelphia, 1862
Mearns, David C. *The Lincoln Papers,* New York, 1948
Miers, Earl Schenck. *The Web of Victory,* New York, 1955
Milton, George Fort. *The Age of Hate,* New York, 1930
———. *The Eve of Conflict,* Boston, 1934
Myers, Gustavus. *History of the Great American Fortunes,* Chicago, 1911
Myers, William Starr. *The Republican Party,* New York, 1928

Nicolay, John G., and Hay, John. *Abraham Lincoln: A History,* 10 vols., New York, 1904
Nixon, Raymond B. *Henry W. Grady—Spokesman of the New South,* New York, 1943

Oakes, R. A. *Genealogical and Family History of the County of Jefferson, New York,* 2 vols., New York, Chicago, 1905
Official Records of the War of the Rebellion,
Series I, Vol. X, Part I
Series I, Vol. XIV
Series I, Vol. XVII, Part II
Series I, Vol. XXVIII, Part I, Part II
Series I, Vol. XXXV, Part I
Olmsted, Frederick Law. *A Journey in the Seaboard Slave States,* New York, 1856

Palmer, John M. *Personal Recollections of John M. Palmer,* Cincinnati (Ohio), 1901
Pearson, Elizabeth W., ed. *Letters from Port Royal Written at the Time of the Civil War,* Boston, 1906
Phillips, Ulrich B. *American Negro Slavery,* New York, 1929
Pierce, Edward L. "The Freedmen at Port Royal," *Atlantic Monthly,* Vol. XII (Sept. 1863)
Pike, James S. *The Prostrate State—South Carolina Under Negro Government,* New York, 1874
Pogue, H. W. "Address to Jersey County Historical Society," (Feb. 12, 1916), *Journal* of the Illinois Historical Society, Vol. VIII, pp. 571, 577-78

Pollard, James E. *The Presidents and the Press,* New York, 1947

Quarles, Benjamin. *The Negro in the Civil War,* Boston, 1953

Ransom, Matt Whitaker. Papers, Southern Historical Collection, Chapel Hill (N. C.)
Ravenel, Mrs. St. Julien. *Charleston—The Place and the People,* New York, 1922
Reid, Whitelaw. *After the War—A Southern Tour,* Cincinnati (Ohio), 1866
Reynolds, John S. *Reconstruction in South Carolina 1865-1877,* Columbia (S. C.), 1905

Salley, Katherine Batts, ed. *Life at St. Mary's,* Chapel Hill (N. C.), 1942
Sandburg, Carl. *Abraham Lincoln: the Prairie Years and the War Years,* New York, 1954
Savage, Henry, Jr. *The Santee,* Rivers of America series, New York, 1956
Seitz, Don C. *Lincoln the Politician,* New York, 1931
Sherman, W. T. *Personal Memoirs,* New York, 1891
Shipp, W. M., chairman. *Report of the N. C. Commission to Investigate Charges of Fraud,* Raleigh (N. C.), 1872
Simkins, Francis B., and Woody, Robert H. *South Carolina During Reconstruction,* Chapel Hill (N. C.), 1932
Spencer, Cornelia Phillips. *The Last Ninety Days of the War,* New York, 1866
Starke, Aubrey Harrison. *Sidney Lanier,* Chapel Hill (N. C.), 1933
Stokes, Thomas. *The Savannah,* Rivers of America series, New York, 1951
Stowe, Lyman Beecher. *Saints, Sinners and Beechers,* Indianapolis (Ind.), 1934
Swepson, George W. Papers, North Carolina Department of Archives and History, Raleigh (N. C.)
Swint, Henry L. *The Northern Teachers in the South 1862-1870,* Nashville (Tenn.), 1941

Talley, Robert. *One Hundred Years of "The Commercial Appeal,"* Memphis (Tenn.), 1940
Tarbell, Ida M. *History of the Standard Oil Company,* New York, 1904
Tatum, Georgia Lee. *Disloyalty in the Confederacy,* Chapel Hill (N. C.), 1934
Thayer, William Roscoe. *The Life and Letters of John Hay,* Boston, 1929
Todd, Helen. *A Man Named Grant,* Boston, 1940
Tourgée, Albion W. *A Fool's Errand,* New York, 1879
———. *Bricks Without Straw,* New York, 1880
"Tribute to the Late President" (report of mass meeting in Savannah, April 22, 1865), Savannah, 1865
Wallace, John. *Carpetbag Rule in Florida,* Jacksonville (Fla.), 1888

Wallace, Lew. *An Autobiography,* 2 vols., New York, 1906
Ward, Reverend W. H. *Abraham Lincoln—Tributes from his Associates,* New York, 1895
Wecter, Dixon. *When Johnny Comes Marching Home,* Boston, 1944
Welles, Gideon, Diary of, Boston, 1911
Who Was Who in America, Vol. I, 1897-1942, Chicago, 1942
Williamson, Jefferson. *The American Hotel,* New York, 1930
Wilson, Forrest. *Crusader in Crinoline—The Life of Harriet Beecher Stowe,* Philadelphia, 1941
Winston, Robert W. *Andrew Johnson, Plebian and Patriot,* New York, 1928
———. *It's a Far Cry,* New York, 1937

Woodward, C. Vann. *Reunion and Reaction,* Boston, 1951
Woodward, W. E. *Meet General Grant,* New York, 1928

Yates, Governor Richard. Papers, Illinois State Historical Library

Index